Retail Banking

Retail Banking

The New Revolution in Structure and Strategy

J. B. HOWCROFT AND J. LAVIS

Basil Blackwell

First published 1986

Basil Blackwell Ltd
108 Cowley Road, Oxford OX4 1JF, UK

Basil Blackwell Inc.
432 Park Avenue South, Suite 1503,
New York, NY 10016, USA

BRITISH LIBRARY CATALOGUING IN PUBLICATION DATA
Howcroft, J. B.
Retail banking.
1. Banks and banking
I. Title II. Lavis, J.
332.1′2 HG1601
ISBN 0-631-14932-5

LIBRARY OF CONGRESS CATALOGING IN PUBLICATION DATA
Howcroft, J. B.
Retail banking.

Includes index.
1. Banks and banking – Great Britain. I. Lavis, J.
II. Title
HG2988.H64 1986 332.1′2′0941 86-6140
ISBN 0-631-14932-5

Phototypeset by Dobbie Typesetting Service, Plymouth, Devon
Printed in Great Britain by T. J. Press Ltd, Padstow, Cornwall

To Family and Friends

Contents

List of Tables

List of Figures

Acknowledgements

The authors would like to acknowledge the support of the Midland Bank PLC, and the Department of Management Studies and the Banking Centre at Loughborough University, without whose assistance this book could not possibly have been written.

In particular our sincere gratitude is expressed to David Mills, formerly Assistant General Manager, Marketing, Midland Bank PLC and to Professors Geoffrey Gregory, John Sizer and John Presley, Loughborough University.

In terms of typing the manuscript and displaying patience beyond the call of duty, the authors would equally like to express their appreciation to Kathleen Gibson and Margaret McMillan, Department of Management Studies, Loughborough.

Finally, the authors would like to thank the numerous friends and colleagues who constantly proffered encouragement, guidance and useful advice in the writing of the book.

The views expressed in the text are, of course, those of the authors and are in no way to be construed as reflecting, in any way, those of the organization and individuals mentioned above.

Part I Strategic Perspectives

1 Retail Banking: an Introduction

This book has two purposes. The first is concerned with developing a framework in which to analyse and discuss the strategic issues present in retail banking, and to make some observations about the concept and function of strategy itself. The second is to provide an analytical commentary on the nature and structure of retail banking in the UK and to develop and suggest some practical approaches to these strategic issues. Both retail banking and strategy are relatively new terms in the banking industry and represent a shift towards a more refined definition and considered assessment of its businesses and business options.

Retail banking is a business activity which is subject to evolutionary change and development, as its processes, structure and market-place are all modified. Strategy, however, exists as a methodology for operating the organization within the environment, for analysing the organization and market-place, and for providing a framework for action. It provides a view or a vision against which planning, the allocation of resources and the setting of objectives takes place. The application of a strategic methodology to retail banking as an interpretative and practical exercise is a vital element in structuring and focussing bank energies towards an increasingly complex and volatile business environment.

The value of applying generalized, conceptual thinking to an industry as apparently dynamic as the banking industry is often questioned. It is thought that its long-term view is not justified given the realities of the market-place, with its framework for action precluding effective entrepreneurial responses to opportunities. Strategy should, however, attempt to encompass the totality of business activity and to create a unity of purpose and action out of the interacting elements that make up a business environment.

To create this synthesis requires an approach that is both structural, that is it deals in fixed terms of either methodology or time, and pragmatic in that it is able to respond flexibly to short-term changes which are either organizational or environmental. Clearly the more able a strategy is to deal in a cohesive way with the totality of factors that affect a business the more able it is to accommodate changing patterns of business and provide successful, long-term lines of action.

There are several points to emerge from this. The first is, rather obviously, that there is no finite strategic methodology. Because the mix of factors is so extensive, every organization has to develop its own strategic decision-making matrix. Successful strategy depends on achieving an equilibrium between the organization and the market-place. Because the status of that relationship varies in all cases, either in terms of self-perception, which is a cultural problem, or in practical terms, the shape of the strategic matrix must reflect the peculiarities of that individual relationship.

Strategy implicitly assumes that all change is evolutionary and not revolutionary. In fact it is worth making the point that revolution only takes place when a situation is not strategically managed. The time spaces between evolutionary phases vary depending not only on environmental factors but also on the nature of the industry itself. The inertial elements of the market-place, the number of variables within the processes of the industry itself, are all critical in forming the strategic decision making structure.

In retail banking, for example, evolutionary changes are much slower than in the corporate market, simply because the market is so large and the number of environmental factors relatively few. But against this is the fact that in a slow moving industry, decisions tend to be cumulative and irreversible, so although the decisions are fewer and more temporally spaced out they tend to be more fundamental and critical.

Although strategy formulation brings its own rules to the analysis of business problems, represented by a slowly developing vocabulary of analysis and scenario building, strategy as an activity intrinsic to the organization itself should be built on an understanding of the idiosyncratic aspects of the business. For just as successful strategies are built on finding a point of equilibrium between the organization and the market, so also an organization must find an equilibrium between the cultural and political aspects of itself and the more positivist and rationalistic requirements of product market strategies, business portfolios and so on.

At the most advanced level, strategy formulation extends beyond the analytical and conceptual aspects of the organization–environmental fit towards tailoring strategies based on the 'psychology' of the organization. Strategies for cultural change are a concomitant of this, where the purpose of the strategy moves towards identifying what might be called the strategic focal point, that is where the organization has to get in order to succeed, and developing a mix of business and politico-cultural strategies to reach that point.

At this stage strategies characterize the 'rational' requirements of the market-place and the subjective tendencies of the corporate culture. It is evident that within successful firms a corporate culture is a vital ingredient of success. The implications for the banking industry, which has just begun to adopt strategic planning, are enormous. The simple adoption of systemized thought and action across competitive groupings of banks will lead to pressure for increasingly sophisticated policies and organizational structures to carry out those policies. The first step is towards defining the nature of the relationship between the bank and the market, represented in an embryonic form in the concept of retail banking itself. The second step is towards actually modifying the organization, but this can only be done after analysing the market-place and finding the business and functional strategies required to succeed in that market-place.

Given some of the complexities outlined above, it is clear that any attempt to provide a strategic perspective on retail banking should try to be methodical, establishing a foundation of categories and definitions from which to establish a reasonably accurate picture of the market place, and of the evolutionary trends taking place.

As this study is industry based, and not geared to analysing and developing the individual strategies of clearing banks, the following discussion will be largely general, touching only upon some of the politico-cultural problems of strategy formulation. Indeed, in general terms, it is highly questionable whether the tools, other than those of intuition and insight exist on which to form such an analysis.

This book breaks the problem into three parts: the establishment of a structure for analysing the retail banking market in strategic terms; the analysis of the components that make up the retail bank environent; and an examination of the principal strategic issues facing competing institutions in the retail bank environment.

2 Retail Banking: the Strategic Context

Retail Banking: a Definition

The term retail banking represents an imprecise category of activity; devised in the past fifteen years and now used extensively, it tends to represent any banking which is not wholesale based. It tends to encompass any business that is conducted through a branch network and which is focussed mainly towards the personal sector. But it does not represent just one industry; to be accurate, 'retail banking' should encompass all institutions who provide a related range of banking services – money transmission, deposit and credit services and some form of financial advice. The nature of the market-place means that a variety of different industry groups, for example clearing banks, building societies and finance houses, are competing for different segments of the market-place. All display different structural and behavioural characteristics, and it is this breadth and richness of activity and interaction that has created the highly dynamic 'retail banking' industry of today.

For our purposes, retail banking will mean a financial service or group of services offered through an institution to personal customers. Although primarily branch based, the category will include any method of delivering financial services to the personal customer. Finally our framework for analysing strategies in retail banking will be concerned with the following principal components:

—the personal sector market
—environmental issues
—the industry groups
—the services and products
…stems

…oviding strategic perspectives is to provide a

—aid the formulation of organizational goals and objectives for the retail banking business
—identify major issues and trends taking place in the industry
—help co-ordinate and integrate the different elements of the organization in the pursuit of such a strategy.

There are three levels to this process – analytical, developmental and implementatory. The first is concerned with tracing the pattern of interaction between the organization and the environment, the second in developing strategic lines of response and choice based on the preceding analysis, and the third is concerned with implementing the business and functional strategies, through introducing the right processes, strategies and structures and by manipulating the politico-cultural aspects of the organization. Our main concern is with the second point, namely, to provide the basis for the development stage.

Strategy and Structure

Within any organization there exists a hierarchy of action and decision making which, in a complex business such as banking, can be divided into the three levels of corporate, business and functional decision making.

The organizational structures of the LCBs* reflect these three distinct levels, from the bank group level, to business level represented in domestic and related services to the functional level in computer operations, marketing and so on. However, there is no explicit business level organization for retail banking. This is due to its traditional interconnectedness with other banking activities. None the less, retail banking should be considered to belong to the business level. This separation of the strategic idea and function and organizational form is due to historical processes.

Retail banking activity is closely linked with other categories of banking business; delivery systems, most especially branch networks, are shared. as are the staple resources of manpower and deposits with other business sectors and their objectives, meaning that the management of retail banking, at best, is conducted on a sectoral rather than an explicit business basis.

Corporate management's function within an LCB should be primarily concerned with business mix, resource allocation and contribution. The

* The term LCB will be used throughout the book to refer to the 'Big Four' banks, namely Barclays, Lloyds, Midland and National Westminster, or the 'Big Five' which also includes Williams and Glyns, now incorporated in the Royal Bank of Scotland.

business level should be concerned with segmenting the market by product and delivery system, and in achieving competitive advantage. Business level strategy should attempt to produce advantages of synergy through establishing the right mix of product, market and distribution.

The third level within this hierarchy, the functional, is concerned in retail banking with two main forms of strategy: marketing and operations. The function of marketing is to establish the relationship between the market-place and the organization. Its concerns revolve around the choice of markets and market segments, product lines, pricing policies and communication/promotion programmes. Operating strategies are geared to the 'manufacturing' of services and their distribution, and should complement marketing strategies at all costs.

At the functional level the strategic concern of matching the strategy to the structure is again evident. Centralized product management techniques can integrate marketing and operational decisions, although with the retail banking approach used by the LCBs this will be compromised by a variety of considerations emanating from other business sectors.

Even at this stage, the centrality of strategic considerations in developing retail banking business becomes clear. The complexity and spread of its markets and the influence of environmental factors all exert pressures which have to be resolved through strategic mechanisms and which are ultimately realized in organizational structures. Structure follows strategy, with growth strategies acting as the main motor behind most structural change. Changes in the market or the industry as it reaches maturity have the same influence, providing motives of managing the market better, and in so doing maintaining market share.

In the retail banking market the organizational structures of the LCBs reflect preoccupations with lending activities, traditional forms of money transmission and the corporate sector. Divisionalization of activity has taken place as previously mentioned on established market distinctions (e.g. merchant banking, international, domestic, finance house, etc.) rather than through organizational structures created in an integrated way to reflect sectoral divisions by market (e.g. the corporate and personal sector).

A rational structuring of the corporate organization into divisions and ultimately into strategic business units (SBUs) which reflect the nature of product–delivery system–make relationships, allows for an integrated planning, control and reward system. This facilitates the formulation of a range of policies tailored to the needs of the busines unit, and allows processes and systems to be matched to the businesses' strategic requirements.

For although the LCBs businesses are highly integrated in organizational terms, those businesses are in themselves becoming highly diversified as they are now evolving in different ways as the business grows more complex and as markets are increasingly segmented. This means that the business in mangement and staff terms begins to expand beyond their cognitive limits. At a general management level this can lead to a lack of agreement over goals. The overall effect is to make the organization inflexible and inefficient. The problem of its resolution is not only an organizational but also a cultural problem and it requires the development of politico-cultural strategies.

The advantages of a division of the corporate structure into business units which reflect the segmentation of the businesses by product and market are that it allows for the proper formulation of corporate level strategy. Businesses can be managed on the basis of rational objectives and resource allocations. Individual business strategies can be pursued consistent with the demands of the market. The businesses within the hierarchy can be managed almost as an integrated portfolio, reflecting an optimized mangement based on business growth, product market evolution and industry position at the business unit level. As the banking business becomes sectorally more fragmented, the introduction of such SBUs becomes crucial, leading, not only to the separation of corporate business from the personal sector, but also an integration of the currently diffuse range of subsidiaries dealing in the personal sector.

A Model for Strategic Analysis

Introduction

The preceding discussion was intended to raise some broad issues about strategy, its function and scope, and the ways in which the organization of retail banking for strategic purposes was difficult to achieve because of its historical development and status within the LCBs business structures.

The following model for strategic evaluation is, to assist analysis, at an industry level, although it can be applied to the individual bank level. As our concern is with the LCBs, discussion of environment, industry structure, competitive strategy and so on will focus on the LCBs treating other groups as competitor groups.

A Model for Strategic Analysis and Evaluation of the Retail Banking Industry

Environmental Analysis

- Financial trends of personal sector

—sources and uses of funds

—borrowing ratio to personal disposable income, and purposes of borrowing
—savings ratio, and application of savings by instrument and maturity
—choice of institution and investment
—size of market for product groups
—financial behaviour.

- Social trends

—demographic
—attitudinal
—cultural.

- Political and regulatory

—government monetary policy
—regulation by institution
—protection of the consumer.

- Technology

—influence and impact
—scope and scale
—trends.

Analysis of Competing Industry Groups

—development
—structure
—markets
—evaluation of current situation
—assessment of future trends.

Analysis of the Key Business Issues and Strategic Choices

- Generic product groups

—payment systems
—lending products
—deposit and savings instruments
—ancillary services

and by pricing policies

- Delivery systems
- Organization structure and issues

—management
—structures
—corporate culture
—image.

The Idea of Industry Evolution, Industry Groups and Business Strategy

The discussion has touched upon the concept of stages of evolution within an industry (reflecting on a larger scale the life-cycle characteristics of products), the concept of industry groups competing within the larger dimension of the 'retail bank' market-place and the notion that retail bank strategies belong generally to the business as opposed to corporate level decision making. The purpose of this section is to amplify these issues since they are central to obtaining a strategic vision of the retail banking industry.

Industry Groups

These are groups of organizations who display similar approaches to the market. Their position can be plotted on a table which shows their market position and competitive strengths and weaknesses. Figure 2.1 illustrates the point.

Each group also has strength as well as market position and a range of similar distinctive competences, key success factors and constraints. These elements constitute the mobility barriers within an industry, preventing other groups from moving into new market positions. Barriers to entry are established on the basis of building up distinctive competences, but these may conversely act to reduce the ability of an organization to respond to new market possibilities because investment in infrastructure precludes movement; these are known as exit barriers.

The banks' money transmission oligopoly illustrates all these concepts. The banks have made huge investments in cash and cheque based payment systems. The oligopoly provides them with a ready source of new business through which they can sell other profit-making services. It is clearly in the interests of other groups to join or supplant that industrial group. But in the absence of the capital or technical know-how to establish new payment systems, or indeed in the case of the refusal of the clearing banks to allow

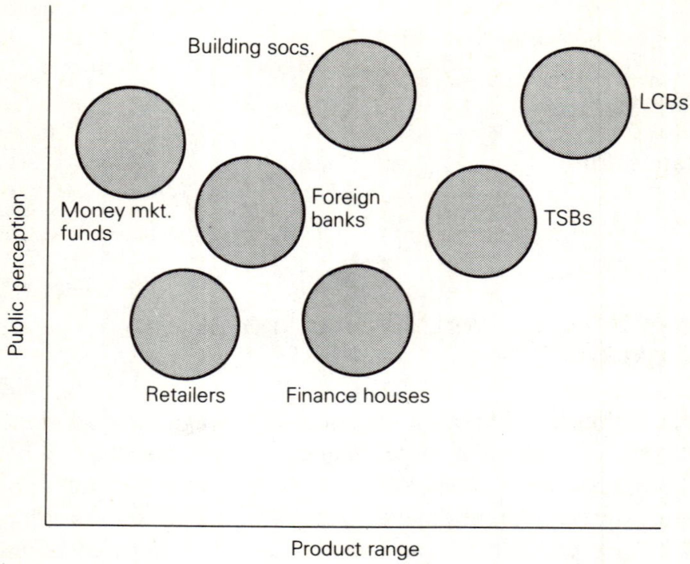

FIGURE 2.1 Market positions of major industry groups

them to join the clearing house oligopoly, a barrier to entry is created. Similarly the LCBs' investment in payment systems makes them vulnerable to new payment system processes, and acts as a barrier to exit, and possibly also as a mobility barrier.

The nature of industry positions in terms of exit and entry barriers, and the vulnerability of established positions in a market made more dynamic by technological and competitive pressures, mean that it becomes increasingly important to devise strategies based on the precepts of market position and the exploitation of mobility barriers.

Industry Evolution

In terms of the retail banking market it is more appropriate to talk in terms of industry group evolution. Although each group is competing in the same market, the different product/market/distribution strategies separate them as industry groups and give them different levels of business potential.

Evolution is analogous to the product life cycle, going through the phases of development, take off, growth, maturity, saturation and shake out. Each industry group experiences different evolutionary patterns, albeit that these are connected in a competitive sense. At a particular level, the building society industry group is still in a growth stage, finance houses in a shake out phase and LCBs are at a mature stage in their evolution. The retail bank market as a generalization, however, can be characterized as a mature market.

Evolution is caused by a number of interacting elements, not only those of competitive forces. Demographic influences, influencing the structure and preferences of customer segments, expansion or contraction in industry capacity, process and marketing innovation leading to different cost structures and government policy change are all instrumental in evolutionary change.

The state of evolutionary development influences the types of strategy that can be adopted, and the time spans within which they must be implemented. For instance the features of a mature market are slow growth and increasing competition for market share, more sophisticated customers, greater emphasis on cost and service and problems of industry overcapacity. In this situation, it is pointless gearing up an organization for growth. Not only do business strategies change, but so also do the functional strategies of marketing and operations.

A mature market requires a much more careful and analytical approach to problems; in the growth phase, strategy tends to be much more externalized and market orientated. At maturity, strategic problems become more internalized as the issues revolve around making the organization more efficient. As margins contract and competition increases, cost analysis and explicit, cost recovery pricing should become the norm. Competition also acts to focus the organization's sense of its own place in the industry, since the broad and sometimes diffuse approach to the market of an organization in its growth stage can be ineffective and inefficient as competition grows. An organization will therefore choose a market position, serving particular segments to maximize its investment.

A typical response of an organization at maturity is to attempt to maintain market position through introducing new products which compromise or supplant existing products, although those existing products provide the key to maintaining market position. This can lead to a serious decline in financial performance and may also affect the stability of management as it endeavours to adopt new strategies. It is part of an action that does not meet competition directly, but avoids it through attempting to create an independent market position. Action unrelated to market forces is often disastrous.

Central to the changing strategies and direction of an organization at the mature phase of evolution are organizational, management and personnel issues. The organizational dimension requires new structures and processes to meet changed circumstances. A multi-divisional structure at the corporate level to serve the different product market groups has been mentioned as an obvious way of serving the market more effectively and efficiently. The system permits not only a more focussed approach to marketing and operational problems but also permits the use of a variety of different business level strategies through the organization. The use of dedicated management and personnel within the framework of an integrated business level strategy should maximize the advantages to be gained from a concentration and specialization of resources.

To match the changed organizational structure the dynamics of management have to be changed. In a mature industry this entails greater attention to operating and controlling the organization and to marketing considerations. Management has to change its attitudes (and skills) to managing the new set of problems facing the organization. In the LCBs, a logical outcome of this process is to divisionalize domestic operations on the lines of personal, business and large corporate business, and to establish business units to serve those different broad market groups, treating each as a separate profit-making business. The present situation of an integrated but cross-subsidizing set of businesses operating a set of compromised strategies which attempt to achieve co-ordination leads to non-specific, unfocussed and inefficient lines of action.

At the personnel level in a mature industry, the problems are in scaling down expectations for business growth and financial performance, and also in career advancement. The strategic problems revolve around the creation of a cultural climate that reinforces corporate loyalty and facilitates the changes in business style that have to take place. The development of a corporate ethos to reinforce management and personnel attitudes is critical.

Business Level Strategy

Although the scope of LCB retail banking activity often tends to belong more to the corporate level, it is essentially, within the corporate matrix, a business level activity. At the business level, strategic concerns are marketing and operations based. The industry structure and its evolutionary stage will, as discussed, influence the marketing strategies that the business is able to operate.

At the operational level the concerns are to create systems that will provide the capacity and the flexibility required by the organization (i.e. computer systems that are able to process payment transactions rapidly and in large volume), which provide the basis for the 'manufacture' of a range of products/services, create economies of scale and provide a sufficiently wide range of methods of delivering products and services. The operations level creates the primary cost structure (plus the cost of raw materials) on which the pricing strategies are based.

It is the purpose of marketing strategies at the business level to choose particular market segments which appear most promising in profit terms to the organization. The choice is based upon the availability and quality of resources and existing distinctive competences, existing customer relationships, competition for segments, the potential of segments based on size, growth and business potential, measured in terms of needs, tastes and usage characteristics of that segment.

To serve those selected segments requires the organization to serve them at least as well as its competitors. Quality of service and corporate differentiation are key aspects of this, as are product quality, type and mix, selection and mix of delivery systems for those products, the application of technology, business and product branding and pricing policy. An organizational determinant of segment choice is the relationship it has to the overall choice of market strategy and other product market strategies.

Strategy Evaluation and Choice

The preceding discussion has outlined how different strategies are appropriate for different organizational levels and how, within an organization, different types of strategy can be employed, depending on the scope of product market choices, which are in turn a reflection of organizational structures and strategies. Organizational structures and strategies should be based on realistic appraisal of industry structure and the opportunities inherent in it, due to stage of industry evolution, and the underlying economics of operating in that market.

The critical aspect of strategy formulation is the final choice of a strategy for each level of the organization. An organization can have several competing strategies, but naturally they should at all levels complement the set of corporate objectives and goals represented in its strategy.

Strategy formulation is an analytical and creative process whose primary purpose is to maximize profit. To achieve this it has four priorities:

—Eliminate or minimize weakness
—Avoid threats
—Build and defend strengths
—Take advantage of opportunities.

There are six types of broad strategy that can be adopted, but which broadly depend on the stage of industry evolution:

—Share increasing —Growth	growth phase
—Profit —Consolidation	maturity

—Turn-around
—Liquidation } saturation and shake out.

Porter in his book on *Competition Strategy* identified a more refined view of the types of strategy that could be employed, suggesting that in essence there were only three generic types of strategy. These can all be employed at the different strategy phases just described, although their individual appropriateness between stages will vary. These are

—cost leadership
—differentiation
—focus.

Overall Cost Leadership This necessitates establishing economies of scale and building market share to benefit from potential scale economies. Anything which threatens those scale economies has to be abandoned. Product and customer strategies that avoid wasteful proliferation and specialization have to be pursued. Price competition to build market share is a feature of this generic strategy.

In the retail banking market there are a number of factors that make this strategy untenable amongst the LCB industry group. The maturity of the market in terms of account holding and industry structure means that the emphasis is placed more on profit maximization than growth. However, other industry groups, such as building societies who are expanding their market, are able to apply this strategy within their own industry group and in competition with other industry groups. An interesting feature of the retail banking market is that competing industry groups are oligopolies, which reinforces the intensity of interindustry group competition. Against this, however, price competition in the monetary sector can threaten economic stability, so it will always be controlled at some level by the authorities.

Differentiation This is based on image building through the use of technology, high quality of service and product design, and a good distribution/ delivery network. In the mature oligopolistic environment described above it probably represents the most attractive generic strategy. Costs, although remaining important in maintaining competitive parity, are not a prime strategic concern.

Focus This requires the concentration of resources on particular buyer, product or geographic groups. This may require cost leadership, differentiation or both. The scope of the LCBs' activities mean that at the generic level this is not a viable strategy, although at the segment level, or as a functional level strategy, it can be used. At the industry level this can be used by small, single product groups such as money market funds who have a far higher degree of flexibility than that possessed by the LCBs and building societies.

There are two subsidiary types of strategy that can be used. The first of these is diversification strategies, where the organization sees advantages in extending the scope of its activities by integrating into other service areas. The shift of the LCBs and building societies towards estate agency is a good example of developing existing mortgage business. Diversification has many advantages; it can reduce product costs or improve the quality of the product, help the organization move to a new industry position, improve its image and make greater use of the existing infrastructure. The LCBs potential entry into the life assurance market would bring all these advantages. Diversification strategies, to succeed, should be aligned with the distinctive competences and attitudes of the organization, and should fit in with the overall corporate/business strategy. The field of ancillary services represents the main potential growth area for LCBs.

Another strategy type is that of segment retreat, where an organization successively withdraws from the low-margin high-volume segments towards higher margin segments. However, it, exposes an organization to aggressive competitors or new entrants. It is a short-term profit strategy, and untenable unless, within the corporate business portfolio, the intention is to 'harvest' profits while gradually withdrawing from the market, or alternatively to use the profits for reinvestment in other segments.

These generic strategies provide the basis on which to identify strategy alternatives and to make decisions about a strategy choice. As generic strategies they represent very broad but distinct lines of action.

KEY FACTORS IN THE LCBs' RETAIL BANKING BUSINESS

This section is designed to provide an outline introduction to the following discussion, as well as a summary of the main management issues.

The LCBs' retail banking activities are subsumed under their general banking role serving a multitude of markets throughout the UK. Their infrastructures are used commonly between different business sectors. The cost structures of the different business sectors are difficult to ascertain because of the function of the LCBs as financial intermediaries between sectors. Management and control systems have been based on principles of a generalized and cross-subsidized approach to the market. Organizational biases are towards the traditional corporate business; with the emphasis on career progression being lending and branch based. The corporate cultures are not attuned to the structural shifts required by industry maturity and changing business patterns.

The LCBs, however, represent a cartelized oligopoly which is slowly beginning to fragment under competitive pressure. The patterns and styles of business have evolved through a long time span; the massive investment in these infrastructures means that the LCBs have a major commitment to remaining in those businesses (exit barriers and mobility barriers are high). The influence of these infrastructures at the management level is pervasive, limiting strategic thought and action.

The time spans for strategic decision making in the industry, because of the scope of the business and the concomitant levels of investment in infrastructure, are long. Decisions and choices although temporally spaced out are cumulative, i.e. a decision is largely determined by the preceding decision and represents a commitment that is difficult to reverse. Strategic time frames for planning purposes are therefore extended with strategic horizons extending for as long as a decade.

Strategy specific to the retail banking area is becoming more crucial for the following reasons.

- Competition is slowly undermining the LCBs' retail market position and in so doing affecting their performance in other areas due to increased cost of funds and overheads.
- Financial performance is generally worsening (due to competition and the stage of industry evolution).
- Technology is influencing the form, control and delivery of product groups, which in turn is affecting the competitive strengths of different industry groups and creating the realistic possibility of new entrants in the retail bank market.
- The overall level of risk is increasing at all levels of activity; products, pricing and market position are all vulnerable.
- There are limitations on the amount of resources available to protect and maintain traditional market positions. In addition, the need to invest in new technology, undertake new product launches and develop new businesses are all making major demands on capital.
- The ability to implement strategy is becoming more difficult given prevailing organization forms, corporate culture, management styles, distinctive competences and the costs of communication and education.

Given these factors the following categories and the potential influence they will have on the LCBs, and the LCBs' strategic response to them, will largely determine their future success.

Influence of Regulation and Legislation This will influence industry structure, the ability of industry groups to compete and will affect the profitability of the LCB industry groups.

Developing Competitive Structure Increasing competition amongst individual LCBs and between industry groups, and the threat of new entrants are producing significant changes in patterns of behaviour, and in the strategies required.

Technology Technology is bringing with it the need to introduce specific strategies, such as whether to be a leader or a follower. Its influences are potentially substantial. It is likely to increase competitioin through altering the present power equilibrium between industry groups, and in so doing increase or decrease profitability. The cost and speed of introduction will depend on competitive pressures, that is LCBs may opt for co-operative, rather than overtly competitive, technological strategies. It will certainly change labour patterns, increasing productivity and contributing to the need for cultural change within the LCBs.

Financial Performance The costs of developing and launching new products and introducing new technology will increase while simultaneously cost of funds will rise and margins contract. There will be an increased need for capital to finance change and growth; the cost of this will have to be measured both in market and opportunity cost terms.

Funding The size, mix, stability and cost of the retail deposit base relative to other sources of funding and the LCBs' share of the personal sector savings market will be crucial in influencing long-term profitability.

Lending Market share, margins and risk loan periods on a portfolio basis will require considerable management attention to maximize profitability.

Payment Systems Two principal questions will be related to payments systems. How far to invest in new systems, and secondly whether to invest in these on a co-operative basis with other operators in the market-place, or whether to operate on a purely proprietory and competitive basis, using branding techniques to establish market differentiation.

Delivery Systems The mix of delivery systems by number type and geographical location represents a key question to retail banking management. The future of branch networks in terms of size and function lies at the centre of this problem. Usefulness measures against other delivery systems and the opportunity costs of its operation and renewal in a period of pressure on profits represent a significant management dilemma.

Market Strategies The choice of which markets to operate in, and the choice of unique strategies for each segment based on a mix of product, price and delivery system and promotional package offer the chance to optimize profitability in a period of market maturity.

Management The dynamics measured in quality and knowledge terms, and its attitude to the retail banking sector will naturally determine the level of corporate resources dedicated to the market. In addition, its ability to work in a higher risk environment and to learn new skills underpin the LCBs' ability to introduce the organizational and cultural changes required by changing business patterns.

Part II The Environment

3 Financial Trends: the Personal Sector

Introduction

Amongst the environmental factors that determine the market position and business options of retail banking institutions, economic trends represent the most important element. Not only do they act as a quantitative measurement of market size and institutional market shares, but they also suggest the underlying dynamics of the market-place, which ultimately influence the structure of the industry and industry groups.

The financial trends, reflected in the distribution of liabilities and assets of the personal sector between financial institutions, are a combination of economic, competitive and regulatory factors. The degree of interdependence is considerable; for instance the inequality of fiscal advantages has contributed to institutional performance and moulded institutional differentiation. Personal sector behaviour is determined not only by competitive and marketing activity between institutions and industry groups, but also by a rational interpretation of the benefits that industry groups can offer in economic terms.

Traditional business biases also determine the nature of competitive response that an industry group will make, and the degree of influence it will be able to wield in the market. The LCBs have acted as financial intermediaries between sectors since their inception, acting to balance out personal sector surpluses with corporate and public sector deficits. The growth in the size of these surpluses and deficits has had two effects; it has emphasized the LCBs' reliance on the personal sector and has committed them further to corporate sector financing as that sector's reduced retained earnings and raising of funds on the capital markets have driven it to the LCBs, amongst others, for funds. The structure of the LCBs' balance sheets and the strategic commitments implicitly contained in them means that at a general level the LCBs cannot operate as flexibly in the personal market as the building societies. The structure of their asset and liabilities portfolio for example, together with differing regulatory and prudential controls has led to an entirely different maturity transformation and liquidity profile compared to that of the building societies resulting in an entirely different and less flexible cost structure.

The portfolio preferences of institutions are particularly important being largely responsible for institutional differentiation. Not only do they determine the type of service offered, but also rate of return, risk, access and period of investment. Consequently, a highly liquid form of investment offering a high degree of access, such as the low risk LCB seven-day account, does not offer the same rate of return as a term account at a building society. When entering a new market, institutions are consequently matching their own portfolio preferences with those of the potential customer. Moreover, success in maintaining market share or, indeed, of increasing it is similarly determined by the ability of institutions to provide products that satisfy the changing preferences of customers. The LCBs have failed to achieve this relative to building societies. However, it must be recognized that certain fiscal advantages associated with industry groups, such as life assurance and pension funds, building societies, unit and investment trusts and National Savings and government bonds have aggravated the situation by contributing to institutional differentiation and attractiveness, thereby influencing market choice.

Banks' business is philosophically established on making money out of interest rate differentials. The size of their operation allows them to benefit from economies of scale in the processes of collecting retail deposits and in lending, in maturity transformation and the lowering of risk to investors (and themselves). The role of financial intermediation between sectors has tended to lead to one sector benefiting at the cost of the other. Historically, the corporate sector has gained in two ways. Firstly, banks have geared the basis of their competitiveness towards corporate lending rather than funding strategies, being primarily concerned with asset formation rather than actively accumulating retail deposits. Companies have gained because banks have been prepared to compete for lending business on rate. Depositors have taken second place because there were always enough funds available from one source or another (the development of the wholesale money market was related to this) to fund competitive assset formation, depressing the rate the banks were prepared to pay for deposits. The assumption that the payment services they offered served partially to discount the rate paid on retail deposits added to the relatively low return awarded depositors. Secondly, this sectoral and rating structure in a period of high inflation means that even with negative real rates of interest, as experienced up to 1981, a sector with a surplus will subsidize a group which is a borrower. Tables 3.1 and 3.2 illustrate this clearly. The LCBs' attitude towards their role as financial intermediators and their contingent rate structure has meant that they have subsidized the corporate sector at the direct cost of the personal sector.

This approach has had various effects: the building societies who act as financial intermediaries to just the personal sector are in a much better

Table 3.1 Notional loss/gain on real value of net monetary assets/liabilities by sector: 1970–81 (£ billion)

	1970	1971	1972	1973	1974	1975	1976	1977	1978	1979[a]	1980[a]	1981[a]
Sectoral net monetary assets (+) liabilities (–) mid-year estimates												
Personal sector	39.4	43.3	45.7	47.8	52.9	58.7	65.8	73.9	81.3	93.6	110.6	122.3
Company sector	– 5.5	8.0	– 8.8	– 10.7	– 14.8	– 15.6	– 14.4	– 13.8	– 11.8	– 15.1	– 24.0	– 24.9
Public sector[b]	– 38.0	– 39.1	– 40.8	– 42.5	– 45.7	– 52.9	– 63.8	– 72.5	– 78.2	– 85.8	– 95.1	– 108.5
Total domestic sector	– 4.1	– 3.8	– 3.9	– 5.4	– 7.6	– 9.8	– 12.4	– 12.3	– 8.8	– 7.2	– 8.5	– 11.2
Overseas sector	4.1	3.8	3.9	5.4	7.6	9.8	12.4	12.3	8.8	7.9	8.0	8.5
Change in consumers' expenditure deflator (Q4–Q4) (%)	7.2	8.0	7.7	9.7	20.2	23.4	14.3	12.4	8.5	16.8	12.9	10.9
Notional loss on net monetary assets (gain on net monetary liabilities)[c]												
Personal sector	– 2.8	– 3.5	– 3.5	– 4.6	– 10.7	– 13.7	– 9.3	– 9.2	– 7.0	– 15.8	– 14.3	– 13.3
Company sector	0.4	0.6	0.6	0.8	3.0	3.3	1.5	1.9	0.9	3.2	– 3.9	2.4
Public sector	2.7	3.2	3.1	4.0	9.3	11.9	7.5	9.4	6.7	14.5	12.2	12.0
Total domestic sector	0.3	0.3	0.3	0.3	1.5	1.5	0.3	2.0	0.6	1.9	– 1.7	1.1
Overseas sector	– 0.3	– 0.3	– 0.3	– 0.3	– 1.5	– 1.5	– 0.3	– 2.0	– 0.6	– 2.0	– 1.5	– 0.4

[a] Bank estimates. The sectoral estimates of net monetary assets in these years are not wholly consistent.
[b] Since December 1978 gold in the official reserves has been valued taking account of market prices, and is hence treated as a non-monetary asset from that date.
[c] The notional loss or gain is not equal to the product (sign reversed) of sectoral net monetary assets/liabilities and the change in the consumers' expenditure deflator, because of the different deflator used for foreign currency denominated monetary assets and liabilities (shown above). For such assets and liabilities, the rate of change of the consumers' expenditure deflator is taken net of the percentage change in the effective exchange rate (expressed in terms of foreign currency per unit of sterling).
Source: Bank of England Quarterly Bulletin, June 1982

Table 3.2 Total financial transactions: 1973–83 (£ billion: 1983 prices) (Increase in assets (+) Increase in liabilities (−))

	1973–77[a]	1978–82[a]	1983
Public sector	−13.6	−11.3	−11.1
Financial sector	− 0.8	− 1.3	− 0.6
Industrial and commercial companies	− 4.4	− 0.5	+ 2.6
Personal sector	+16.3	+16.7	+10.3
Overseas sector	+ 2.5	− 3.6	− 1.2

[a] Annual averages.
Source: BEQB, June 1984

position to achieve a more equal distribution of favours between borrowers and savers, and as a direct consequence have benefited more in terms of market share. Cost structures and fiscal advantages have also helped the situation. Customers of building societies are able to borrow money to fund house purchase, an investment which throughout the 1970s, in capital growth and utility terms, has outstripped any other investment. Consequently, the personal sector as borrowers were able to benefit from its own sectoral financial assets. As investors they have been increasingly rewarded by the building societies in terms of rate, to attract funds away from competitors. The building society philosophy, unlike that of the banks has been based principally on retail deposit based funding strategies rather than funding asset formation.

Three factors, then, have contributed to the building societies position:

- Their exclusive involvement in the personal sector.
- Their ability to offer equally attractive (and connected) advantages to both borrower and saver.
- A philosophy of putting the emphasis on the collection of deposits and competing on that basis, rather than competing on asset formation and funding in a retrospective spirit. The influence of this on funding mixes and costs are significant.

Building societies gain in another way from the nature of their business. Banks rely on sectoral surpluses (e.g. the personal sector's savings ratio) for funds, whereas the building societies, mediating between savers and borrowers in the personal sector, are much less dependent on such surpluses. When building societies lend to the personal sector, for example, they also increase the volume of funds available for reinvestment to that sector and these can be used for reinvestment with financial institutions. To take a specific example, a building society may make a loan of £10,000 to a borrower who pays it over to a vendor who promptly deposits it with a building society. The sources and uses of funds in the personal sector and of banks have increased by £10,000, but the overall position of the sector is unchanged as is the savings ratio. The building societies by remaining almost entirely within the personal sector are relatively unaffected by changes in the savings ratio, which is a measure of the extent that funds of individuals are available for investing in other sectors.

Finally banks are disadvantaged further by having to suffer more than any other financial industry group from financial control. This has taken a number of forms such as capital adequacy requirements based on the type and mix of assets for prudential reasons, and a fixed ratio for monetary control reasons. This is largely because since bank deposits form the basis for most popular definitions of money supply, the banks are seen as the main propellants of money supply. As a consequence of these measures and other economic conditions the banks have not been able to operate a systematic long-term strategy towards asset/liability management. PSL2 which in addition to bank deposits includes savings deposits with building societies and the National Savings Bank has not been used as an official definition of money supply, leaving building societies in particular outside the ambit of government monetary control.

Overall, a variety of circumstances, historical, competitive, regulatory and fiscal have contributed to inequalities within the market-place. Differences in business philosophy have exacerbated these trends. It will now be worthwhile to analyse the trends on a quantitative basis to show the financial trends of the personal sector, and to illustrate causal connections between those trends.

Financial Trends of the Personal Sector

The balance sheet for the personal sector given in table 3.3 shows the broad disposition of the sectors assets and liabilities. Dwellings are the single most important asset, followed at some distance by consumer durables. Financial assets' most important elements are equity in life assurance and pension funds. Ordinary shares still form an important component of the sector's assets, although there has been a steady decline in its importance in the sector's portfolio. Indirect holding of company equity through assurance companies and pension funds has become more preferable, with some concern now being shown by the authorities for the distortions this may be inducing in the supply of capital to industry. The removal of fiscal incentives on life assurance and the reduction on stamp duty on share dealings is a step towards correcting these trends.

Table 3.3 Personal sector balance sheet (£ billion)

	1975	1980	1981	1982
Physical assets				
Property	137.5	300.7 (est.)	273.3	
Consumer durables	38.2	50.0	86.3	N/A
Other	33.9	71.5	72.3	
Financial assets				
Notes and coin	4.8	8.4	8.9	9.3
Bank deposits – sight	8.1	14.2	15.6	20.1
– time	11.3	23.2	25.9	31.6
Building society deposits	22.2	49.4	56.7	66.9
National savings certificates	8.0	12.1	18.2	21.8
Savings bank	2.8	7.6	6.1	5.4
Central and local government: debt and loan	9.0	14.5	14.7	20.1
Other financial institutions	0.2	0.2	0.3	0.3
Trade and other debtors	6.9	8.6	14.4	14.2
Unit trusts	1.9	3.2	3.2	4.6
Life assurance – pension funds	33.5	89.0	105.0	135.0
Shares, debt and loan stock	26.2	40.9	46.8	55.8
Other	5.6	9.9	12.7	12.9
	140.5	281.2	328.5	398.0
Financial liabilities				
Bank loans	5.8	14.7	18.5	25.2
Instalment credit	2.1	5.0	5.3	2.8
Loans – house purchase	25.0	52.2	61.7	76.0
Domestic trade and other credit	4.8	9.8	9.9	10.0
Other	1.9	3.3	3.3	3.9
	39.6	85.0	98.7	117.9

Source: Report of the Committee to Review the Functioning of Financial Institutions, Central Statistical Office (*Financial Statistics*)

Liquid assets make up approximately a third by value of financial assets. These are principally placed with building societies and banks. By the end of 1982, the two accounted for £118.6 billion, with building societies accounting for 56 per cent of this.

National Savings has substantially increased its share of the market from £12.1 billion in 1980 to £21.7 billion in 1982. The twin incentives for this are to reduce the fiscal burden and to avoid recourse to the banking sector, which would in turn increase money supply.

Table 3.4 Percentage growth 1980–82 on selected categories of personal sector savings

	1980–81 (%)	1981–82 (%)
Bank deposits – sight	9.9	13.6
– time	11.6	5.6
Building societies	14.0	17.0
Assurance and pension funds	18.0	28.0
National savings	50[a]	19.0

[a] Government funding policy turned towards the use of personal sector savings; in 1980–81 national savings certificates attracted £6.1 billion, to take their share to £18.2 billion or 5.5 per cent of the total saving market, compared to the banks sight and time deposits of £15.6 billion and £25.9 billion respectively.
Source: Central Statistical Office

When percentage increases by sector between the periods 1980–81 and 1981–82 are analysed (Table 3.4) they show that in a period of high savings the LCBs and other banks in the personal sector failed to maintain market share, since the growth of their deposit base has not been commensurate with the growth in the market.

On the liabilities side, the single most important element, complementing the sector's investment in housing, is loans for house purchase. Building societies had, at the end of 1982, £56.9 billion outstanding out of a total of £75.9 billion; banks had lent £10.7 billion. In the post-1980 period, with the relaxation of credit controls on the banks, and the removal on term and deposit controls on HP agreements and car loans, there has been a major growth in lending for borrowing other than housing.

Personal disposable income (PDI), which is income after deductions for tax and national insurance provides a key basis for judging trends in the personal sector. In figure 3.1 the graph shows how borrowing for house purchase has become the central feature of the personal sector, reaching a peak in 1982 at 7.6 per cent of PDI. The substantial rise may in some measure be attributable to the fall in interest rates during 1982 (see figure 3.6), but this acts only to reinforce broad trends. Other borrowing has tended to imitate the increase in borrowing for house purchase, although remaining lower than in 1972–73. Figure 3.2 reinforces the points made in figure 3.1 showing how borrowing for house purchase is the most important element of the personal sector's liabilities, and how, despite growth in the borrowing for other purposes, it is assuming an ever greater proportion of the personal sector's liabilities.

Viewed in strategic terms, and taking into account the market role of building societies discussed in the introduction, it becomes clear that if the LCBs had remained outside the house finance market their role in the personal

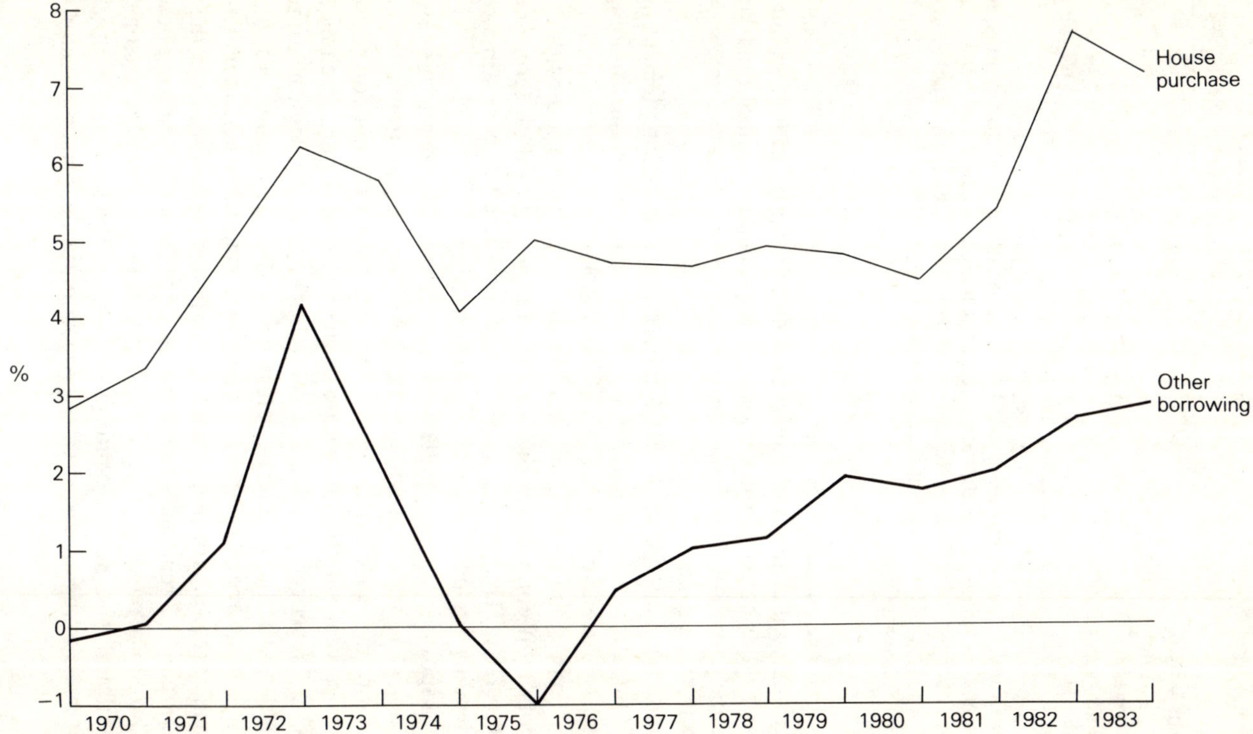

FIGURE 3.1 Ratios of borrowing to PDI: 1970–83
(*Source:* Central Statistical Office)

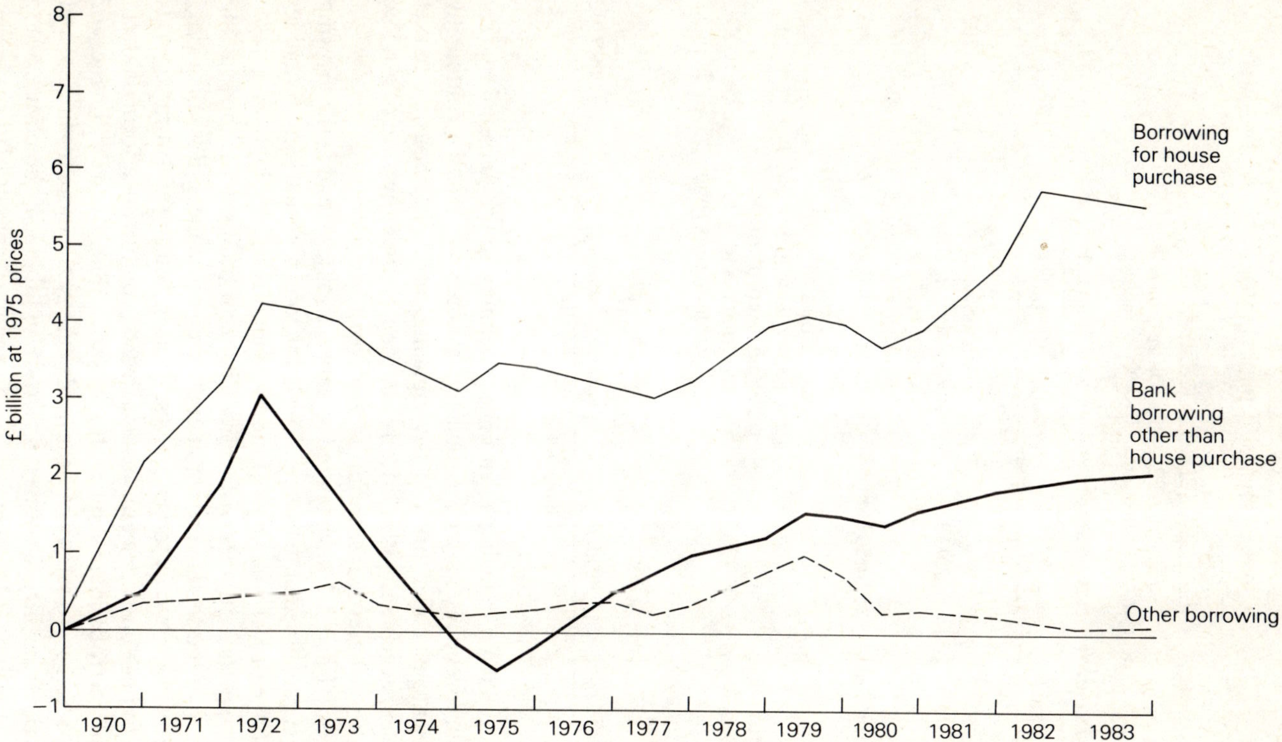

FIGURE 3.2 Borrowing in real terms: 1970–83
(*Source:* Central Statistical Office)

Table 3.5 Personal sector debt ratio

1975	1980	1981	1982
53.4	50.8	59.1	62.9

Source: Central Statistical Office (*Financial Statistics Economic Trends*)

Table 3.6 Personal sector – sources and uses of funds: 1983

Sources of funds		Uses of funds	
Saving	22,257	Taxes on capital and transfers	1,302
Capital transfers	2,439	Investment in fixed assets and stocks	15,423
Borrowing for house purchase	14,594	Acquisition of liquid assets	17,065
Other borrowing	5,720	Acquisition of public sector securities	– 41
Accruals and unidentified	– 36	Acquisitioin of life assurance and superannuation funds	15,171
Sale of company securities etc.	3,946		
Total	48,920	Total	48,920

Source: Central Statistical Office (*Financial Statistics*)

sector would have diminished even faster. Lending to the personal market for other purposes does not grow as quickly, is more volatile and is continually either subject to or under threat of government control. The housing market is socially very acceptable, is politically immune, representing long-term low risk assets for whatever institution is involved.

As figures 3.1 and 3.2 have tended to show, a major trend is the growing level of the personal sector debt ratio. This is the total personal sector liabilities as a percentage of PDI. It is now standing at an historically high level (table 3.5). This suggests a number of factors. The most important is the growing sophistication of the personal sector in organizing its finances. It is borrowing, as table 3.6 shows, not only to make investments in housing and durable goods but also to finance investment in financial assets, conducting a form of asset/liability and portfolio management. It also shows the growing willingness of the sector to borrow to satisfy present needs against the more traditional and prudential thrift instinct. However, as shown in table 3.6, the nature of the investment decisions in housing and in financial instruments offering higher returns or different liquidity characteristics tend to be almost wholly rational.

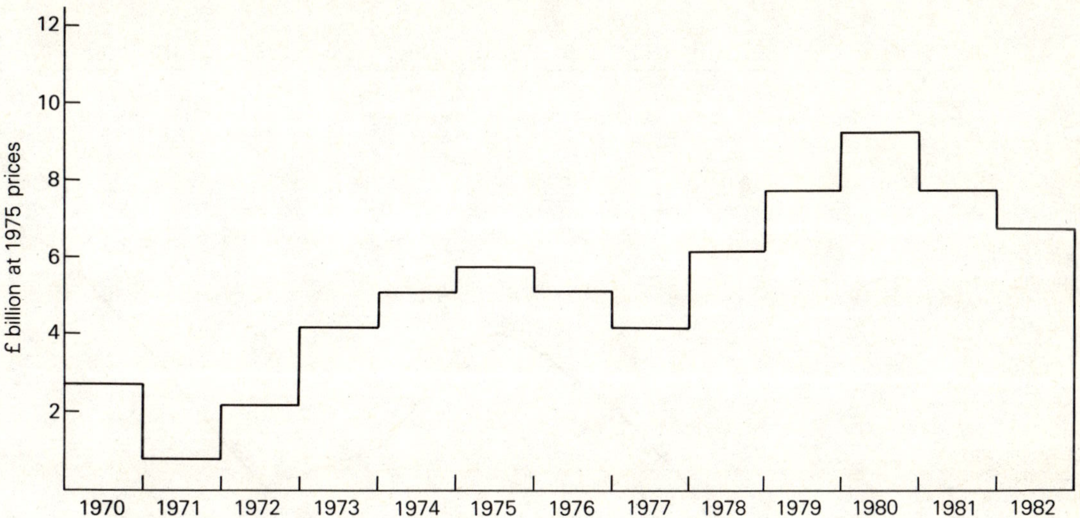

FIGURE 3.3 Net acquisition of financial assets in real terms: 1970–82
(*Source:* Central Statistical Office)

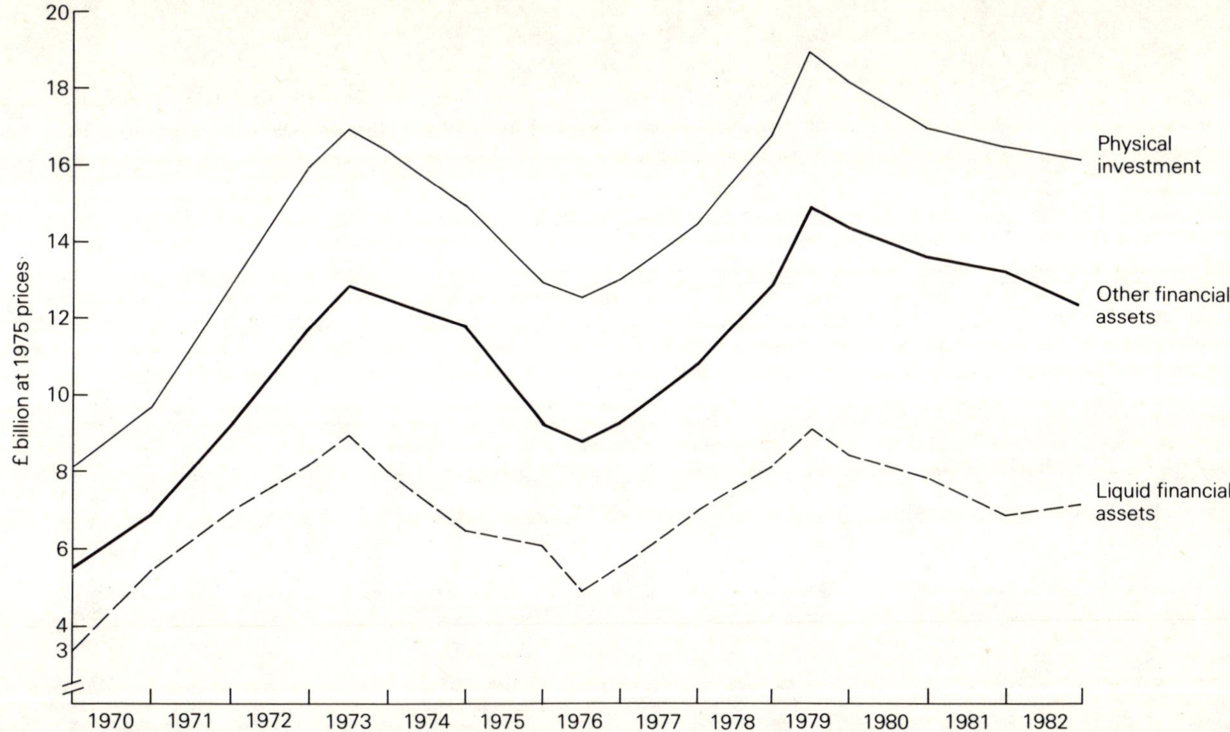

FIGURE 3.4 Gross acquisition of financial and physical assets in real terms: 1970–82
(*Source:* Central Statistical Office)

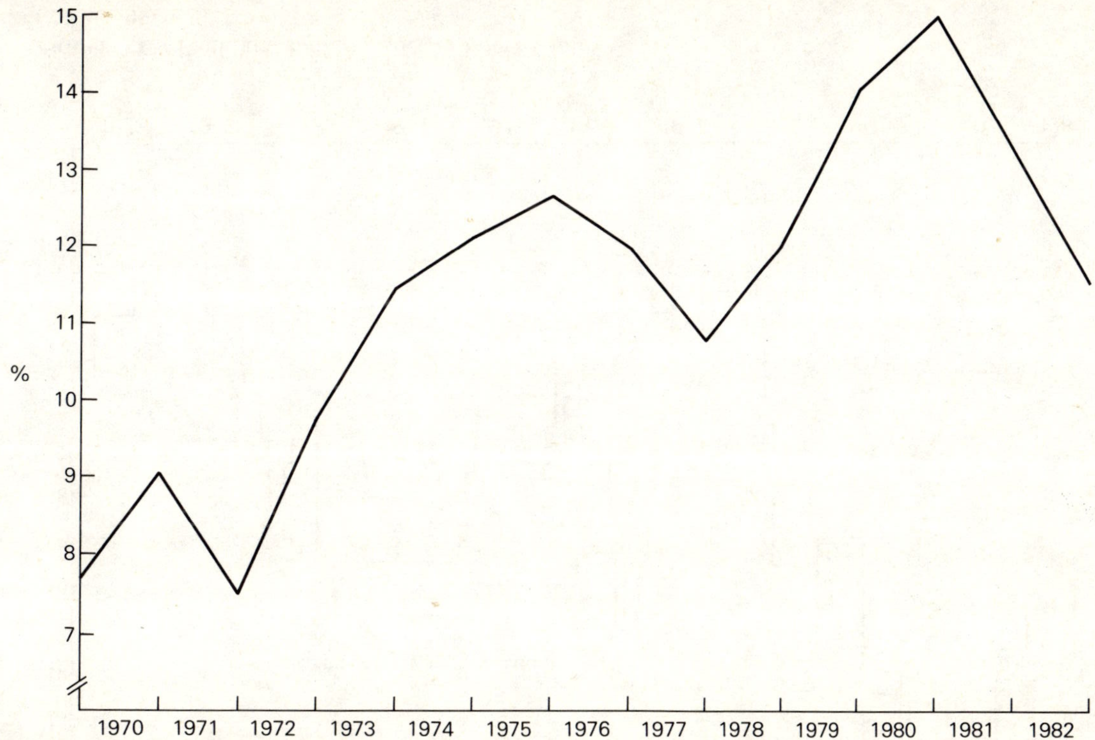

FIGURE 3.5 Savings ratio: 1970–82
(*Source:* Central Statistical Office)

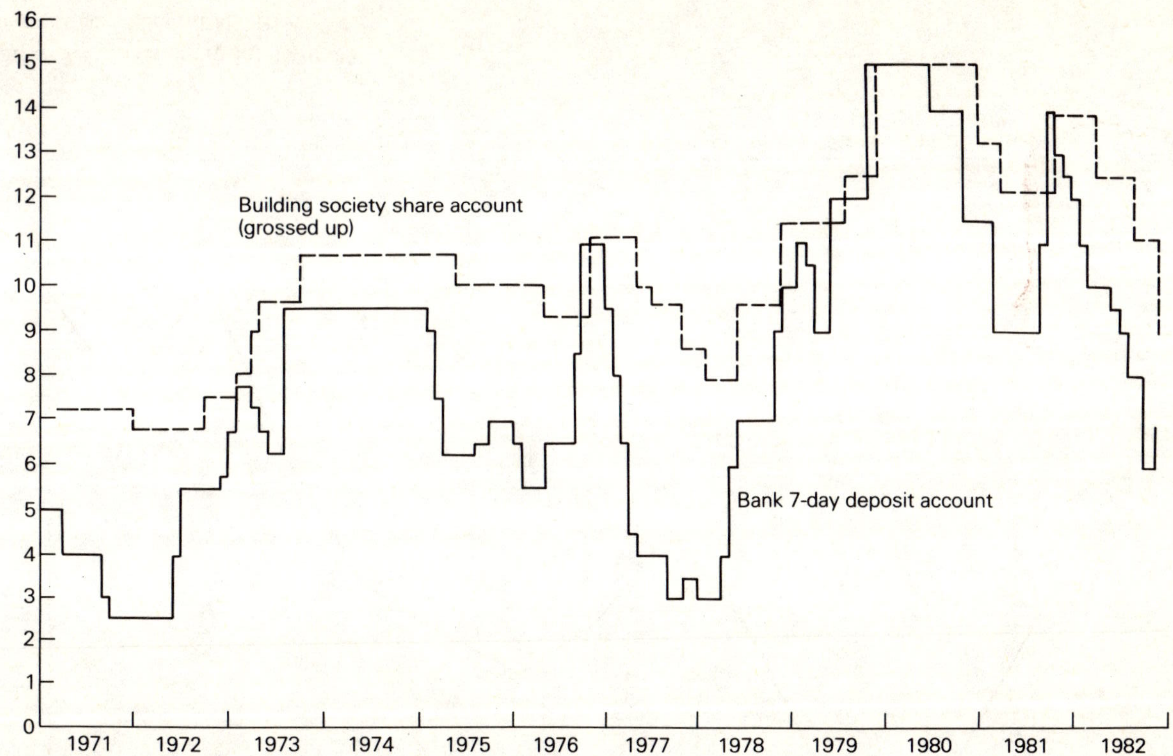

FIGURE 3.6 Bank and building society interest rates
(*Source:* BEQB)

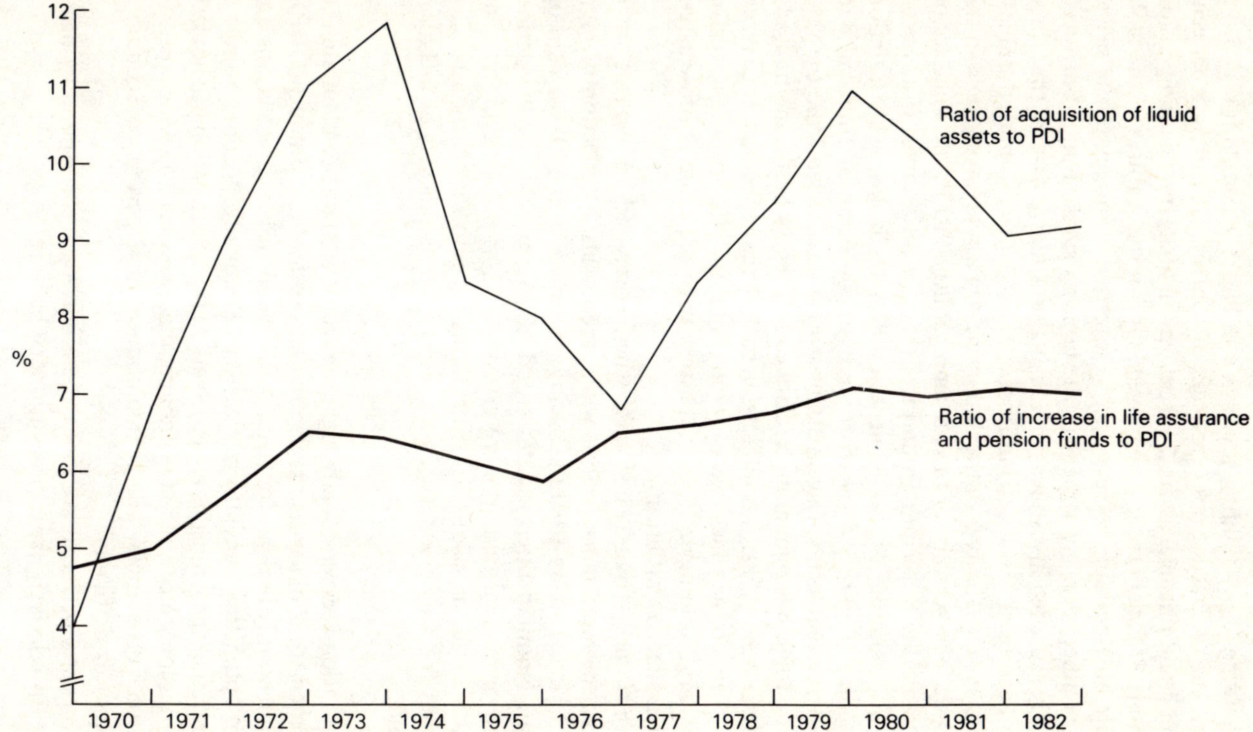

FIGURE 3.7 Ratios of acquisition of financial assets to PDI
(*Source:* Central Statistical Office)

Table 3.6 shows that savings accounts for only 45.5 per cent of the sector's funds. Borrowing from building societies and banks accounts for 41.5 per cent and the sale of shares for 8.0 per cent of sources. Of this 34.8 per cent is invested in liquid financial assets, 31.0 per cent in life assurance and pension funds and only 31.5 per cent in fixed assets. One of the features of the table is to indicate how building societies act as a source of money to the sector for purposes other than investment in the housing stock. Funds borrowed have regularly exceeded investment in housing; it is fair to assume that these funds have been used for acquiring financial assets or consumer durables.

On the assets side (figure 3.3) the real monetary assets have grown in the period 1970–82. The reasons for this are ambiguous; either the personal sector has been attempting to recoup ground lost through inflation or it has been attempting to maintain a ratio of new liquid assets in line with inflation adjusted income. Figure 3.4 shows the gross acquisition of financial and physical assets in real terms. Levels of investment have fallen from the very high levels of 1979, but remain high relative to the early 1970s, maintaining trends set during the 1970s. It is interesting to note that considerations other than purely economic ones were responsible for the personal sector maintaining large holdings of financial assets when the value of those assets were being eroded by inflation.

The savings ratio (figure 3.5) has, when compared to interest rates responded to the high interest rates, which are in turn a reflection of high rates of inflation. During 1980 the savings ratio stood at 14.8 per cent or £23.7 billion. Nominal interest rates stood at 15 per cent. In the period 1980–81, however, real savings were assessed at £4.5 billion or 6 per cent of adjusted income, most of this being funnelled into monetary assets.

The reasons for the personal sector's response to high levels of inflation are threefold.

1 When inflation is exceptionally high, the sector attempts to maintain the level of their stock of saving in relation to gross domestic product (GDP). This is not wholly logical, for reasons discussed earlier. The reasons are based on optimism or an illusion created by nominally high interest rates: optimism, since there must be an anticipatiion that the inflation will not last long, or illusion, since it might be thought that real wealth is being created.
2 Precautionary balances will be maintained in a period of economic uncertainty or difficulty.
3 Where incomes per head are lower there may be a corresponding need to build up relatively large precautionary balances.

When committed and discretionary savings flows are analysed over the period 1970–82 (figure 3.7) it shows that movements in the savings ratio to PDI have important influences on the money available to the financial sector. The trend shows that despite a fall-back in recent years it has been rising from about 7.5 per cent in the late 1960s to about 10 per cent in 1982.

This can be chiefly attributed to the growth in contractual savings, chiefly in payments into life assurance and pension funds; these have risen from 4.6 per cent of PDI in 1966 to 7.1 per cent in 1982. The trends, if uncorrected, suggest that this element would grow even stronger through time, with the effect of disturbing the overall balance of savings in the personal sector, since precautionary and speculative aspects of savings would have been increasingly covered by this group. However, the removal of the fiscal benefits enjoyed by life assurance policies and the growing encouragement of the personal sector to invest directly in shares should have two effects. Firstly, it should lead to some redistribution of the personal sector's savings amongst institutions, and secondly, it will encourage direct investment in shares, reversing post-war trends.

The acquisition of liquid assets has by comparison been more volatile, with a substantial increase taking place in the early 1970s, when it rose from 4 per cent of PDI to 12 per cent of PDI in 1973 when an explosion in money supply and credit availability took place. How far this was an abnormally high share, that would have been dissipated by normal market forces without the economic crisis of 1973, is debatable. The period 1973–76 saw a return to a more normal state of affairs, but the rise in the period 1976–79 is not so closely correlated with bank borrowing as it was in 1973, but reflects a real growth in PDI. (This was probably a contributory factor in 1969–73.) The periods of a declining real value of PDI between 1973–76 and 1979–82 are reflected in falls in the accumulation of liquid financial assets. The logical inference is that the accumulation of such assets is something of a luxury for the personal sector. The implication for banks is that competition for deposits will intensify in a period of low PDI growth, reflected in high interest rates.

The personal sector's borrowing requirement, especially from banks, also acts to reduce the availability of financial assets, and depresses the savings ratio. As figure 3.1 shows, the ratio of borrowing to PDI was low during the late 1960s; this was due to quantitative lending controls. The sharp rise of 1971 was due to competition and credit control, but was brought back to low levels by the mid-1970s by the twin elements of recession and supplementary special deposits (SSDs). The removal of SSDs in 1980 saw banks readjusting and expanding their portfolios, mainly in the area of house loans. Loans for house purchase recorded the highest ever increase relative to PDI in real terms in 1982.

Liquid savings as a totality are volatile and rate sensitive when compared to life-assurance and pension funds (figure 3.7). The components of liquid savings (table 3.7) also reflect particular responses to interest rates.

Table 3.7 Net discretionary savings through liquid assets as a percentage of PDI

	1979	1980	1981	1982
Notes and coins	0.4	0.4	0.2	0.3
Bank deposits	4.7	4.1	2.3	2.0
National savings	0.8	0.8	2.4	1.8
Building societies	4.3	4.5	4.1	5.4

Source: Central Statistical Office.

Non-interest savings as a percentage of PDI peaked in 1971 and 1977 when 7-day deposit rates were 3 per cent. When MLR began to rise, the proportion of sight deposits to PDI fell; in 1980 when MLR stood at 15 per cent, this proportion fell to an all-time low. *It appears that the growth in current account balances is inversely proportional to the level of interest rates, and have, in fact, grown at only half the rate of inflation.*

The period when bank deposits and building society share rates were at the same level, in 1979, the shares of PDI attracted were respectively 4.7 per cent and 4.3 per cent (although the proportion of bank sight deposits to time deposits was 27 per cent).

The relationship between interest rate and share of deposits gained as a percentage of PDI emphatically demonstrates that the savings market is highly rate sensitive. With 45 per cent of building society accounts standing as premia accounts, the banks' position has correspondingly worsened. National savings certificates offering highly attractive, fiscally boosted rates further support this argument.

Conclusions

An analysis of economic trends demonstrates the weakness of the banking sector in the savings market. There are numerous reasons for this, but central to the banks' situation is a structural and rational shift in the portfolio preferences of the personal sector.

The factors are related to the banks' financial role in the personal sector, to their business philosophy and attitude towards the retail sector and retail deposits, as well as the rational, economic choices of the personal sector. The banks have treated retail deposits as a cheap source of funds, without reciprocating by historically providing relatively cheap home loans and personal lending facilities. Retail deposits were seen as a sectoral surplus to be lent primarily to the corporate sector; additionally the banks competed on the asset side of the balance sheet, being primarily concerned with funding loans rather than collecting deposits. This was reflected in the rate structure for corporate loans and retail deposits. Building societies, however, provided a balanced service to the personal sector, providing increasingly good returns to investors and relatively cheap home loans. The societies benefited from effectively creating their own market, with interest rate strutures related to this equilibrium and the simplicity of a market position which was concerned only with the personal sector.

The competitive disparity between banks, building societies and other institutions can be adduced to other factors. The personal customer seeks a combination of convenience, access, maturity, rate and security in its choice of savings instruments. Sensitivity to rate has been demonstrated in the liquid assets of the personal sector. Nevertheless, banks have consistently failed to compete on rate, competing for deposits on the basis of other services provided. Payment systems have predominated in this thinking, with non-interest bearing sight deposits and cheque-book accounts being one of the most important elements in their funding strategy. In the sector's mind, transaction balances are utility balances; building society investments are much more a luxury item, offering higher interest rates but reduced access and convenience. Banks tend to hold money for cash-flow purposes, building societies for investment; the distinction accounts for the difference in volumes attracted by the respective industry groups.

The preference for national savings and building society investments over banks for investment purposes is helped by fiscally boosted interest rates. Contractual savings schemes are similarly helped by fiscal incentives.

Ostensibly, a distinction exists in the market between long-term and short-term liquid investment. The growing preference for contractual savings schemes will, arguably, affect flows of funds to the liquid assets sector, which will become progressively more a 'luxury' preference. Building societies are the most vulnerable to such a squeeze, unless they begin imitating the utility services of banks, which they are beginning to do.

However, there is a wider implication from this trend, which is an attitudinal one. If a distinction is drawn between long-term and short-term savings, as banks and building societies see themselves pursuing only the liquid savings sector, they are limiting their strategic options in the savings sector. It must be, increasingly, a prime strategic concern of banks and building societies to gain access to the long-term saving markets.

In general terms, the personal sector is becoming more sophisticated, making rational decisions about portfolio content and exercising simple forms of asset–liability management in their borrowing for house purchase and for investment in financial assets. Housing, however, is the key to this behaviour, and essentially any institution, to optimize its presence in the personal market on both sides of the balance sheet, should be involved in this market.

Banks, however, find themselves in an invidious position on the basis of this analysis.

- They cannot offer fiscally boosted interest rates.
- They suffer from regulation which makes competition more costly and disrupts long-term strategic planning.
- They have developed a business philosophy and role which militates against a successful presence in the retail market.
- Their cost structures as a result of their intersectoral financial intermediation role are different from their competitors.
- They are not perceived as savings institutions, but providers of payment services that require transaction balances, not investment.
- They are not well placed to exploit the structural shift taking place in the savings market.

The LCBs are faced with a number of considerations. These include:

- Becoming more fully involved in the personal sector, offering an integrated range of products on both sides of the balance sheet.
- Extending the dimensions of competition in the savings market beyond the liquid savings category.
- Shifting the balance of reward away from borrowers to depositors, and competing more on the basis of funding strategies than asset formation.
- Using existing systems to attract greater volumes of retail deposits, e.g. paying interest on current accounts.
- Being prepared to pay higher rates of interest on deposits, as competition for personal sector savings intensifies.

4 The Personal Sector Market

Introduction

The economic background to the personal sector has illustrated the broad trends taking place. This chapter will first review the characteristics of the market in socio-economic terms, and the distribution of wealth by socio-economic category. It will then analyse the market in terms of the proportion of the population who have accounts, by institutions, supplementing that information by looking at patterns of wage and salary payments, and sources and uses of cash.

The change in the distribution of wealth shown in table 4.1 is connected with economic, political and structural changes which took place throughout the period in question and induced changes in the distribution of personal disposable income (shown in table 4.2).

The gap has narrowed between skilled and unskilled workers due primarily to trade union power. This has increased prosperity amongst the C2/D groups mainly at the cost of the C1 groups. Overall, increasing prosperity and the redistribution of wealth and income have brought many people into income groups that make them attractive to the banks as potential customers; however, changes in the distribution of wealth have been marked not only by structural shifts in the patterns of employment, from primary and secondary industries to tertiary (service-based) industries, but also by the increased financial sophistication of the average man in the street.

Consequently, the banks too, when attracting and satisfying existing and new customers in the personal sector have had to adopt more increasingly sophisticated services and marketing techniques.

Account Holding in the UK, and the Use of Financial Services

The changed social structure, the redistribution of wealth, the growth in competition linked to the pursuit of profit and changing attitudes and needs

Table 4.1 Distribution of wealth

	1966 (% of wealth)	1979 (% of wealth)
Most wealthy 1% of population	33	24
Most wealthy 2% of population	42	32
Most wealthy 5% of population	56	45
Most wealthy 10% of population	69	59
Most wealthy 25% of population	87	82
Most wealthy 50% of population	97	95
Least wealthy 50% of population	3	5

Source: Annual Abstract of Statistics

Table 4.2 Changes in the shares of total personal income: 1959 and 1976–77

	Income shares			
	1959		1976/77	
Quartile group	Before tax	After tax	Before tax	After tax
Top 1%	8.4	5.3	5.4	3.5
Top 2–10%	21.0	19.9	20.4	18.9
Top 11–50%	47.5	49.7	49.7	50.0
Bottom 50%	23.1	25.0	24.5	27.6

Source: Diamond Commission, Report No. 7

in the market-place have led to a substantial growth in the numbers of 'banked' people in the UK.

An analysis of the banked population shows that the UK does not match North America or France in terms of the adult population who have bank accounts. This has occurred due to three factors: firstly, unlike France, for instance, there has been a singular lack of government involvement in promoting the banking habit; secondly, legislation in the UK, particularly the Truck Acts have reinforced workers' conservative preferences for wage payments in cash; and finally, the perception of financial service needs and the contingent attitude towards financial institutions has remained myopic and anachronistic. Hence building societies, who traditionally provided a linked and simple range of services, have been preferred by large sections of the population who neither want the full range of services provided by the bank and worse, tend to be intimidated by the very notion of a bank.

Nevertheless the growth in financial institutions is partly a function of the growing financial needs of the population and a change in their attitudes.

Table 4.3 Account holding in the UK: 1982

	Types of account		National	
Total population	Bank current account (%)	Bank deposit account (%)	Building society (%)	Savings bank (%)
	63 (45)	31 (30)	51 (30)	20
Male	68 (50)	33 (32)	52 (31)	22
Female	55 (40)	30 (39)	49 (29)	25
Age				
16–24	50	24	50	
25–34	75	30	64	
35–44	75	35	47	N/A
45–54	65	37	47	
55–64	58	36	61	
65+	46	32	35	
Socio-economic class				
AB	89	32	69	29.1
C1	80	33	59	24.9
C2	59	33	48	21.3
D	37	29	41	20.8
E	17	27	21	20.9

Figures in brackets indicate 1976 position.
Source: Adapted BRMB and IBRO

The apparent failure of the banks to seize a larger proportion of the population is partly due to their own inability to change and adapt to the needs and demands of the new market and to the simple fact that large proportions of the market, as demonstrated by the first two tables, remain commercially unattractive.

Table 4.3 shows how much the financial institutions have made inroads into the population in the last six years, with the main thrust of expansion occurring amongst the upper socio-economic classes and amongst the working population.

When the unbanked are analysed by demographic feature (table 4.4) it appears that the potential for growth in bank account holding is limited to the youth market and women. The female component is, however, compromised since many of this group are unemployed or have access to a husband's account. Of the 16.5 million 'unbanked', 23 per cent have a bank deposit account, 21 per cent have a post office/NSB account and 40 per cent have a building society account. Many of those who do not have an account will have access to an account. Given these facts, the idea of the UK having an unbanked market appears to be a myth.

Table 4.4 Demographic features of the unbanked: 1981

	%
Total unbanked	16.5 million
Male	39
Female	61
Age	
16–24	24
25–34	12
35–44	10
45–54	13
55–64	15
65 +	26
Socio-economic group	
AB	5
C1	12
C2	32
D	30
E	21
Employed	39
Unemployed	61

Source: BRMB + IBRO

Table 4.5 Market shares of banked population of UK banks: 1983 (£ million)

Bank	Current a/c	Retail deposit	Time deposit	Wholesale deposit
Barclays	5,929 (26.2)	5,929 (29.2)	N/A	13,594 (71.4)
Lloyds	3,943 (17.3)	4,582 (22.6)	6,358 (35.5)	N/A
Midland	5,977 (26.3)	4,290 (21.1)	N/A	5,447 (28.6)
National Westminster	6,817 (30.1)	5,487 (27.1)	11,529 (64.5)	N/A
	22,666 (100.0)	20,288 (100.0)	17,887 (100.0)	19,041 (100.0)

Percentages shown in parentheses.
Source: Compiled from annual reports

The distribution of the banked population amongst the major UK clearing banks is shown in table 4.5. Despite the dominant position of the LCBs, the provision of a full range of banking services available to all account holders has not been sufficient to stave off very substantial competition for deposits, particularly from building societies and national savings. Although the success of these latter two sectors was partly due to their 'privileged' position, it was

Table 4.6 Consumer credit – balance outstanding 1978–82: 31 December 1983 (£ million, current prices)

	1978	%	1979	%	1980	%	1981	%	1982	%	1983	%
Banks[a]	4,741	57.9	5,618	57.4	6,742	58.9	8,792	63.1	12,655	81.8	15,085	78.8
TSBs	84	1.0	160	1.6	239	2.1	331	2.4	N/A	–	N/A	–
Finance houses	2,017	24.7	2,441	24.9	2,767	24.2	3,039	21.8	1,202	7.8	2,929	15.3
Insurance companies	248	3.0	240	2.5	271	2.4	295	2.1	N/A	–	938	4.9
Retailers durable goods, dept. stores, others	641	7.8	774	7.9	711	6.2	742	5.3	813	5.3	192	1.0
Mail order	460	5.6	554	5.7	716	6.2	744	5.3	782	5.1	N/A	–
Total	8,191	100.0	9,787	100.0	11,446	100.0	13,943	100.0	15,452	100.0	19,144	100.0

[a] Up to 1981 includes consumer companies recognized as banks. From 1982 includes consumer credit companies licensed to take deposits.

Source: CSO Financial Statistics; Business Monitor SDM6, SDM8

equally due to the LCBs' obsession, throughout the 1970s, with wholesale money and their commensurate neglect of the retail money market.

The banks, however, have performed better in the consumer credit market, holding a share commensurate with their current account penetration of the UK population, at about 65 per cent.

However, when it is considered that much lending by value will be to higher socio-economic categories, of which the banks have a much higher share, then their performance compared to finance houses and to a lesser extent retailers appears less assured. The reasons for their failure to achieve a more substantial market share, at least commensurate with the potential suggested by account holding, are attitudinal and historical: attitudinal, because the banks have suffered from the same image problems as in the savings market – people have tended to dislike going to a bank to ask for a loan, and have preferred the more covert methods of obtaining a loan through a finance house or at the point-of-sale either through a retailer credit scheme or a finance house; historical, because the government has traditionally placed restitutions on the banks' involvement in consumer credit. Limiting the banks' presence in the market, and stimulating disintermediation through finance houses, has induced a traditional preference for the corporate lending market. With the relaxation of controls, banks, as shown in table 4.6, have begun to increase their share of outstandings in the market quite dramatically.

Consumer credit outstanding at the end of 1982 was £15,452 million (£19,144 million in 1983) a small amount compared with the personal sector's liabilities for housing loans which at the end of 1982 were £76.0 billion. Until 1980 this was a market that the banks had largely stayed out of, despite its size and central role in the public sector's finances. In strategic terms this was an abnegation that meant the banks could only have a peripheral involvement in the sector, except in the provision of payment services through current accounts.

Table 4.7, however, shows how the banks' entry into the market had the effect of boosting the market rather than diminishing the building societies' involvement. This growth not only reflects the effects of increased competition

Table 4.7 Volumes of mortgage lending by institutional group: 1978–82 (£ million)

Year	Total	Building societies	Local authorities	Insurance companies	Monetary sector and TSB	Other
1978	38,533	31,715	2,900	1,623	1,805	500
1979	45,010	36,986	3,193	1,854	2,403	574
1980	52,296	42,708	3,654	2,117	2,996	821
1981	61,759	49,039	3,906	2,204	5,441	1,169
1982	75,914	56,894	4,447	2,365	10,714	1,494

Source: Annual Abstract of Statistics

Table 4.8 Tenure of dwellings (millions of dwellings)

	1960	1970	1980
Rented from private owners and other tenures	5.24	3.77	2.80
Rented from local authorities or new town corporations	4.40	5.85	6.82
Owner occupied	6.97	9.57	11.91

Source: Abstract of Statistics and Long Range Planning, October 1982

Table 4.9 Media by which workers in UK received wage and salary payments (%)

	1969	1976	1979	1981
Bank Giro Credit and other	15	29	32	41
Cheque	10	12	14	15
Cash	75	59	54	44
Total workers (millions)	25	25	25	23.5

Source: IBRO

in a market that had traditionally operated a cartel, but also the social and political trends towards house ownership in the UK. This is clearly indicated in table 4.8.

Wage and Salary Payments

The banks' prime institutional role in the personal sector, is the provision of a money transmission service. To provide an optimum service both to themselves, and to the economy at large, would entail the efficient use of bank accounts by all economically active adults. A significant step in this direction would be heralded by the introduction of electronic fund transfer systems on a significant scale thereby reducing reliance upon cash and other paper bases and the revocation of the Truck Acts, thereby encouraging major employers to pay directly into accounts and workers to open such accounts. As the tables 4.9, 4.10 and 4.11 show, the patterns of wage and salary payment still remain biased towards cash and to weekly payment, although there is

Table 4.10 Frequency of payment (%)

	1976	1979	1981
Monthly	33	36	42
Weekly	67	64	58

Source: IBRO

Table 4.11 Distribution of payment types by socio-economic category: 1981 (%)

	Other	Bank Giro Credit	Cheque	Cash
AB	5	70	16	9
C1	5	56	19	20
C2	5	32	15	48
D	1	38	7	54

Source: IBRO

a gradual shift towards more efficient payment media. Conservatism is mainly demonstrated by the C2 and D social groups; although redistribution of wealth means that these groups are better off, the volume and value of their spending patterns together with their payments profile substantially undermines the advantages gained from obtaining those accounts.

Given the economics of operating payment systems, there is a point where the benefits of obtaining new accounts are counterbalanced by the disbenefits of processing large volumes of low value payments emanating from those newly gained accounts.

Without strong competitive pressure, it would still be rational for economic factors to lead to greater account holding and the more efficient use of payment systems. The development of more economic and efficient payment systems, to service what were regarded as marginal business areas, would complement this process. To an extent, this seems to be taking place but the competitive pressure to maintain market share in an expanding market will inevitably result in moves downmarket, forcing the speed of change and resulting in the banks taking on unprofitable business until payment systems and technology can catch up. The dilemma that banks face today is one of preparing for the future (but it may be that new accounts gained now will never be profitable) and simultaneously establishing a profitable basis for business in the present. Whatever happens, a primary concern remains to make the use of payment systems more efficient.

SOURCES AND USES OF CASH

A direct corollary to the efficient inpayment of wages and salaries is the use that bank customers make of their accounts and the requirement that they have for cash. Cash handling is costly, impinges upon the banks' efficiency and profitability, and requires substantial investment simply to provide that service. It is estimated that cash costs the banks some £500–700 million per annum, being highly expensive relative to other payment media. The value and volumes of cash transactions going through banks have increased substantially in the last five years, due to inflation and an increase in the number of banked, who maintain a strong preference for cash over other bank payment media. In the period 1976–81, the flow of cash from employers to employees has fallen commensurate with greater account holding, while amounts of cash obtained from banks and post offices has increased commensurate with the increase in state benefits. It is predicted that this will begin to decline by 1986 for the following reasons.

- A growth in the banked population, linked to increasing financial sophistication of the banked market.
- A slow trend towards cashless pay.
- With growing affluence and sophistication an increased use of bank payments media. Indeed the average bank account holder made about 40 per cent more bank media payments – cheque, credit card, direct debit and standing order – in 1981 compared to 1976. However, between 1976 and 1981, the amount of cash provided by banks increased from £18 billion to £24 billion, accounting for about 30 per cent of the personal sector's cash requirement.

As the banks' payment burden grows within the economy, their will be an onus to improve the quality, cost-efficiency and convenience of the systems. The strategies for achieving this will be founded on automation and establishing economies of scale, often in co-operation with other institutions.

5 Social Trends

Introduction

The greater the level of market penetration achieved by financial institutions the more susceptible they become to broad social changes reflected in changing attitudes and behaviour. But more pertinently competition means that as the institutions become more actively involved in marketing themselves and their products so they must in turn take greater account of customer behaviour if they are to succeed.

Analysis and reaction to social trends is generally encapsulated in market research. But the responses formulated tend to be reactive and short term, without helping an organization to make the long-term structural changes for sustained success in the market. There is a need for a strategic view of social change which should, along with analysis of other environmental factors, lead to an integrated organizational response. It should also be emphasized that social change is something which affects the internal substance of an organization just as much as its adaptation to the market place. Cultural change within an organization is an adjustment which encompasses not only a different philosophical and management perception of how the organization should be operating in the market place, but which should also accommodate fundamental disparities of cultural outlook amongst personnel working inside the organization. These are complex issues; strategy can be fudged by not assessing the implications. Organizations can become outdated simply because they lack the ability to adapt and conform to the requirements of society. In a competitive market the pressure for change becomes greater, and the urgency to find the right solution paramount. But even without pressurized competition, cultural change is important since it affects the organic health of the organization and its place in the market.

Social Change and Trends in the UK

With social change there is a particular difficulty in assessing the relationships between cause and effect. There is a similar difficulty in matching quantitative data to valid comment. Retrospective social analysis is difficult; to hypothesize the impact on business conditions of current trends is even more problematic. However, there is a difference between broad evolutionary change which can take decades, and mercurial switches in fashion. Financial institutions have to ensure that their organizational reactions are based mainly on social change not changes in taste. It is the job of marketing to control and implement short-term responses.

In the UK there are some major quantitive changes taking place that will in a straightforward way influence business policies: changes in the demography of the population by age, employment and regional distribution. Changing distribution of wealth and income of house ownership have already been analysed, but belong to the same process of shifts in the social structure. The following details illustrate the nature of these quantitively measured social changes.

The birth rate declined between 1964 and 1977, with the birth rate in the 1970s being the lowest in the century. At the other end of the age spectrum, increased life expectancy has increased the proportion of elderly people. The proportion of males to females in the population in 1980 is given in table 5.1.

Regional distribution of population has changed little in the past 20 years with the South-east having the largest proportion of population. The changes in regional distribution and the distribution of wealth have significant implications for branch and marketing segmentation strategies that the banks employ. Movements within regions are also highly significant. Although the places of employment have tended to remain linked to city centres (especially with the emergence of tertiary industries) and to new towns, residences have systematically shifted to suburban and rural areas away from city centres. For instance the population of Greater London fell from 8 million in 1961 to 6.8 million in 1980. Educational changes have a marked influence on the attitudes and sophistication of the market. One of the major changes of the last twenty years has been the explosion in graduate numbers, with the growth in numbers of universities. Throughout the 1970s numbers of undergraduates rose from 192,700 in 1970 to 252,000 in 1980. The overall effect has been

Table 5.1 Population of UK by age and sex: 1980 (millions)

	Under 16	16–29	30–44	45–64	Over 64	Total
Males	6.6	6.0	5.4	6.1	3.2	27.3
Females	6.3	5.7	5.3	6.4	5.0	28.7
Total	12.9	11.7	10.7	12.5	8.2	56.0

Source: Annual Abstract of Statistics

to produce a more discerning market, and has contributed to changing patterns of financial behaviour, seen in more sophisticated financial requirements, greater price sensitivity and a lowering of customer loyalty.

However, against trends which can be measured, there have taken place unprecedented social changes in the past 25 years that have fundamentally altered the individual's perceptions of the society he lives in and the way in which he behaves within that social context.

There are certain elements that are more responsible than others for these changes. They are naturally all interrelated. The emergence of the mass media, the growth of education, the decline of religion, the birth control pill and technology have all contributed to a repatterning of social mores and attitudes. Inflation and unemployment have added to this combination of factors, contributing to patterns of social behaviour such as the propensity to save and acquire houses.

The development in communication and especially social and environmental awareness have led to society beginning to fragment, to perceive itself as made up of distinct, separate groups. The western liberal tradition has contributed to the establishment and acceptance of pluralistic beliefs. The ideas of distinct groups sharing equally valid, though different viewpoints has not only exerted internal pressures on society, but has given it an impulse for change. The multiplying of 'issues' is a feature of the age; environmentalism, consumerism, sexual and political equality, minority groups and nationalism are a few examples of this.

At the individual level there exists a view that the established hierarchy of power, found within society as a whole and within institutions, is not credible. This has had some radical affects: a gap has emerged between the expectations of the individual in terms of better wages, working conditions and job fulfilment, and the failure of the system to deliver them, has produced a disenchantment and distrust of government and the large, impersonal organization.

Individualism, always a recurrent feature of western culture, has manifested itself in the way an individual seeks greater involvement in determining his job, and in the quality of response he expects from service organizations such as banks.

Social change at the cultural level will be matched by a changing working environment. This is seen in the high unemployment continuing with the restructuring of the industrial base. The restructuring of the working environment, coupled to the cultural factors outlined above, will lead to earlier retirement and a shorter working week, although this trend will be constrained by a requirement for higher productivity. As technological change helps to change the patterns of work, it will bring about ageing of skills or the need to renew existing skills to keep pace. Education in mid-life will progressively feature in social life. It is difficult to evaluate the impact of these factors. It is important to stress that social issues will be as imporant to the internal workings of retail banking institutions, as to their role in the market. Changes in attitude, behaviour, in cultural and work expectation will influence the way business styles, organization structures and personnel planning and training adapt to strategic requirements. In the relationship with the market, the retail banks will have to face a more demanding client base. The range and quality of services, and the style of the institution will all have to reflect this. To overcome the problems of competing in an increasingly fragmenting market, institutions will have to pursue segmentation strategies increasingly based on attitudinal and behavioural rather than socio-economic characteristics, providing marketing policies attuned to those chosen segments' needs and wants.

Finally, public relations skills and the activity of retail banking institutions will have to become correspondingly much more sophisticated, to match the segmentation based business strategies and to create and communicate images to meet those segmentations' expectations of an institution.

Throughout, the retail banks, as service institutions in an increasingly service orientated society, will have to evolve at the same speed as the society in which they operate.

6 The Political Condition: Regulation, Legislation and Control

Introduction

The concern in this chapter is to view the impact of politics on the retail banking environment in the widest sense, ranging from governmental policies to the protection of the individual user. The effect and level of strategic consideration will be measured in structural terms; namely the influence these have on the way competition has evolved and on the way the individual institution has responded and is able to respond.

Political belief and action pervades the whole retail banking environment. It ranges from the macro-control of the economy to the quality of service received by the individual. These can be analysed as follows:

—monetary control
—supervision and regulation
—protection of user.

As retail bank deposits form a significant element in most commonly used definitions of money supply, retail banking typically finds itself frustrated by deflationary measures instigated by government monetary policy. This frustration is further compounded by unfair and conflicting government directions which, for instance, have conferred special tax advantages on building societies in the past and still exclude their deposits from money supply definitions. The market, already volatile because of competitive and technological factors, is also at the mercy of changes in government policy.

The purposes of political action are based on ideological premisses about how institutional structures should work, In France this has assumed an extreme form with nationalization; in the UK, nationalization has been a recurrent theme through the mid-1970s but has largely dissipated itself into a number of smaller concerns related to the operation and control of market mechanisms. This concern with institutional activity is reflected in ensuring the system will carry out government economic and social policy, such as the control of inflation through money supply. The maintenance of confidence in the system by ensuring its stability and security is a prerequisite of this. The last aspect of government's policy concern is to ensure that the individual user obtains the best service out of the system.

The clearing banks have a central role in the fabric of economic activity. Not only does the financial structure rest on them, but as prime agents in the creation of credit and money growth they are the most vulnerable to government policy and intervention. Building societies who have encouraged home ownership have conversely been shielded from government action and encouraged by fiscal measures in their activity. Likewise, life assurance funds and pension funds have received fiscal support, and the government's own borrowing through gilts and national savings has been given a boost through fiscal incentives. The government therefore is free to introduce substantial distortions into the market in the pursuit of its policies.

Background

The past 20 years have been a period of considerable innovation and change, but with the banks' place within the system alternately encouraged and curtailed. Between 1965 and 1971 lending ceilings were imposed on the LCBs inducing them to concentrate on priority borrowers, and remain largely outside the consumer sector (although the first credit card appeared in 1966). During this period the banks were encouraged to disclose their true profit figures and reserves, a move which accelerated their commercial development.

In 1971, the introduction of competition and credit control heralded the breaking up of the self-protective cartelized oligopoly of the LCBs. As part of a government plan to 'kick-start' the economy, direct credit controls were also abandoned in 1971. Credit ceilings were abolished, controls of instalment credit were suspended and tax deductability of personal interest payments were restored.

The reasoning behind these measures was to ensure that credit growth was controlled by cost rather than rationing. However, the market showed itself insensitive to cost; the banks reverted increasingly to wholesale money markets and to sophisticated techniques of liability management. The result was that the relationship between money supply and interest rates was overturned. Not only did the authorities fail in their prime objective of controlling money supply, but the resultant high rates of interest had undesirable side-effects throughout the economy. Resort was made to direct controls, the most notable, perhaps, being the 'corset', the supplementary special deposit scheme, which was introduced at various times between 1974 and 1980. Such measures not only had little impact in controlling the growth in bank balance sheets but were not conducive to the spirit of competition and credit control.

Throughout this period the banks persisted with the same business philosophy as before, namely concentration upon the relatively cheaper money in the wholesale money markets and a relative avoidance of the personal sector, arguably encouraged by the Bank of England directives, and reinforced by term and deposit controls on certain categories of consumer lending. The consequence of this was that on the asset side of their balance sheets the LCBs did not pursue a rational portfolio policy. This resulted not only in frequent disturbances in the provision of bank credit but also enabled less powerful institutions, particularly finance houses and later Building Societies, to profitably exist and gain significant footholds in the provision of credit in the personal sector national savings schemes. This also affected, to a more limited extent, the growth and nature of the banks liability preferences.

Supervision and control within this context were synonomous, ensuring that balance sheet growth was not excessive. But controls that are primarily designed for prudential purposes are closely intertwined with monetary control requirements. So, in addition to the issues outlined above, the banks have been in the position of finding themselves constrained from two directions. The history of supervision complements the development of the LCBs' business. In the period before 1971, the static market for credit meant that there was little need for a highly developed system of external supervisory regulation. Self-regulation and the informal directives of the Bank of England were sufficient to maintain adequate standards of liquidity and capital adequacy. Liquidity was important as a process of meeting depositors calls on money, the maturing of liabilities and to meet running costs. Capital was seen as important to absorb losses, to provide risk capital, vitally to give confidence in the system and to provide a mechanism to control unreasonable growth.

In a relatively simple environment, broad brush gearing and quick asset ratios were sufficient to fulfil all these functions. However, as liability management became more sophisticated, and portfolios of assets and liabilities requiring extended degrees of maturity transformation more complex, then emphasis became focussed on liquidity rather than capital.

Today capital adequacy still represents a prudential requirement, having replaced the basic reserve asset ratio, and is calculated individually for each LCB, utilizing three principles: free capital (funds employed less net fixed assets, trade investments and current liabilities); gearing (loan capital as a percentage of total capital employed); and risk asset ratio (the banks' quantification of the different level of risk appertaining to different types of asset and relating these weighted risks to the banks' available capital). Nevertheless, capital adequacy, despite its lessening importance in prudential terms, still plays a central part in determining the scale and mix of portfolio choice, and acts as a key feature in strategy formulation through the allocation of resources.

There is now also a requirement on the LCBs to maintain a ratio of liquid or near liquid assets to eligible liabilities. The system introduced in 1981, replacing the reserves asset ratio, means that the banks have to maintain a rolling average of 5 per cent of eligible liabilities with the London Discount Market, in addition to a non-operational, non-interest bearing balance with the Bank of England representing a half per cent of eligible liabilities. Clearing banks have also to maintain an operational balance for the purposes of clearing. The holding of these assets not only constrains the lending activities of the LCBs but also increases their average cost of funds relative to non-eligible competitors.

The overall growth in supervision and control of the LCBs is a direct consequence of the growth in their business and the impact they are able to make in the economy. Although these controls have been applied to the LCBs' total operations, they directly affect the nature and competitiveness of their retail banking operations. The availability of credit, the freedom to exercise balance sheet management and the overall cost competitiveness of their position are all influenced by monetary and prudential considerations, and undermine to an extent their ability to implement and operate coherent long-term strategies.

Governmental influence has extended to other areas of the retail banking environment, again acting to develop market conditions inimical to the free development of competitive strategies. Building societies have been largely favoured by successive governments. Capital gearing and liquidity requirements are much less severe with the societies. Monetary authorities have focussed on the monetary aggregate M3 which is primarily composed of bank deposits, rather than PSL2 the aggregate including building society deposits in their control of money supply. They have also benefited from considerable fiscal advantages: they pay a lower corporate tax than banks; traditionally have paid a composite tax rate on deposits which gives them an approximate 1 per cent advantage in price competition for deposits; and pay no capital gains on increase in property value. The building society movement has grown almost as an inevitable consequence of these 'privileges'.

Fiscal advantage is used as a common governmental method for stimulating certain sectors: National Savings Bank has offered non-taxable interest on the first £70. Life assurance and pension funds gain considerable benefit from lower rates of taxation imposed on subscribers. The effective distortion in free-market prices is compounded by the government's willingness to sell public debt at relatively high rates of interest. The influence of all these measures is to produce a situation where the competitive equilibrium has been disturbed by government, and hence politically based action.

Government has also worked to introduce new groups into the competitive environment in an attempt to stimulate greater competition, make the system more efficient and to provide a greater range of choice to the individual. The full effect of these measures has yet to be felt. The Page Report of 1973 encouraged the formation of a third force in banking through the phased diversification of TSBs, and the Post Office (Bank Services) Act 1976 encouraged National Girobank. Today both the TSB and National Giro are regarded as substantial competitors in the retail bank market and have the potential to make even more significant inroads into the market.

On a wider scale the government-led restructuring of the stock market and its intervention in the Lloyd's insurance market point to a situation where political belief, when it is not satisfied with existing 'market' conditions, will act to deregulate, demonopolize and restructure the market to create more 'perfect' conditions.

The implications of this are manifold and profound at the industry level. For the political system will act to create new balances of power to serve itself and the market better. It will be discriminatory, favouring certain groups over others, but the overall impact of a 'free-market' philosophy is to create a situation where the fastest moving and fastest thinking will benefit most. It should also move towards removing the competitive anomalies outlined earlier. The National Consumer Council report on *Banking Services and the Consumer* (1984) for instance, recommended the removal of the building societies' advantageous composite tax. However, rather than abolish composite tax, the government simply extended its application to interest bearing bank deposits in 1985.

Traditionally there has always been an apparent contradiction between the efficient functioning of the financial system and political intention manifest in monetary and financial control. For example, the banking system regards capital and liquidity as being essentially associated with the diversification of activities and the amelioration of risk, but the authorities regard them as essential components in controlling monetary aggregates.

The changing tenor of the market towards greater competitiveness has a number of significant implications for both banks and supervisors: the emphasis on liquidity as a function of balance sheet management and maturity transformation will become greater as competitiveness increases interest rate sensitivity, especially amongst the retail deposit sector. Substantial investment in new fixed assets to facilitate competitiveness and efficiency will raise questions against the traditional role, value and adequacy of capital.

The nature of supervisory authorities will also become increasingly more complex as groups of financial institutions become less homogenous. For instance, the Registrar of Friendly Societies does not have the responsibility nor the power to control building societies if they diversify into the provision of banking services. The Bank of England and Department of Trade and Industry will need much closer co-operation to monitor and control the interconnection of insurance companies and banks. Technology itself will allow some institutions to avoid the Banking Act because they will not take deposits, thereby necessitating the need for some alternative form of supervision.

There are political penalties and responsibilities for increasing the scope of the market, and this must be primarily seen in equality of treatment between industry groups. Whilst this does not occur the LCBs, for example, will suffer discrimination to the direct advantage of new and existing competitors in the retail banking area.

THE POLITICAL ASPECT AND THE INDIVIDUAL

Political influences on the system outlined above occur at the macro-level, affecting the individual institutions and industry group's role and ability to compete. At the micro-level this is found in the very governmental agencies campaign for change for the best interests of the individual consumer. The legislation most pertinent to the retail banking sector is the Consumer Credit Act (1974). Also, the activities of the National Consumer Council and the Office of Fair Trading are highly influential in forming government action.

The Consumer Credit Act is intended to provide consumer protection in all credit transactions. It belongs to a general pattern of consumer legislation – the Trade Descriptions Act, 1968; Fair Trading Act, 1968; Supply of Goods Act, 1973; and Unfair Contract Terms Act, 1977. The principles behind it, concerned with providing a comparative pricing system, fair advertising and limitations on canvassing and the methods used in persuading the consumer, are straightforward and laudable. The details of the Act, however, have proved to be complex and expensive to implement. Designed to protect the consumer from rogue firms, it has produced blanket legislation which means bona fide operators such as the LCBs have been as restricted as the small peripheral operators. But the restrictions extend only to credit providers and exclude building societies, insurance firms, and so on.

The 1984 NCC report on *Banking Services and the Consumer*, following on from its earlier *Consumers and Credit*, makes a wider range of recommendations to the government and banks concerning the operation of the retail banking environment. The recommendations to government favour equalizing the competitive situation by abolishing institutional and fiscal inequalities between building societies and banks, such as extending the societies' activities, abolishing the recommended rate system and imposing equal corporate tax treatment between banks and building societies. It makes direct recommendations about derestricting the LCBs' virtual monopoly on money transmission. It also recommends direct and indirect interventionist activity to improve the service and choice available to the consumer, such as a government sponsored small-saver scheme, raising the £50 cheque guarantee limit and ensuring that the terms and conditions of electronic payment systems are equal to the existing systems.

The existence of such reports, whilst at one level contributing to the quality of service received by the individual, do encourage the development of the market-place at a rate which may be beyond its structural capabilities. They also illustrate the inherent tensions and paradoxes of an industry that has to serve and function within an environment that is commercially motivated and yet, as an instrument of monetary policy, be bound by the ruling governments 'free market' principles. Finally the industry has to service consumers within a mandate increasingly shaped by idealist consumer organizations, which are themselves fulfilling a mixture of government dogma and liberal belief.

CONCLUSIONS

Political influence in the retail bank environment is wide-ranging, affecting the strategic direction of financial institutions at the macro-level through a variety of control measures. The effect in the past has been to alter the balance of power within the market.

The present trends, seen at both the macro- and micro-level, are towards direct intervention or influence through the appropriate authorities to achieve a more efficient structure; this entails removing restrictions in the market-place to providing greater levels of service to the customer. The dichotomies of the political decision mean that a variety of purposes have often to be fulfilled through single lines of action, e.g. monetary control and prudential supervision. The regulation has tended to be unilateral rather than multilateral, leading to an inequitable distribution of competitive power between institutions. The current political trend, however, is interventionist towards creating free-market mechanisms, in the spirit of 1971 and competition and credit control, rather than towards manipulating the market towards more overt ideological ambition, such as directing the flow of funds and controlling institutions directly. Political influence in this respect has become positive and market associated. The institutions that respond to this will gain the greatest advantage.

The strategic implications for the LCBs, and other commercial operations within the retail bank market are as follows:

- Long-term strategies are highly vulnerable to government action. It means that such strategies have to be flexible enough to accommodate such changes.
- The history of government action shows that banks are often used for overtly political purposes in a pragmatic way, rather than as a direct consequence of their own activities. It would seem that the banks' strategies should be less politically sensitive and more commercial.
- The LCBs are the most vulnerable group, partly as a consequence of the spread of their activities and partly because of their economic function. Until equal fiscal and regulatory treatment of competing industry groups becomes a reality, the LCBs will always be suffering competitive disadvantage.
- The increasing complexity and homogeneity of the market-place will not only lead to greater problems for the regulatory authorities but, in the long-term, it should also lead to a more equitable political treatment of competing groups in the retail market.

7 Technology

INTRODUCTION

The critical questions surrounding technology revolve around whether it should be seen as a means or an end, a threat or an opportunity, a revolution or an evolution. The breadth of its application through an organization, the choice of technologies and the speed of its introduction are questions fundamental to the competitive posture and organizational structure that institutions will be able to adopt in the future.

The impetus for the adoption of technology is determined almost wholly by competitive considerations. As competitors grow more efficient and the structure of the competitive market changes, operators in that market-place in terms of quality, breadth and price of service, need to respond. The threats and opportunities, implicit in new technology are based on managing the organization and its place in the environment better. Fundamental to this idea lies the efficient management of costs and profitability. Cost structures are based on the efficiency of the organization in its distribution and use of resources. These impinge upon the size of its net profit figure and contribute to the flexibility of strategic and marketing response the organization can make in a competitive sense. Profitability, however, is mainly a function of competitiveness measured in terms of the quality and attractiveness of a service, its distribution and its price. Technology is in a position to provide the mechanisms to solve these questions. Improved efficiency in processing and in the distribution of resources, a greater use of those resources such as the customer base through more refined application of management information and a rationalization of the infrastructure through using technology to supplant or improve existing techniques can all help modify and improve cost structures. Competitiveness can be improved through technology adding to the features of a product, its distribution and its delivery. It becomes feasible, for example, for a financial organization to deliver a wider range of complex products to its customers outside the limitations imposed by the existing infrastructure.

Against the apparent advantages offered by the new technologies, there are a number of considerations which should act as a brake on the speed of innovation. At the core of these dilemmas is the whole question of customer preference; there are limits to the speed with which customers will adopt new, technology driven services. There is always a danger that an expensively developed service may have no place in the consumer's set of potential needs or desires. This single factor should influence the level of capital investment, measured in terms of payback and opportunity cost, and the timing and the degree of risk an organization may be willing to accept.

Other extrinsic factors that influence the speed and nature of technological innovation include the type of response required by an organization in answer to developments being made by existing competitors, or indeed new entrants whose appearance is almost completely due to technology. The effect of technology in disturbing the established regime of regulation and legislation requires a high degree of prudential care in introducing new systems or services, so that security against fraud and abuse and protection of the customer's interest are maintained.

Intrinsic considerations are tied up with the nature of the current status quo. The introduction of technology may prematurely negate or undermine organizational investment in infrastructure. Branch networks are commonly perceived as the single most important element responsible for raising organizational costs; technology may well replace, to as yet an unascertained level, their function; but branches will remain a highly successful method of occupying the market and attracting business. The phasing out of the networks will raise problems of maintaining customer relationships and loyalty, and ultimately of building satisfactory levels of corporate differentiation in a market that will increasingly seem to deal in commodity-like products.

The introduction of technology will inevitably have a substantial impact on the entire question of organizational design, corporate culture and, within that, management style and direction, personnel training, career structuring and motivation. In a management sense there will be the additional problem of maintaining a balance between the tradition-based business philosophy of banking and the potentialities of technology.

Technology is a fundamental concern of management; the speed and scale of its introduction should be based on a balanced assessment of the implications it has in organizational and competitive terms.

Background

An analysis of the current and intended uses of technology show changing patterns of influence on the business structure. The uses it has been put to in the last 20 years have been geared up to transaction processing, accounting and providing financially based management information. Branches have been equipped with 'intelligent' terminals that are connected on-line to mainframe computers. Computers have tended to be unobtrusive, administrative and back-office based.

At another level, but again used in the bulk processing of payments, the LCBs established an automated clearing service called BACS. Offering an EFT system between banks it provides for automated credits such as salaries and pensions, and automated standing orders and direct debits. An extension of this idea of using electronic signals instead of paper is cheque truncation, where paper-based information is translated into electronic signals and communicated in that form to another bank. Cheque truncation remains an experimental but very fruitful idea.

The administrative aspect of technology being used to complement existing styles of business by reducing costs and increasing efficiency is seen in the introduction of more sophisticated branch terminals into branches such as Midland Bank's Nixdorf controller. These can store information and control a variety of subsidiary operations within the branch, ranging from an ATM to a front-office terminal, an enquiry VDU or word processor to the established input/output functions of a branch terminal.

The future administrative applications of technology potentially promise much greater levels of individual efficiency in the handling of information. The electronic office offers integrated word processing, electronic mail, electronic filing, executive work queue management, information retrieval systems and data base management and interrogation facilities. It complements, at the executive level, the reduction of mechanical tasks of processing ever-increasing volumes of payments. The automation of the organization is a central aspect to controlling cost structures through reducing unit costs and maximizing resource use. It represents the application of technology which the banking industry is attuned to understand and can accommodate. It does not require significant structural changes in terms of organization or business philosophy, and its impact at staff level is gradual.

However, the change in emphasis which has slowly emerged in the last ten years, with the introduction of increasingly sophisticated ATMs, marks a fundamental new direction. Previously technology remained relatively unobtrusive. Currently technology is being used increasingly to alter the terms by which business is done. Product and service design, and the method by which it is distributed and delivered, are changing not only the industry structure but the orgaizations operating in that environment. Technology is increasingly seen as the key in developing the relationship with the customer and gaining competitive superiority.

The reasons for this are twofold: firstly, the reduced costs per unit of the technology and secondly, general improvements in the telecommunication channels across which financial data can be transmitted. Financial information is essentially nothing more than alphanumeric data; therefore, technology has suddenly become capable of apparently revolutionizing the structure of retail banking, especially if financial transactions are seen as nothing more than an exchange of electronically based information. The industry structure also becomes susceptible to the arrival of a variety of new entrants. Traditional business demarcations and styles of business are no longer valid or operable if the infrastructures responsible for these divisions are reduced to a common and simple basis. It is this idea of competition, manifested in different ways that is pushing the industry into the new technology. Response to competition is seen in building barriers to competitive entry, or by consolidating existing positions. ATMs are the first example of this, although it should be stressed that ATMs, in common with new delivery systems, belong also to the 'administrative' approach to technology as they reinforce the existing business style through reducing unit processing costs and improving cost structures. Nevertheless, ATMs have altered the very nature of the competitive position through providing a cheaper alternative to branch teller positions. Offering a variety of services in addition to cash dispensing, such as balance enquiry and statement and cheque book ordering, they provide a service which is not necessarily constrained by time or branch location (although at the moment most ATMs are located at branch sites). Competitive advantage can be gained by an institution or industry group possessing these in such numbers as to pre-empt competitor action, and by employing them as a complementary delivery system to the branch.

ATMs represent a half-way step, however, in the evolution of distinct and deliberate business actions based on technology. The tendency towards network sharing tends to relegate ATMs back towards the administrative function of technology. It is this theme of co-operation or competition in the use of technology which is a primary dilemma in the retail banking area. The preference for co-operation over competitive advantage arguably reflects the essentially risk-adverse and conservative characteristics of the banking fraternity. Co-operation does have much to recommend it. It reduces capital investment and the risk of going down the wrong road. It also reflects what is the often essentially co-operative nature of institutions in the payment systems area. Point-of-sale electronic funds transfer (EFT/POS) dramatically illustrates the need and preference for competition within a co-operative framework. The sharing of development and implementation costs and the universality of proposed systems will reduce the risks and costs of a major transformation of the payment system.

EFT/POS will permit a person carrying a debit card to pay for goods electronically rather than using cash or a cheque. The retailer has the advantage of having payment authorized and confirmed by the system but the banks are in the best situation: the process of debiting accounts, making payments and recording transactions will be automated and, providing overall transaction volumes justify the cost of installation, much cheaper than the traditional money transmission mechanism. It will also reduce fraud, a major consideration in payment systems. However, EFT/POS has a number of negative aspects that are suggestive of the overall problems associated with the introduction of technology. Using packet-switching technology recently introduced by British Telecommunications and a range of hardware and software provided by IBM, the manner of allocating the cost of installing thousands of card-reading terminals in retailers and establishing the overall framework has yet to be decided upon. Although the system will reduce unit processing costs, the creation of an alternative payment system to the clearing house means an effective duplication of systems and costs, and it means that the authorities will be in a position to deprive the clearing banks of their oligopoly by insisting the system is open to all. In addition, as this is essentially remote from the bank branch based payment system, as with the ATM, it lowers the banks' direct involvement with the customer, and may in turn ultimately affect the patterns of customer loyalty.

There are questions not only over the readiness of customer and retailer to use the system, but over how much they will be prepared to pay for its use. The banks will not, under an Office of Fair Trading directive, be able to differentiate pricing solely to encourage its use at the expense of existing payment systems. The banks may therefore be in the invidious situation of perhaps having to pay for two sets of loss-making payment systems. The administrative motive in introducing technology may also have jeopardized itself, especially as EFT systems will also require considerable organizational back-up in addition to the capital costs.

Alternatives to the on-line EFT/POS system are found in the memory card and transaction telephone. The transaction telephone consists of a hand-set, an automatic dialling service, a card reader, a display screen and a keyboard. Again using packet switching technology, a card can be connected to a computer at a credit card company where the intended payment can be authorized. This simpler and cheaper technology, as opposed to the more complex account debiting and funds transfer aspects of EFT/POS, has been investigated by the already highly automated credit card subsidiaries of the clearing banks, as well as the American owned Amex and Diners Club and a company has been established and is now operational.

The memory card can use a variety of technologies, but is commonly used in connection with cheaper off-line computer systems; possessing a microprocessor with an indelible or erasable memory, they are fraud resistant. Using card readers and PIN numbers, account and transaction details are taken and later transmitted to bank computers either by cassette or through the packet-switching network. The memory card is currently undergoing extensive trials in France.

Home banking represents the last and most radically influential of the three main innovations in the delivery of bank services. Based on television-based viewdata technology available in the UK through the Prestel system, it permits interaction between the service-provider and the customer by means of the Gateway software system. One commercial scheme is already available in the UK through the Nottingham Building Society and Bank of Scotland. It provides the customer with statements, allows him to pay bills, transfer funds, check and book holidays, or purchase goods and use Prestel's other services. The slightly more advanced home banking system offered by the German Verbraucherbank allows the customer, in addition to Nottingham's services to establish and amend standing orders. None, however, allows direct cash withdrawal.

The development of cable television networks, using optic-fibre technology, provide a major alternative to Prestel which is based on established telecommunication technology. But, whatever the technology, the development of home banking on a large scale will produce connect-time and peak characteristics different from the existing telephone use. The development of large-scale home banking will depend, therefore, on the improvements in existing telecommunication systems, developments incidentally which are in hand, but which are unlikely to be completed until the next century. For example, British Telecommunications System X is scheduled to be fully introduced by 2015, although the main part of it will be in place by the end of the century.

As with the other uses of technology in a business-getting context, a number of strategic questions surround the development of home banking. What will be the demand for the services it offers, what competitive edge will it provide, what cost and what return and what part will it play in the overall payment system mix? As with POS and to a lesser extent ATM, home banking is a remote service, therefore introduction will also have to be considered in terms of the effect it has on the existing infrastructure: not just the economics of running the entire organization but the level of corporate differentiation and customer retention/attraction it will offer.

POS and home banking are set, at some stage, to be offered by some and probably the most important institutions. The administrative and competitive justifications for their introduction have to be measured in terms of their opportunity cost and the possibilities of managing the changes required in organizational terms. Multiplicity of technologies when there has only been one type of technology administratively applied before, suggest different strategic solutions based on the economics of the individual organization operating in a diverse market-place.

Technology, Regulation and the Consumer

Technology creates problems for both the institutions and the consumer, in ensuring that its adoption does not breach in any way standards of protection against fraud, against abuse and most especially of the confidentiality of the customer's account. All previous legislation concerned with banking has grown at a slow pace in line with the gradual development of the system. Technology creates an entirely new framework for business; it is bringing in its wake products like the debit card, for which there is no existing legislative protection, and the creation of electronic data bases which are not protected by the customary security of the bank branch. The systems are, in addition, prone to errors and omissions, improper controls, inadequate system design and fraud and defalcation.

To overcome these potential difficulties, the NCC's report on *Banking Services and the Consumer* has recommended the creation of an 'EFT' statute, which would provide the appropriate legal framework. It recommends amongst other things that:

- Legal safeguards should be as stringent for debit cards as for cheques and credit cards.
- There should be certainty and uniformity as to the respective rights and obligations of banks, customers and third parties.
- A written record should be provided for each transaction.
- Liabilities for lost or stolen debit cards should be on a similar basis as those for credit cards.
- There should be a guarantee of the customer's right to privacy.
- There should be an amendment to the Bills of Exchange Act to facilitate cheque truncation.

This set of considerations acts as a very substantial brake to the speed of innovation. The relationship with the customer is central to banking activity and a major component in that is the integrity, security and quality of the service offered. Any system which is introduced must be seen to fulfil these factors.

Organizational Implications: Management and Personnel

A key aspect of technology outlined at the beginning of this chapter was whether it should be regarded as a means or an end in itself. As the discussion has shown, the main thread of bank thinking has principally been to see it in 'administrative' rather than strategic terms. The advent of EFT/POS and ultimately home banking has altered this philosophical approach quite fundamentally, but the effects on the business culture will not be apparent until the end of the decade.

None the less, even at the administrative level, the effects are considerable. Automated or electronic processing of volumes of payment transactions has controlled the growth of clerical staff. The systems generate considerable quantities of management information; hitherto this has been accounting based, but progressively it is being used to provide marketing information. In personnel terms these changes mean a shift away from a clerical-based culture to a greater emphasis on analytical and decision-based skills.

In structural terms, especially with the introduction of new delivery systems, the appropriateness of the existing infrastructure is questionable. Why have extensive branch networks when their function is replaced by electronic media? A reorientation in the way the infrastructure is managed necessarily means new organizational structures, probably shifting away from geographic towards segmentation based management and ultimately towards product/technology management. This shift presupposes that management is actually able to control the process of change and develop workable structures around the new concepts.

At the personnel level the effects will be greatest. Changes in organizational structures and management styles will include

—redistribution of labour
—new career structures
—new recruitment policies
—greater emphasis on specific types of training.

The bank unions are deeply suspicious of the new technology: a mixture of conservatism and justifiable concern over job security suggest their opposition to change. Overcoming this will represent a key strategic challenge to management.

The management culture itself, to survive, will have to develop new skills, become more sophisticated in the management of people and situations, become less risk adverse and change its style of management from authoritarian and hierarchic, to a more open, marketing based style.

CONCLUSIONS

There are a mixture of problems and potentialities in the increasing use of technology within retail banking. Its adoption is inevitable, both by reason of improving efficiency and controlling costs. Moreover, response to intensifying competition will necessarily require either the consolidation of market positions or in response to a more direct competitive threat the use of technology. An incidental but important facet of this is that strategies will be constructed and adopted on the basis of assumed changes in the environment.

However, it is surrounded with uncertainty; the massive investments required may not produce the expected returns. The time spans and the dynamic elements of the new technologies are difficult to forecast; there is the danger of investing too soon. There is the existence of counter-pressures which will slow down its introduction; management attitudes, union opposition, legal and other regulatory constraints, and of course the customer's willingness to use new technology. Change will bring with it the need to introduce new systems alongside existing systems, and then manage them simultaneously. The need for capital and expertise to introduce new systems will have two effects. Firstly, it will reinforce established co-operative structures, and secondly, it will then move to new alliances and power groupings as the accent in the industry moves towards greater competition.

Technology represents, undoubtedly, the single greatest challenge to management in the retail banking environment. It also represents a focal point in the strategy-making process as strategies will increasingly have to see technology as a principal rather than a supporting feature of their operations, and will have to introduce lines of action accordingly.

Part III Industry Groups

8 The London Clearing Banks

INTRODUCTION

The environmental chapter has illustrated the trends asserting themselves in the retail bank sector, and has suggested a number of possible reasons underpinning those trends. Although economic and regulatory factors have especial significance in determining the conditions of the market-place, a still more powerful factor belongs to the nature of the industry group itself; historical and functional factors are responsible for determining the nature of its market position, and by that its ability to respond to changing economic and competitive patterns.

This chapter will be primarily concerned to show how the LCBs'* current market position has been the consequences of a combination of changes in the market-place and the responses made by LCBs on the basis of an historically and functionally determined role. The validity of considering the LCBs as an industry group is seen in the way the LCBs have suffered and responded to change almost as a single organism.

THE EVOLUTION OF THE BANKS' FUNCTION

1955 represents the watershed in the LCBs' evolution. A cartelized oligopoly of banks held 85 per cent of commercial lending, and possessed a sterling deposit base three times greater than the building societies. Lending and borrowing rates were fixed by collective agreement allowing for a comfortable margin between deposit and lending rates. The banks' product range was simple; all deposits were by way of seven day deposit account or 'free' current account money and all lending was by overdraft. Official credit controls compounded the situation by constraining the growth of the banks' balance sheets. The banks were, therefore, underlent, tending to act as a government fund-raiser.

* LCB will refer to the 'Big Four', unless otherwise stated.

The banks' function was to act as a financial intermediary. This required two things; the first was to attract deposits from sectors that had a financial surplus and then lend these to sectors who were running a deficit; the second was to provide the mechanism to allow this to take place and to provide an incentive for both borrowers and lenders to do business with the banks. Money transmission was the key to this. But the development of these functions had taken place over a long period. The LCBs' market position reflected in the nature of the cartelized oligopoly and its functional role was not the result of planned management, but as an often pragmatic reaction to market forces.

The LCBs' role as providers of money transmission facilities reinforced the co-operative nature of the cartel through the joint ownership of the clearing house. But although the cartel may have been supposed to have created a comfortable situation, blunting the competitive edge of the LCBs, it can also be argued that the cartel acted as a forum for intense but self-regulated price competition. Uniform prices exist either as a consequence of a monopoly or of perfect competition. The competition was not manifested in prices (the regulated environment ensured that with limited opportunities for asset growth and a limited supply of funds, price competition would be useless and self-destructive), but in non-price competition – the establishment of large branch networks and in ensuring that cost structures and business styles were broadly the same. The consequence of this was the development of a particular attitude, a cultural philosophy towards the market-place which still exists, its persistence being largely reinforced by the way the market has not dramatically changed in the period after 1955. If the LCBs' present situation is seen largely in terms of this management attitude and by the evolving nature of the bank market both in the characteristics of the personal sector and by the LCBs' own actions, then the trends seen in the economic analysis become more explicable.

Throughout the 1960s the authorities adopted a stop–go approach to the regulation of the LCBs. Lending ceilings curtailed their growth and acted to reinforce the conditions of the 1950s, delimiting innovation and expansion. But by the end of the 1960s two things were happening: the oligopoly was restructuring itself through a process of mergers between its members. The appearance of the 'Big Four' in some ways modified the nature of the competitive situation, but more importantly consolidated the introspective cartel mentality. The disclosure of true profits and reserves perhaps reinforced this, as competition between the LCBs was intensified. The second factor, 'competition and credit control' of 1971 changed the external rules of the game by encouraging price competition, and through abolishing credit controls and restoring tax deductability on interest payments encouraging balance sheet growth.

No longer a cartel, but still an oligopoly through their control of payment systems, the banks still operated uniformly on deposit rates but competed against each other on asset formation, fuelling their growth (when retail deposits proved inadequate) through the wholesale money-markets.

As an incidental point, the availability of funds through the wholesale markets tended to reduce the importance of retail funding strategies, with retail deposits seen as an incremental structural feature of their clearing bank operations.

It was their reliance on the money-markets which was responsible for the failure of the 1972–73 experiment in monetary control and the imposition of a further set of controls on bank growth. It was thought that cost would determine the supply and demand for credit. The consequence was an explosion in bank lending which the market revealed not to be price sensitive, at least in the short term. The banks' use of the wholesale money-markets destroyed the connection between interest rate and money supply. The monetary authorities, therefore, looked to control money supply by limiting the LCBs' ability to create credit through inflicting penalties on deposit growth through the 'corset'. The LCBs, however, managed to circumvent most of the effects of the 'corset' by providing acceptances on bills of exchange. Controls on consumer lending, furthermore, tended to make the bulk of asset growth take place in the corporate sector, a trend reinforced by the growing reliance of that sector on bank borrowing rather than on the capital markets or retained profit for growth purposes.

All these factors compromised the LCBs' role in the personal sector, which although remaining central to their funding was serviced through the mechanisms of non-price competition, the branch networks and the money transmission services, rather than by the aggressive marketing campaigns based on price, promotion and new products. Their market as a direct consequence was limited, with less than half the adult population being banked in the mid-1970s. The combined influence of these factors helped to contribute to the growth of the LCBs' main rivals, the building societies.

The building societies saw their asset base, consisting almost entirely of house mortgages, grow by five times between 1955 and 1980, and their deposits grow a third larger than the banks. Their role as virtual monopoly suppliers of house mortgage finance, coupled to their ability through the cartel to regulate the supply and demand of funds by controlling prices, helped this growth considerably. The simplicity of their function, with one lending product and a limited range of retail deposit products, made their management easier and cost structures cheaper than the LCBs. When a range of fiscal advantages was added, the competitive superiority of the building societies was assured.

FUNCTION OF THE LCBs

The functional role of the LCBs is based on the service they provide to a range of depositors and borrowers across different sectors. Financial intermediation between sectors is founded on four basic functions:

— Taking in savings
— Providing credit facilities
— Providing savers and borrowers with instruments to meet their differing needs
— Operating maturity and risk transformation through economies of scale loans can be provided on a long term basis, but permitting a high degree of liquidity to depositors; margins are established on the advantages to both depositors and borrowers.

The needs of borrowers and savers are very different. Savers demand varying degrees of convenience, security, liquidity and return. Borrowers may need

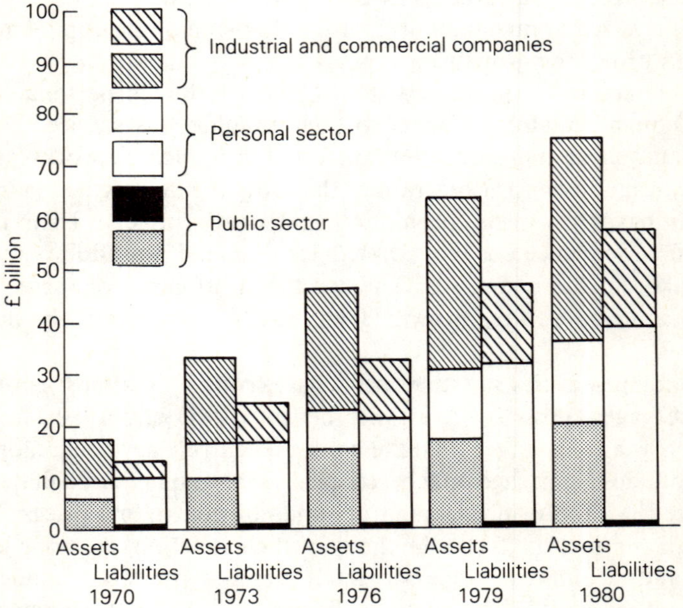

FIGURE 8.1 UK banking – main structural features 1980: assets and liabilities (*Source:* Bank of England)

accessibility to funds as required, require different loan periods, and may be concerned with price.

This market situation and the portfolio preferences of different customer groups is complemented by the different portfolio preferences of the financial institutions themselves. These preferences will be based on maximizing profitability and, as a concomitant of this, reducing risk in the long term. Portfolio preferences will be based to a certain extent on the infrastructure, established connections with the market-place and the attitudes of senior management. All these tend to be historically determined and, in the absence of a radical upheaval, subject to slow change.

The LCBs' portfolio is complex; their assets are split between the public corporate and personal sectors and their liabilities across retail deposits and the wholesale market. An analysis of UK banks' assets and liabilities (figure 8.1) and their sterling advances (figure 8.2) illustrates the nature of the banks' situation. When these are seen against a sectoral analysis of the flow of funds (figure 8.3 and table 8.1), the central role of personal sector deposits in the LCBs' financial intermediation function is apparent. Retail deposits are highly attractive because they complement the LCBs' established infrastructures. The attractions that they provide to savers means that the deposits are discounted against the advantages of access, liquidity and low risk.

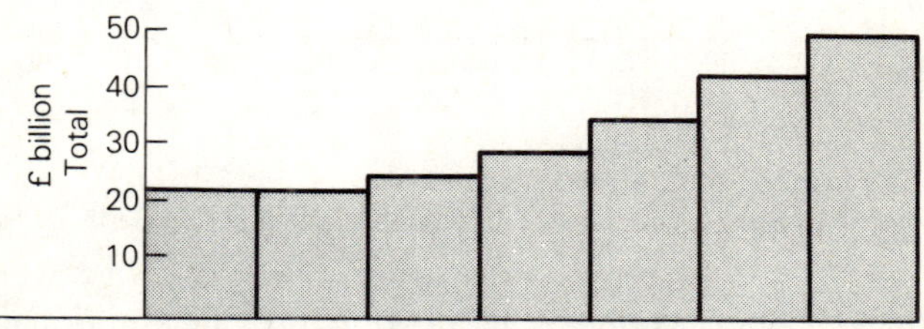

Year*	1975	1976	1977	1978	1979	1980	1981
% Share	%	%	%	%	%	%	%
Manufacturing	28	25	28	27	28	27	24
Other Production	13	13	13	13	13	13	13
Services	22	24	25	27	28	29	31
Personal	17	18	17	18	18	19	20
Financial	20	20	17	15	13	12	12
Total	100	100	100	100	100	100	100

* All data relate to May of each year

FIGURE 8.2 UK banking – main structural features 1980: classification of sterling advances
(*Source:* Bank of England)

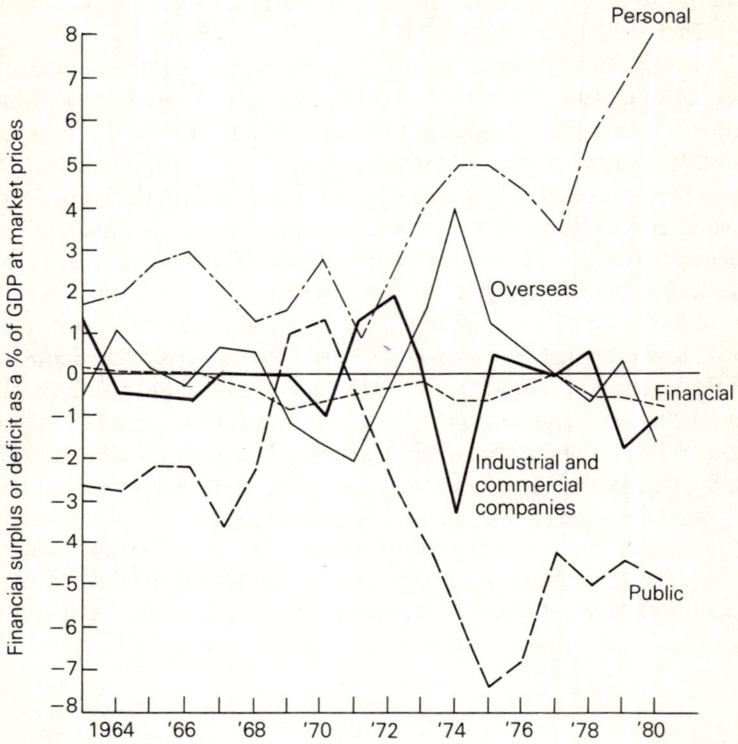

FIGURE 8.3 Flow of funds – sectoral analysis
(*Source:* Bank of England – UK Flow of Funds Accounts and Quarterly Bulletin)

For example, cheque accounts generally only provide a notional interest to depositors; the seven-day account provides a relatively low interest rate because it provides depositors with certain advantages. Unfortunately, for the LCBs this emphasis on using established infrastructures and historically based business policies for attracting retail deposits is undermined when other industry groups such as building societies and life assurance funds are competing for the same market on the basis of different cost structures and different pricing policies, which are a direct reflection of very different portfolio preferences and market functions.

The LCBs' involvement in the retail banking market has meant that substantial investments have been made to enhance existing business styles. The branch network has been maintained and made more efficient by the introduction of computer technology. As inflation and competitive action have made an impact, the pressures to realize the economies inherent in this

Table 8.1 Flow of funds – sectoral analysis

Sector flows – financial surplus or deficit as % of GDP (at market prices)

	Sector				
Year	Public	Financial	Industrial and commercial companies	Personal	Overseas
1963	−2.7	+0.1	+1.2	+1.7	−0.4
1964	−2.8	Nil	−0.5	+1.9	+1.1
1965	−2.2	Nil	−0.5	+2.7	+0.1
1966	−2.2	Nil	−0.7	+3.0	−0.3
1967	−3.6	−0.1	Nil	+2.2	+0.7
1968	−2.2	−0.4	−0.1	+1.3	+0.6
1969	+1.0	−0.8	Nil	+1.6	−1.1
1970	+1.3	−0.6	−1.1	+2.9	−1.6
1971	−0.5	−0.4	+1.2	+0.9	−2.0
1972	−2.4	−0.3	+2.0	+2.3	−0.4
1973	−3.8	−0.1	−0.1	+4.1	+1.4
1974	−5.7	−0.5	−3.2	+5.1	+4.0
1975	−7.3	−0.5	+0.5	+5.1	+1.4
1976	−6.7	−0.1	+0.2	+4.5	+0.7
1977	−4.1	−0.1	Nil	+3.6	Nil
1978	−4.9	−0.4	+0.7	+5.6	−0.6
1979	−4.3	−0.4	−1.7	+6.8	+0.4
1980	−4.7	−0.6	−1.0	+8.2	−1.4

Sources: Bank of England, UK FLow of Funds accounts and Quarterly Bulletin

infrastructure, through obtaining high volumes of business, have intensified to the detriment of their overall business strategies, e.g. the move downmarket in the personal sector. Portfolio preferences became orientated towards using the infrastructure to its fullest potential and obtaining the greatest return through asset–liability management. Although apparently complementary, the two strategies can be incompatible, since the first pursues volume and the second is dependent on careful segmentation, which is often antipathetic to volume strategies.

The LCBs' situation is complicated by several factors. The first is that the infrastructure, which was developed to provide money transmission facilities and attract retail deposits, is no longer adequate to meet this goal. Although a changing market-place and the pursuit of greater economies of scale has led to the LCBs providing current account services to a greater proportion of the UK population they have not attracted a commensurate level of deposits. This suggests a failure of a business strategy based on historical precedent. The market position, chosen as a consequence of portfolio preferences which are in turn based on a variety of factors such as the demands of infrastructure and traditional function and management attitude, not only limits the flexibility of competitive response but also the type of markets available.

Profitability is based on gaining the widest margins between assets and liabilities and by ensuring cost structures do not erode that income. Competition from, for example, building societies and amongst the LCBs themselves will contract margins and mean that available economies of scale will not be fully used, thereby raising costs. As the situation grows worse with the intensification of competition, so the worst affected banks will begin to adopt further rationalization and segmentation strategies. The LCBs' competitive position is further constrained by capital requirements, regulation and by the fiscal advantages enjoyed by other industry groups.

The cartel and then oligopoly in the money transmission area meant that the LCBs were primarily concerned with competing amongst themselves; the main thrust of competition was in establishing market share both by numbers of current accounts and by assets, mainly in the corporate sector. Retail deposits were a function of the infrastructure. The influence of other industry groups offering different and sometimes better mixes of return, liquidity, convenience and security has undermined their cartel principle, and is progressively undermining their traditional market position. It is for this reason that the banks will have to evolve distinctive and specific strategies in the personal sector.

The Evolving Situation

During the early 1960s almost all deposit money was on seven-day deposit account, at an average cost of 3.3 per cent. When current account money was included into this, average cost of funds fell to 1.75 per cent. Without the benefit of 'free' capital, under the cartel, base rate was 6 per cent, providing a generous margin to the LCBs. Retail deposits have not matched the needs of the LCBs' asset growth. The gap has been filled by wholesale deposits, whose cost is related to money-market rates, so raising funding costs.

High interest rates, limited growth in personal disposable income and increased competition for the personal sector's savings have contributed to the relative failure of the current account to provide retail deposits. In 1983, current accounts in aggregate accounted for only 11 per cent of bank group deposits compared to 19 per cent in 1980. These trends did not seem critical in the 1970s because average interest rates were climbing faster than the

Table 8.2 London clearing banks – number of branches

	Barclays	Lloyds	Midland	Nat. West.	Total
1972	3,099	2,345	2,649	3,416	11,509
1982	2,959	2,284	2,441	3,253	10,937
1983	2,912	2,276	2,345	3,226	10,759

Source: Annual Reports

deterioration in the deposit mix. However, with the recent fall in interest rates the average cost of funds has grown faster than yields, compressing margins.

The LCBs, to counterbalance these trends, have done three things. Firstly, because the value of current accounts attracting deposits has grown less, and since the cost to the banks of operating money transmission facilities is substantial and growing, the LCBs have moved towards obtaining greater cost recovery through higher and more widely imposed tariffs. Secondly, the LCBs have, aided by derestriction on consumer lending and the abandonment of the 'corset', begun to change their portfolio of assets, to give them higher margins, by lending more extensively to the personal sector and by entering the house mortgage market, to give them a block of countercyclical lending. (This lending becomes more profitable in periods of declining interest rates because mortgage rates lag behind.) Thirdly, the banks have begun to control their costs, so that profitability is enhanced, thereby improving their competitiveness in the long term. In this third area, the branch networks have come under close scrutiny. One of the effects of the series of mergers was to expand some of the clearers' networks beyond a reasonable level; although some rationalization has been undertaken, the networks were essentially too large and were supportable only in a period of high margins. Now profitability is the key, and since it appears that the branch networks are no longer fulfilling their primary function of attracting retail deposits on the scale required, then their future, especially with the advent of technologicl surrogates, is under scrutiny. Table 8.2 shows the pace of branch reduction. Some, notably Barclays and Midland, have embarked on long-term programmes of rationalizing networks both by closure and by changing patterns of use.

Tables 8.3–8.7 show how changes in the funding mix and interest rates have affected overall profitability of the four major clearing banks. The divergence in net interest margins shown in table 8.3 is attributed to differences in deposit structure. Lloyds and Barclays have the highest proportion of current accounts and consequently the widest margins.

The shift away from retail deposits (table 8.4) and a lower average base rate (11.9 per cent against 13 per cent) combined to produce universal

Table 8.3 London clearing banks – profit and loss items as a percentage of average interest-bearing assets: 1982

	Barclays	Lloyds	Midland	Nat. West.	Industry average
Net interest income	5.3 (6.0)	5.7 (7.0)	3.4 (3.9)	4.2 (4.9)	4.5 (5.2)
Less					
Fixed costs	4.9 (5.4)	5.4 (6.3)	3.8 (4.0)	4.0 (4.5)	4.4 (4.8)
Bad debts	0.5 (0.3)	0.6 (0.3)	0.3 (0.2)	0.5 (–)	0.5 (0.2)
Plus					
Fees and commission	1.6 (1.5)	1.8 (1.9)	1.1 (1.1)	1.4 (1.4)	1.3 (1.4)
Gilt trading profit	0.2 (–)	– (–)	0.2 (–)	0.1 (–)	0.1 (–)
Operating profit	1.7 (1.8)	1.5 (2.2)	0.6 (0.8)	1.1 (1.8)	1.2 (1.6)

1981 figures are shown in brackets.
Source: Annual Reports

Table 8.4 Composition of London clearing bank funding (deposits % 1982)

	Barclays	Lloyds	Midland	Nat. West.	Industry average
Current accounts	25 (27)	26 (32)	17 (18)	22 (25)	22 (25)
7-day and other small savings	28 (33)	29 (37)	15 (16)	18 (22)	21 (25)
Wholesale and other	47 (40)	23 (10)	24 (24)	26 (23)	30 (26)
money-market related currency	– –[a]	22 (20)	44 (42)	34 (29)	26 (24)

1981 figures are shown in brackets.
[a] Structure of Barclays Bank means that parent bank has no recourse to currency money-markets.
Source: Annual Reports

reductions in net interest margins. The extent of the decline in individual cases is related directly to the change in the deposit mix.

Although interest margins became worse (table 8.5), the yield on interest-bearing assets and the average cost of deposits widened in almost every case.

Although, in the case of all banks, cost restraint has been exercised, it has not covered the decline in interest margins (table 8.6). At Barclays, National Westminster and Lloyds, overheads took in about 90 per cent of net interest income and Midland's overheads exceeded net interest income.

Midland's problem comes from having a small retail deposit base in relation to the expense of running a money transmission service. The unit cost of collecting retail deposits is 15 per cent higher than for the rest of the industry. The problems posed by this deterioration in the funding mix is illustrated in table 8.7. A redistribution of 3.5 per cent would lead to funding costs being reduced by £155 million, and net interest margins 0.2 per cent higher.

Table 8.5 Interest spreads: 1982

	Barclays	Lloyds	Midland	Nat. West.	Industry average
Yield on interest-earning assets (%)	13.4	13.5	13.6	13.4	13.5
Average cost interest-bearing deposits	10.7	10.9	12.0	11.7	11.5
Spread	2.7 (2.6)	2.6 (2.7)	1.6 (1.4)	1.7 (1.5)	2.0 (1.9)

1981 figures are shown in brackets.
Source: CLCB Statistics

Table 8.6 Clearing bank fixed costs as a percentage of interest income

	Barclays	Lloyds	Midland	Nat. West.	Industry average
Fixed costs as a % net interest income	91 (89)	94 (90)	112 (102)	97 (92)	98 (93)
Unit cost of collecting retail deposit 1982	85 (79)	86 (80)	103 (95)	89 (84)	90 (84)

1981 figures are shown in brackets.
Source: CLCB Statistics

Table 8.7 Changes in funding mix

	%	Average £m volumes ×	rate	+ cost £m	%	× rate	= cost £m
Current a/c	31	19,000	–		32.5		
7-day a/c	30	18,300	6.5	1,190	32	6.5	1,287
Wholesale	39	24,400	10.1	2,464	35.5	10.1	2,212
Total		61,700					

Source: Annual Reports

The change in deposit structure accounts for about half the decline in interest margins, with most of the remainder being attributed to a reduction in the value of current account money through lower interest rates. One response to this problem is to widen the spread between seven-day deposit rate and base rate; when much of the competition for retail deposits is based on rate this solution seems wrong-headed.

From this it may be judged that the clearing banks' response to the retail bank market remains largely pragmatic, determined by historically formed factors.

CONCLUSIONS

The period from 1955 has been marked by considerable structural change. The retail bank market was very stable, with little change and apparently little need to embark on competitive strategies. The cartel mentality promoted a view that saw the market defined by those who had a bank account or had the potential to own a bank account. This market was competed for by the clearing banks, generally on the basis of non-price or implicit price competition, such as providing a range of services through a large branch network. The prime objective of the clearing banks was to provide finance to an increasingly cash hungry corporate sector.

What has happened to alter this is the emergence of new industry groups, competing with great effect in an increasingly homogeneous market. When commentators suggest that institutional boundaries are disappearing, what they are actually seeing is growing competition by institutions for the same markets. Building societies and banks are now competing openly on both sides of the balance sheet, whereas before it may have been felt that the nature of competition was limited to just the retail deposits area, and even then the nature of competition was covert and carried out in an indirect way. The appearance of the TSBs and National Girobank in particular have intensified pressure in the bank market and overall, regulation and control have undermined the banks' self-determination. The LCBs' assumption that the retail market was stable is reflected in the comparative lack of innovation when compared against the corporate sector. Although the credit card made its first appearance in 1966, its impact was small compared to the development of liability management or corporate lending products. It was thought, instead, that traditional business methods would continue to operate effectively; and indeed they did in the circumscribed clearing bank market, increasing the numbers of the population who had a bank account. But as money transmission was seen as a means to an end, i.e. the attraction of retail deposits, and was palpably failing to achieve this end, then it became apparent that other industry groups and other business strategies were proving more effective. The assumption of stability was disproved and the ideas of competition and change were implanted.

It was found that the changing market-place was a response to, and had indeed induced, more sophisticated portfolio preference especially amongst personal sector savers, who had become more discriminating in what the institutions were offering and more rational in their choice of institutional products. The implications of this change of focus are great, yet even in itself this change may be flawed. The reasons why the LCBs are attracted to retail deposits are because they are cheaper, less volatile and longer term (easing liquidity needs). Yet increased competition may change these advantages to disadvantages by increasing the cost of funds and making them more rate sensitive and so more volatile.

The implications are, however, reflected in a changed competitive philosophy and strategic view of retail banking.

Since competition is now taking place on the macro-level then bank competitiveness has to be judged at the macro-level, not the clearing bank level. Markets have to be seen in categorical not hybrid forms, i.e. deposits, payment systems and lending entail separate strategies which may be used beneficially to support each other. Therefore, all should be seen as deliberate profit-making business sectors. It also, of course, entails a much more even-handed approach towards corporate and personal sectors, to ensure, as with product groups that no cross-subsidization or mixed business objective asserts itself.

The implications for the LCBs are:

- To reduce fixed costs, most especially in the branch and processing areas with a very clear idea of what the costs and benefits are at the broad strategic level and the sectoral and product level.
- To improve asset quality; this may mean a shift away from the fine margin lending to the corporate sector to the higher margin personal sector, incidentally exploiting the economies of scale inherent in branch networks.
- To become more differentiated at the macro-market level, for example, by pursuing competitive strategies which are not dictated by the conditions of the clearing bank oligopoly.
- To become more marketing based, in fulfilling the personal sector's portfolio preferences more directly, especially in the savings sector.

9 Building Societies

INTRODUCTION

The so-called building society movement, described here more accurately as the strongest and most homogeneous industry group in the retail bank market, is demonstrating characteristics analogous to the development of the LCBs during the 1970s. The situation is complicated, however, by the fact that the dimensions of the building society industry have widened as a direct result of their own endeavours and by the internal and external pressures on the clearing banks which have made the retail bank market more universal and less segmented by institution.

The impact of these pressures has been to quicken the pace of industry evolution, so that the societies will become, as they grow increasingly commercial in their outlook, more sophisticated at the business level. Their growth in the past has been a direct consequence of economic, regulatory and institutional phenomena. However, their future success will increasingly depend on their ability to manage the business. It seems that this fact has been recognized both by the societies and governments as evidenced by the Spalding Report and subsequent Green Paper.

BACKGROUND

The building societies have steadily moved to a position of pre-eminence in the personal sector. Chapter 3 highlighted the trends on both sides of the balance sheet, and gave some reasons for those trends. Nevertheless it is worth reiterating the fact that the societies had, at the end of 1984, 49 per cent of personal sector liquid assets, compared to the banks' 35 per cent, and despite the considerable volume of bank lending for house purchase, they maintain about a 75 per cent share of the market. The trends are self-evident, and the explanations in market terms are simply that the societies more adequately fulfilled the needs and expectations of the personal sector.

Underlying that success, however, are structural factors that belong to the building society industry group and enabled them to obtain a pre-eminent market position. Much of this growth was linked to the mutual status of the societies and to their cartel structure. Designed to fulfil a social function in providing housing finance, they benefited from governmental support in the shape of fiscal advantages and in being able to operate in a competitive market but without the same levels of commercial pressure facing their competitors. Building societies, above all, have most crucially benefited from the relative simplicity of their operation: having one lending product for which not only was there an almost insatiable demand but a demand that the societies could manipulate by being monopoly suppliers, and having savings schemes which exclusively tapped the personal sector, offering rates dictated by the cartel mechanism and which were linked directly to their management of house mortgage supply. Although the societies were involved in balance sheet management and maturity transformation, the simple relationship (when compared to the LCBs) between assets and liabilities and the virtually risk-free aspect of their lending made the management of their business relatively easy. The societies' principal balance sheet concern is to maintain sufficient liquidity to meet investors' requirements. The historical stability of retail funds over wholesale funds makes this a relatively minor concern, and again contributes to the strength of the societies' position.

The nature of the business was reflected in the prudential regulations governing the societies, permitting very high gearing (although the nature of building societies' balance sheets with a large number of share accounts makes this a small consideration), low levels of supervision for control or monetary purposes and positive advantages in the form of lower rate corporate tax and being allowed to pay investors taxation liabilities on a composite basis. In addition the housing market gained from considerable taxation advantages. In essence, therefore, both the supply and demand sides of their business are given advantages by central government. The cartel, as with the clearing banks in the 1960s, acts as a device which creates the conditions of competition amongst its members, and should act to protect the cartel group from competition by safeguarding margins. A cartel can only operate effectively, however, when its members dominate the market. With the changing structure of the market-place changing the balance of power, such a cartel can end up being a handicap preventing a flexible response to changes at the macro-level. However, the building society cartel is a direct outcome of the social purposes of the societies; it acted benevolently in distributing benefits equally between investors and borrowers. Mortgage rates were always relatively low, while investors were able to obtain good returns. The cartel simultaneously acted to provide the societies with assured and good margins between deposit and lending rates. This in turn had the effect of fuelling the structural growth of the societies, protecting the smaller and the less well-managed societies from the ravages of competition, and permitting substantial investment in non-price competition which principally took the form of rapidly expanding branch networks and costly advertising campaigns.

There is also a causal relationship between a cartel and the stage of industry evolution. The pace of growth seen through the 1970s reflected the way the industry group structure could develop steadily without having to develop the more sophisticated business and competitive strategies associated with industry maturity. The evidence seems to suggest that, in terms of the industry group, the societies are now entering a mature phase of development and, at the market level, the societies are involved in an emphatically mature market. However, the legacy of their business function and cartel will ensure that they remain highly competitive, since their cost bases are much lower than the banks, enabling them to enter a period of price competition in the savings sector with a marked advantage.

Structure and Current Developments

There has been a steady consolidation of building societies, the number declining from 456 in 1972 to 227 in 1982. There are five nationwide societies, all with assets over £3.5 billion, and a further 11 regionally based with assets between £900 million and £3.5 billion; the top 16 societies own 83 per cent of all building society assets.

The building societies have some 25 million investors (57 per cent of all UK adults), 73 per cent of whom have a bank account. The most important group of investors by value are the 36–65 + age group, who hold 87 per cent of society deposits by value, but there are 10 million investors in the 16–34 age bracket with only 13 per cent of savings. There are 2 million children investors, which shows the strength of the societies' appeal across the family life cycle.

On the other side of the balance sheet, societies had, in 1983, £62.5 billion house mortgages loaned out to 5.6 million borrowers, which represented some 80 per cent of total assets. There had been an increase of 1.5 million borrowers in 1982, which accounted for the spectacular growth in lending of £10.5 billion which took place in 1981–82. This growth occurred at the same time as the LCBs' entry into the market. The remainder of societies' assets is made up of £13.3 billion cash and investment and £8.1 billion of government securities. The decision to tax capital gains on gilts will have a substantial impact on the structuring of their assets, with a transfer to certificates of deposit being most likely.

The most tangible element in the societies growth has been the expansion of branch networks in key retail areas. In the period from 1972 to 1982 there was a growth from 2522 to 6479 branches. Although the pace of this growth has begun to slow down it has played a part in non-price competition amongst cartel members and attracted, through physical representation, a major proportion of personal sector savings.

To ensure that this growth could be maintained, the societies have, however, tended to rely heavily on price competition to attract deposits, partly as a consequence of increasing competition for deposits, and partly to increase the overall stock of personal sector savings by making investment appear more attractive than consumption. The effect has been to make the societies' funding costs more expensive. The cartel operating through the BSA recommended rate system applied firstly only to the main societies, and secondly only to the mainstream savings accounts. Although it heavily influenced rates paid outside these limits it did not control them. Smaller, maverick societies, by paying premium rates found that they could easily attract the required volumes of savings. The larger societies to compete and maintain market share began also to offer premia accounts in 1980. This caused a fairly significant adjustment in the funding portfolio mix. Table 9.1 illustrates this distribution at the end of 1982.

In 1980, ordinary accounts held 80 per cent of all building society deposits. The premia accounts offer between 1 per cent and 1.5 per cent over ordinary account rate, and have become more liquid as time has passed, offering depositors more for less in return. These accounts have broadly succeeded in their intention, helping the societies raise £10.3 billion in 1982. However, the cost to the societies has not yet been fully recognized, either in terms of contracted margins and the subsequent effect on the societies' cost structures, or in terms of liquidity management, since the attracted funds will tend to be more volatile and rate sensitive.

The first part of the break-up in the cartel was seen in 1983, as societies abandoned the recommended rate system in favour of pursuing independent

Table 9.1 Distribution of building society funding by account type: 1982

Type	£m	%
Ordinary	36,510	54.2
High interest	11,400	16.9
Term	15,790	23.4
Regular savings	1,980	2.9
Other	1,740	2.6

Source: Report of the Chief Registrar 1981–82 BSA

pricing policies on both sides of the balance sheet. This was inevitable as increased competition within the industry undermined the cartels principal function in providing an effective mechanism for controlling and enhancing the societies' business.

The evolution of the industry group seen in the initial dismantling of the cartel (although as with the LCBs its spirit will persist for some time) will have a number of important structural and competitive implications for the societies. The benevolent characteristics of the cartel will begin to disappear, as the equilibrium between depositors and borrowers becomes subject to open-market forces. Depositors will receive increased returns on their investments and borrowers will pay more. This will actually reflect a secular trend across the entire market, shifting the balance of power away from the borrower to the investor. In order to fund their growth, which will become asset orientated as the LCBs did during the 1970s, the societies will utilize their powers under the Finance Act, 1983, and increasingly resort to the wholesale money markets. This will increase the cost of funding and increase the complexity of liability management, especially as increased price competition will lead to increased volatility of retail deposits.

The most important effect of abandoning the cartel, however, will be to reduce their 'profitability' by narrowing margins. Economies of scale will have to be obtained and branch networks will have to be made more efficient, as will the overall operation. Inefficient societies will no longer be sheltered by the cartel, and consequently a process of industry consolidation will be quickened in a pattern similar to the LCBs. A developing feature of economies of scale driving consolidation will be increased advertising and promotional expenditure and the need for capital investment in technology.

Industry maturity and generally intensified competition will also bring pressure to improve business and market strategies. New lending products, increasing the range from simple house mortgage finance to new savings schemes and entrance into the money transmission area, all facilitated by the use of new technology, seem to be inevitable together with a general tendency to diversify services.

The societies' institutional structure puts a major block on these developments. The Spalding Committee in 1983 made some radical proposals to allow societies to step beyond the current constraints on their business. Taking a strategic view it saw that financial trends would ultimately erode the societies' competitive position if they were not permitted to extend their business. Those proposals will inevitably undergo some modification, the Green Paper has already indicated this, but they will nevertheless form a central element in the forthcoming Building Society Act.

The major beneficiary of these changes will be the market. Although the cost of a mortgage will be higher, there will be no artificial restrictions on the supply of mortgages. Investors will gain considerably in the quality and rate of return on products as building societies move into money transmission. This will increase the liquidity of some types of investment and will challenge the LCBs' oligopoly, thereby reinforcing the trend towards macro-market rather than internal industry group competitors.

However, all these developments, actual and potential, will challenge the competence of building society management, which has not really created the conditions for success so much as administered them. In future, building society management must become more sophisticated, as it will be concerned with a far more complicated and diverse asset/liability portfolio than previously and growth will be generated to an increasing extent by the extension and diversification of activities. Moreover the conditions for business are not likely to remain constant. As the societies' business becomes more complex and more widely based it will come under ever-increasing scrutiny and control of the monetary authorities. The use of PSL2 as a monetary aggregate for measuring growth is an incidental example of this trend. Increased legislation and supervision will become a function of maintaining the societies' position as public confidence becomes central to their role.

On a wider scale the market is growing more dynamic, suggesting that the conditions of stability that eased the LCBs' movement out of the cartel will not be present to the same extent for the building societies. The financial system is generally becoming less structured as institutions are tending to compete across the market rather than limiting themselves to traditional institutional boundaries. Electronic technology is being used to extend marketing activities through new products and by making cost structures more uniformly competitive. As both a cause and an effect of competition, the personal sector will become more sophisticated and more demanding, undermining traditional assumptions about operating in the retail market and actually making the market more difficult to manage. An incidental effect may well be to remove the traditional distinctions between retail and wholesale business, e.g. the appearance of money-market funds.

In an effort to compete more effectively, particularly against other industry groups (but before they are in a position to transform the basis of their activity), the societies have struck up alliances with banks and finance houses. The logic of this action for the service providers, given the strength of building societies, would seem more pragmatic than strategic. Two societies, the Halifax and Abbey National, have joined with clearing banks to offer cheque book accounts. Two more have begun to offer Access cards and another Visa cards. Other societies have linked with finance houses to provide personal loans. The Leicester Society is offering a Citibank tandem account, selling its services through the post office network, and like the Halifax installing its own ATMs. One very interesting development is the link between the Nottingham Society, the Bank of Scotland and Prestel to provide a home banking service. Unless constitutional changes occur, it is probable that these alliances will become better defined, perhaps moving towards the formation of financial conglomerates.

THE FUTURE

It is apparent that the structure of the building society industry group is undergoing a profound change. The speed of change amongst its components will differ, but overall the effect will be to increase the level of competition amongst the societies themselves and to change the nature of their competitiveness within the market as a whole. This motive will be accentuated by the growing commercial spirit of the societies.

It is very unlikely that the fundamental aspects of building society business will change; the societies, especially the larger ones, will build upon their traditional strengths and extend the range of services they offer to house purchasers, i.e. conveyancing, surveying, estate agency. They will increase the type of lending products available both for house and for other purposes, and increase the range of savings products to incorporate money transmission services.

The capital requirements necessary to provide a broad based service, maintain public confidence and ensure profitability will enforce the move towards consolidation into fewer and larger societies. Management will have to become more competent to cope with all the problems that these changes will bring, and more importantly have to manage a business that will grow less profitable and more risky.

As the building societies' business grows, and competition across the market brings greater equality in competitive, regulatory and fiscal terms, the conditions that made for the almost inevitable success of the societies may well disappear. Their future pre-eminence may, therefore, depend more upon management expertise which could enable the LCBs eventually to regain the initiative in the personal sector.

10 Finance Houses

Finance houses need to be analysed for three reasons. The first is that they do belong to the retail banking market, albeit on a small scale through the operation of so-called 'Money-shops'. These are mainly operated by American-based banks and consumer finance organizations, although a limited presence by British-owned operators has been seen.

The second reason is that finance houses are often substantially involved in consumer finance operations, either through retailers ('indirect' finance) or by providing credit directly either through their branches, through press advertising or through mail shots. To this extent they are an important feature of the total consumer finance market. The main finance houses are owned by the clearing banks: purchased in periods of regulatory control they have acted as good profit centres in their own right, often operating autonomously, on higher margins than their banking parents, and in areas of higher risk. They have, in the past, produced countercyclical profits to their parents since much of their lending is at fixed rate for medium term, and much of their funding is done on three-month wholesale money, with very limited retail deposits.

The third aspect of interest is that, because they operate in areas of higher risk, they have tended to be far more innovative than their parents, or used as test beds by their parents for schemes which are later adopted. It is, however, a curious feature of their operations that the clearing bank owned finance houses have tended not to be incorporated into universal strategies by their parents. Their value is that, just as LCBs and even building societies occupy market positions based on a mixture of economies of scale that can be extracted from their market position and have developed corporate images necessary to sustain those positions, so finance houses offer different cost structures, different economies of scale and different images. These enable them to hold a market position which the LCBs cannot directly fill, and which should be exploited.

History

Finance houses were originally based on the provision of hire purchase facilities to industry and to the consumer. This business has now diversified masssively by taking in leasing business, which accounts for most leading finance houses' profits, and factoring.

The standard finance houses operate through limited branch networks, which act as administration centres for new business representatives. Their location usually detracts from their ability to attract any volume of direct consumer business.

The main finance houses are formed into the Finance Houses' Association (FHA), which has 43 members, accounting for 90 per cent of finance house business. The ownership of primary finance houses is as follows:

Bank of Scotland	North-West Securities
Barclays	Mercantile Credit
Lloyds (61.7%)	Lloyds & Scottish & Bowmaker
Midland	Forward Trust Group
National Westminster	Lombard North Central
Co-op	First Co-operative Finance
Royal Bank (39.3%)	Lloyds & Scottish & Bowmaker
Standard Chartered	Chartered Trust
TSB	United Dominions Trust
Williams & Glyns	St Margarets Trust
Yorkshire	N. British Securities

There has been a move towards concentration in the finance house industry, with business concentrating in the hands of a few major companies, primarily the bank-owned. Despite this, it remains the most diversified and heterogeneous of the three industry groups involved in the retail banking market.

Most finance house consumer business originates at the point-of-sale. To attract this business, finance houses either establish a coterie of connections with manufactures to finance their products or alternatively establish themselves as sole providers of credit at retailers. The connections that Mercantile Credit and Lombard North Central have developed illustrate this:

Mercantile Credit	Automobile Association
	Peugeot–Talbot Group
	Alfa Romeo
	Ace Belmont International

Personal loans are extended on a 'direct' basis, mainly through direct mail. In 1982 such programmes were conducted in connection with Debenhams, British Airways and the British Horse Society.

Lombard North Central	British Leyland
	RAC
	Special terms to the Caravan Club

A specialist finance subsidiary 'Tricity Finance' undertakes all small 'white and brown' good financing.

Additionally, some finance houses operate credit card operations for retailers. This will be looked at more closely in chapters 11 and 12. The most important plastic card 'links' with retailers are as follows:

Forward Trust Group	Club 24, a joint venture with Hepworths, but which provides small value finance schemes at the point-of-sale in the form of branded customer accounts
Citibank	Vantage Card for UDS and Marks & Spencer in the South
North-West Security	Operates the Marks & Spencer's account in the Midlands and North
Welbeck Finance	Has 29 clients, but includes Debenhams and Harvey Nichols.

Table 10.1 indicates by volume the importance of the different categories of consumer lending by the finance houses. It shows the importance of the finance houses' links with manufacturers, distributors and retailers through the scale of their lending for cars and home improvements. There are two further interesting facets to the table. The first is the presence of checks, vouchers and credit tokens, primarily offered by Provident Finance to the least sophisticated consumers

Table 10.1 Regulated fixed sum instalment credit extended at fixed rate classified by purpose in 1984 (excluding charges and seasonally adjusted)

	£ million	%
New cars	966.0	22.0
Used cars	975.8	22.1
Commercial vehicles	115.3	2.6
Motor cycles	62.6	1.4
Caravans	71.1	1.6
Household and personal goods	418.2	9.5
Home improvements	276.3	6.3
Other goods and services	394.5	8.9
Checks vouchers and credit tokens	146.7	3.3
Other fixed sum credit	980.0	22.2
Total	4,406.5	

Source: SDM6 Table 4

Table 10.2 Total credit business of finance houses (seasonally adjusted) (£ million)

	Accounts outstanding		Increase in accounts outstanding
	Fixed sum	Running account	
1980	7,651	796	1,300
1981	8,320	1,030	1,203
1982	9,869	1,289	1,808
1983	12,404	1,653	2,899
1984	14,740	2,029	2,712

Source: SDM6 Table 5

Table 10.3 Money-shop operation in the UK

Name	Parent company	Number of branches	Hours of business
Associates	Associates Corporation	58	Monday–Friday 9.00–17.00
Avco	Avco Corporation	86	Monday–Friday 9.00–17.00 Saturday 9.00–12.30
Beneficial Trust	Beneficial Corporation	70	Monday–Friday 9.15–17.15
HFC Trust & Savings	Household Finance Corporation of America	120	Monday–Friday 9.00–17.30 Saturday 9.00–17.30
Boston Trust & Savings	First National Bank of Boston	14	Monday–Friday 9.00–17.30
Western Trust & Savings	Royal Bank of Canada	29	Monday–Friday 9.15–17.00 Saturday 9.15–16.00
Citibank Savings	Citicorp	41	Monday–Friday 9.00–17.00 Saturday 9.00–12.00

in the UK. The second is the growth in what can be described as 'direct' credit, offered either through branch outlets/money-shops, press advertising or more usually through direct mail to the consumer. Although the table simply shows the scale of this type of lending in the unsecured and secured reducing categories, there is a further type, the revolving credit facility, whose growth is shown in table 10.2. A more sophisticated, longer term and more flexible credit account than the reducing agreement, it, nevertheless, remains a relatively minor form of lending. This reflects both the inability of finance houses to market the product effectively and the reluctance of their customers to use longer term revolving credit facilities.

The business cycles of the finance houses are inextricably tied to patterns of consumer spending, which are prompted by economic and government action. For instance real growth in PDI in 1982–83 coupled to patterns of consumer lending led to a substantial growth (see chapter 3).

MONEY-SHOPS

In addition to the main finance houses there are the American owned 'money-shops' operations. First seen in the UK in 1972, their networks and importance have steadily grown. Indeed they have influenced not only the business policies of their finance house competitors, but have also acted catalytically on the clearing banks' attitudes towards their customers. As table 10.3 shows there are only six main operators in the UK. There was an early shake-out in the business when some companies, faced with the prospect of large capital and management investment and relatively high risk consumer business, pulled out. All offer continuous credit, except Avco, and all provide personal loans and mortgage finance. The types of account available from these operations is fairly uniform. All offer current accounts of one kind or another, but the most sophisticated are offered by Western Trust & Savings and Citibank Savings. Both of these offer interest on current account. All offer savings accounts, and only HFC does not offer a term savings account.

Only two UK owned operators have ventured into the money-shop market, North West Securities, which pulled out in 1980, and Forward Trust Group's Forward Trust and Savings whose growth was truncated in 1981. In both cases a preference for traditional styles of finance house business linked to an unwillingness or an inability to commit capital to a risk venture seems to have determined their actions.

How far the new money-shop operations will be successful *vis-à-vis* their finance house competitors, or indeed to the clearing banks is debatable. All are making reasonable profits from the business, but with investment in new infrastructure, and payments in the form of management fees and interest to their parents, the real position is difficult to calculate.

However, the impact is certainly being made in a qualitative way. Opening hours are longer, and the style of the branches is more comfortable and convenient to customers, breaking away from the institutionalized atmosphere of the clearing banks. Their branches are relatively low cost units, offering a limited product line exclusively to the personal sector; they are in some ways more sophisticated building societies. They have also been innovative in product design and marketing techniques. It is fair to say that their activities have certainly prompted clearing banks to rethink their branch designs, opening hours and marketing tactics. From this point of view their influence has been very positive.

They remain, none the less, relatively small-scale operations, as specialists in the market-place, aspiring to compete against the clearing banks, but crucially not competing really either in terms of rate or overall convenience at the moment. They will represent a threat only so long as the clearing banks do not match the qualitative aspects of their service.

Indeed their strategies at the moment seem geared up mainly for growth. A more likely eventuality concerning the money-shops' operations is that they will be used as the basis for a growth strategy in the consumer sector. Citibank has begun to expand its house mortgage finance facility and has applied for membership to the clearing house. Using a mixture of centralized and branch-based operations it is probable that, with the resources of the American parent, it will make a sizeable impression on the UK market unhindered by the high cost structures of the LCBs. Given a lead, other operators may well follow.

Conclusions

Finance houses generally, and more importantly as subsidiaries of clearing banks, grew as a direct consequence of the banks being shut out of the consumer credit market by regulatory constraints. In a period when the bias in the banks' personal sector profile was up-market they established themselves in the middle- and down-market areas, but also made substantial inroads into banked customer business. They achieved this by providing convenient, accessible credit, albeit at a high cost.

The growth, which in most cases was about 25–30 per cent in 1982, remains very strong, but is still largely based on the provision of indirect finance. Direct finance techniques such as direct mail and press advertising are more widely used. Money-shops or retail credit and savings outlets provide a third and important element in the market. Just as building societies are establishing payment systems on the basis of savings, so finance houses may do the same to provide credit facilities. The attractiveness of the longer term, more sophisticated, revolving credit account provides the finance houses with a more cost-effective form of credit provision. Written also on variable rate terms it is lessening the cyclicality of their profits, and is filling a gap in the consumer finance market just as indirect credit is rapidly declining, and as banks, credit cards and even retailers begin to take a greater share of that market.

There are patterns in the finance house market, however, which are worth reviewing in the light of the clearing banks' involvement in the market, and which should be considered in the formulation of their group level strategic plans.

- Their business is high margin compared to the clearing banks, although now less counter-cyclical.
- It carries a commensurately higher risk, although the finance houses' market position allows them to price accordingly.
- The customer profiles are predominantly middle- and down-market, moving down-market and higher risk as the banks increase their presence in the market. This will be offset to an extent by the nature of the connections some of the finance houses have with retailers and manufactures. It is probable that this factor will be less influential over time.
- Historical and management and infrastructure problems preclude a growing presence in the consumer market by the long-established finance houses. Nevertheless the newer, innovative and more dynamic money-shop operators are demonstrating the growth and profit potential of the market.

The future of finance houses in the consumer market hangs on two factors: the first is dependent on how far patterns of consumer behaviour change and the extent and manner to which competitors fulfil those needs. The second is the ability of the finance houses not necessarily to change their market position but to change their infrastructures and business style to continue to meet market demands for particular types of credit at a profit. The examples of Mercantile Credit's successful marketing and business schemes and of First Co-operative Finance's strategic links with its parents are valuable. They show how a finance house can fill a market position that its parent cannot and also how, by sharing systems, finance houses can fill a strategic group role.

It is in this context that finance houses can maintain a mainstream role in retail banking, through fitting into a coherent Bank Group strategy, by adopting a market position that depends both on direct links with manufacturers and retailers and on adopting segmentation strategies that are not available attitudinally and practically to their parents.

11 Retailers

Introduction

Retailers are included in this book, not so much because of the scale of their activities which are slight, but because they represent an element which has the potential for growth. At present some extend credit facilities to support the sale of their goods; those that do not use finance house companies like Unicredit and Tricity Finance. But it is both here, and in their potential ability to sell financial services, most obviously insurance, through their low cost distribution networks, that they could figure as substantial players in the retail banking market of the future.

There are three distinct approaches to retailers' involvement:

— sell financial services direct
— set up a specialist subsidiary
— invite a specialist outsider to undertake the operation.

An example of the first type is GUS, the mail order organization; the example of the American giant retailing chain, Sears Roebuck, provides an interesting perspective on what might happen. Debenham's finance house 'Welbeck Finance' and Hepworth's Club 24 (in conjunction with Forward Trust Group) are examples of the second type, and Marks and Spencer's use of Citibank and North West Securities examples of the third. The use of credit and charge cards supplements these facilities.

Background

Sears Roebuck provides a fascinating example of how a retailer has gradually evolved to straddle financial services and retailing. It is worth making the point at the outset that the conditions for its growth were size, nationwide coverage and the highly fragmented US financial service market.

It has built its financial services up by applying the Sears imprimatur to financial products, and by then assembling a range of products and selling them through direct mail techniques based on extensive data bases of customer information. The result is that it has 25 million cardholders and 12 million catalogue holders, and is now in the process of building an integrated range of financial services; it has recently acquired the stockbroker Dean Witter, and a very large commercial and residential real estate agent in addition to a savings and loan organization. The importance of financial services are reflected in the breakdown of its turnover and profits; retailing was worth $20 billion in 1982 and produced $350 thousand profit a 1.7 per cent return. Financial services were worth $10 billion turnover, but brought in $500 thousand profit a 5.5 per cent return. (These figures are directly pertinent to banks, not simply as a competitor's activity.) In the UK there were three significant groupings: Debenhams/Welbeck Finance, Hepworths/Club 24 (which has now ended) and GUS. Two smaller operations Burton's Readicredit and House of Frazer's in-house credit scheme account for the the most important groups. There are three main types of credit account offered by these retailers:

—option accounts – similar to Visa cards or Access
—budget accounts – a fixed monthly payment, giving a credit limit which is a multiple of that payment
—credit sales agreement/HP.

Plastic cards, of which there are about 5 million on issue in the UK from retailers, either activate an account in the same way that an Access card does, or acts as a method of authentication and authorization. Table 11.1 illustrates the volumes of credit extended by retailers. It clearly shows the very short

Table 11.1 Credit extended by retailers: 1977–84 (seasonally adjusted) (£ million)

	New credit extended	Accounts outstanding	Increase in accounts outstanding
1977	2,306	1,070	146
1978	2,698	1,257	187
1979	3,020	1,482	225
1980	3,259	1,580	98
1981	3,211	1,612	32
1982	3,447	1,748	136
1983	3,684	1,886	138
1984	3,845	2,002	136

Source: SDM8

life of borrowing by customers, and indicates an erratic and slow growth. This is mainly due to the pre-eminence of other payment methods and the limited scale of retailer-based credit in the UK. Credit cards are responsible for about 25 per cent of all sales, with bank budget accounts and revolving credit accounts satisfying most of the remaining demand for credit. Growth would seem dependent on increased value rather than volumes of goods sold. It appears that retailers use credit schemes for boosting retail sales rather than as another source of profit. This is generally true, although there are some exceptions to this rule. It is, therefore, worth looking at some examples of credit provision through retailers.

Welbeck Finance Limited

Debenhams own 10 per cent of the equity, but obtain the majority of the profit. The company primarily serves the Debenhams group but, through Welbeck Finance, provides services, credit card processing and marketing services to non-Debenham owned companies. It runs 900,000 Debenhams card accounts, and accounts for 32 other retail groups. Welbeck also provides a service to direct response firms sending out advertising material in its mailings to account holders.

Interest charges represent the most important source of income, but the 2.5–3 per cent merchant card charge also brings in significant income. Welbeck provides all three kinds of product described earlier through Debenhams stores, as well as a Homemaker Charge Account, which is a mixture of an option account but with the repayment profile of a budget account.

Table 11.2 shows the importance of credit to Debenhams, with the percentages by volume of transaction sales. Welbeck's main strength is based on a highly efficient computer operation, which gives it an ability to target direct marketing effort on those consumers who are most likely to respond and make purchases.

Hepworths/Club 24

Jointly owned by Forward Trust and Hepworth, Club 24 is largely funded and managed by Forward Trust personnel. It runs budget accounts for 16 companies, with a total issued card base of 700,000, 550,000 of which belong to Hepworths and Dixons.

Table 11.2 Importance of credit to Debenhams: 1982

Cash	45%
Cheques	20%
In-house credit cards	20%
Barclaycard and Access	4%
Hire purchase	5%
American Express/Diners	1%

Credit card customers spend two to three times as much as cash spenders.
Source: IBRO

Club 24 offers simply a budget account, with high volume, low value business. Less sophisticated than Welbeck, it derives much of its income from management fees for card processing rather than from cash investment in consumer loans. Club 24 does not undertake direct selling or endorsed mailings, although this would be in the interests of both Club 24 and the retailers.

Although not as profitable as Welbeck (£8.1 million pre-tax profit in 1982) it still represents a strong investment for Hepworths, although probably primarily regarded as a selling tool for the retail outlets.

Great Universal Stores (GUS)

The tenth largest company in the UK, it has approximately 35 per cent of the UK mail order market, and controls about 2,000 outlets. Mail order represents 40 per cent of GUS's interests.

GUS operates three types of financial service: mail order credit, hire purchase and consumer finance and a small retailer credit card operation. It runs two lines of credit cards, one for itself, and one for Heron's 10,000 customer card base. GUS operates, as part of its mail order activity, a highly sophisticated credit reference and control agency.

GUS seems to be switching more assets to its financial services, which in 1981–82 made a 19 per cent contribution to pre-tax profits along with travel and property. It is not in a position to compete directly with banks, but would be well able to promote financial services through the mail.

Conclusions

The homogeneity of the financial market in the UK, and the established and growing business of banks and credit with their universal acceptability and advantages in terms of marketing and other economies of scale are bound to limit the potential for retailer credit schemes. Indeed the problems and costs of operating credit schemes acts as a major deterrent.

Although Debenhams and Club 24 branded cards account for about 30 per cent by volume of their customers transactions, with Visa and Access for only 5 per cent, changing patterns of retailing and the introduction of EFT/POS may well see a significant curtailment in retailer credit. EFT/POS probably represents the most significant watershed for retail credit in the long term; cards linked to bank accounts or credit card companies will provide customers with instant, guaranteed sources of cash.

EFT/POS will in fact provide retailers with advantages; the merchant fee on credit cards will probably become a thing of the past so extending the use of these facilities to retailers like Marks and Spencer and the John Lewis Partnership who do not use them at present. It will also free them from the limitations of the £50 cheque cards, incidentally making bank accounts more attractive.

With the growing dislocation of credit schemes, it may well be that retailers move more towards the provision and sale of financial services like Sears Roebuck and J.C. Penney in the United States. And it is probable that it is in this sphere that retailers will emerge as mainstream competitors to banks, in what all will see as the most profitable part of the retail bank market.

12 Miscellaneous – Credit Cards and Charge Cards; Money Market Funds and Cash Management Accounts; Travellers Cheques

Credit Cards and Charge Cards

Introduction

In addition to the retailer branded credit cards, described in the previous chapter, more sophisticated national and international organizations have grown up crossing retailer and customer boundaries. There are four main organizations involved in the UK, Visa, MasterCard, American Express and Diners Club, of which the first two are global payment systems, providing credit and to a much lesser extent debit cards, whilst the other two are charge cards organizations.

Background

Plastic credit cards first appeared in the UK in 1966. Issued by Barclays in a link with the then Bank Americard, it subsequently became the Visa network. When launched, its primary purpose was not to create an additional payment mechanism, but to encourage customers to take credit from the bank by adding a delayed payment facility and revolving credit line to guaranteed payment at the point-of-sale.

To combat the dominance of Barclays in this field, the other three main clearing banks issued the Access Card in 1971–72. The Joint Credit Card Company (JCCC) organizes and operates the standard payment system functions of authorization, retailer contact and payment processing with each individual bank having responsibility for marketing the card. To match the international service of Barclaycard, it was necessary for Access to link into similar operations abroad. Finding different partners from Barclays' was a competitive obligation, and so it made arrangements with Eurocard and the

American Interbank Card Association; these were primary contacts, run by banks in regional areas with interests similar to Access. The bilateral arrangements were rationalized into the world-wide MasterCard network.

The Barclaycard operation in the UK, which issued cards to Co-operative and TSB customers has become much more focussed on Barclays' customers and is developing a less complicated and more competitive position in the market. The Co-op and the TSB with its Trustcard have not developed their own Visa card operations in the UK. Visa cards are also now being issued by the Bank of Scotland, the AA, and by some of the money market funds, reflecting Visa's pluralistic market policy.

In addition to the nationally bank owned and internationally affiliated operations, there are two major international travel and entertainment or charge cards operative in the UK market. These are the non-bank owned financial group, American Express, and Citicorp's Diners Club, which in the UK is 49.8 per cent owned by National Westminster, but with Citicorp owning the majority stake.

While the banks possess established and aligned customer bases to market their credit cards, Amex and to a lesser extent Diners Club have to advertise through the media and use mail-shots to attract business, operating very much on a remote scale. Amex is a highly specialized global financial services organization; although it does operate independently from banks in the issue of its greencard, its premium card, the Goldcard, has been issued primarily by Lloyds and also by Grindlays.

The most recent trend in plastic cards are the gold premium cards, marketed by the banks to up-market customers (those earning over £20 thousand per annum) in the 1981–83 period. Although now an established feature of the credit card market, the market is comparatively small. It is estimated that the Lloyds/Amex gold card has about 40,000 customers and the Midland gold MasterCard about 20,000. Figures for Barclays Visa premium card probably fall into the intervening area of about 30,000. These cards are seen as prerequisite of a full service bank serving particular segments. It is questionable how profitable they are, excepting Lloyds, in addressing their limited, sophisticated and cost-conscious market with highly sophisticated and costly products.

Table 12.1 shows the market share of credit cards in 1974–82. In 1982, credit card growth was 25 per cent, with 19.5 million cards issued to 11 million customers, while in 1983 growth slowed to 10 per cent, with 21.6 million cards in circulation, of which 15.6 million were bank issued and 12.5 million were credit cards. The biggest growth has taken place in the blue collar and clerical groups. This trend explains the diminishing market share of Amex and Diners Club. Access and Barclaycard have about equal representation in retailer

Table 12.1 Market share of credit and charge cards in the UK: 1974–82 (thousands)

	1974	1979	1981	1982
Access	3,100	4,300	5,400	6,100
American Express	160	410	700	776
Barclaycard	2,890	4,952	6,113	6,607
Trustcard	–	–	1,540	N/A
Diner's Club	N/A	N/A	260	N/A

Source: Monopolies Commission, Card Companies and IBRO

Table 12.2 Access and Barclaycard – vouchers processed and turnover: 1982

	Vouchers processed (million)	Turnover (£ million)
Access	102.1	2,324.6
Barclaycard	99.1	2,178.9

Source: IBRO

outlets, being accepted in some 192,000 outlets. Amex is accepted in about 67,000 outlets.

Although Barclaycard has more cards issued, Access has overtaken it in terms of vouchers processed and turnover (see table 12.2). In 1981 only 24 per cent of the adult population had a credit card. This increased by 10 per cent in 1982 and 14.4 per cent in 1983 to represent 33 per cent by the year end. Even so, credit cards account for only 24 per cent of all credit transactions, while bank loans have a share of about 40 per cent. The increase in credit card holding is due to a widening of the net and, primarily, the issue of Visa cards by TSB to its large customer base.

This reflects two characteristics. Firstly Access has expanded mainly into its banks' better customers, as shown by the fact that its average credit limit is £625 compared to Barclays £500 (a point reinforced by an average limit of £475 on Trustcard). Secondly, Barclays have more successfully penetrated the market available to them, suggesting that Access will grow larger than Barclaycard through a more thorough exploitation of its available customer bases.

However, although Access may be in a position to capitalize on its economies of scale, it is clear that Barclays has stolen a march on it in terms of marketing. Barclaycard has also been shown to be a major profit earner, gaining some £30 million for Barclays in 1982. JCCC means that although the profits of Access are the same if not larger than Barclaycard, the value to member banks is smaller. It is incidentally interesting to see the marketing of the Access card outside the banks through connections with building societies, namely Midland Access to Nationwide and National Westminster Access to National Provincial.

Barclaycard also benefits from a more unified management vision. Even within the structure of Barclays it is permitted to run virtually autonomously, developing its own strategies in partial competition with its own parent, the benefits being seen in the context of a wider market. Its value as such is seen in the way it is pioneering experiments at Amoco petrol stations, in EFT/POS, and telephone authorization techniques. It has a unity and coherence of purpose that cannot be matched by the JCCC, whose group integrity may come under increasing strain as competitive pressures increase.

One common problem facing all the companies in the UK are losses through credit losses and fraud. It is estimated that these represent about 1 per cent of turnover, of which about 80 per cent consist of credit losses. There are three facets to the problem: whether the card is valid, whether the holder is valid, and finally whether the holder is worthy of the credit request. The companies are employing a mixture of tactics to overcome these problems which can be categorized into both visual and electronic. The visual aspect will revolve around the use of holograms on the card and the electronic around the use of authorization telephones, which is based on using a card reader and an automatic telephone device that will switch through to the appropriate card company. Problems of credit and validity (through hot-card files) should significantly reduce theft. The four main credit and charge card companies are currently involved in setting up a joint authorization telephone company.

Fraud, credit loss and authorization are central pre-occupations of the two global payment systems Visa and MasterCard. As their problem extended to international proportions they are establishing communication networks that will permit cross-border authorization as well as settlement links.

Visa and MasterCard

The issues surrounding the future of Barclaycard, Trustcard and Access cannot be viewed outside the global activities of the larger organizations, Visa and MasterCard. It is in the development of payment systems that they will gain national and then international acceptance with relative ease and economy. It is improbable that clearing banks will develop their own individual payments systems, but much more likely they will affiliate to the product ranges and contingent broader ambitions of the global payment systems.

Visa Visa possesses a highly streamlined connection into the UK market through its links with Barclays and TSB. However, Visa has ambitions that may subordinate the objectives of member organizations to its own operations: it intends becoming the dominant international consumer payment system by establishing the first global electronic payment system. Size and market dominance is central to this because it entails a total commitment to EFT/POS when the remainder of the international payment systems possess and believe in offering a variety of payment mechanisms.

To achieve this dominance requires that its own market remains relatively fragmented; its belief in pluralism against the trend of consolidation is a will to ensure that it maintains a power equilibrium in its favour. Unlike MasterCard, it decentralizes power to regional boards and through those arranges partnerships with foreign organizations.

Its extremely ambitious strategy is to have an electronic communications system, accompanied by credit or debit cards, which will reduce fraud. The economics of this approach are questioned by MasterCard, who cannot see 80 per cent of transactions taking place over electronic terminals.

However, it is well advanced in its desire to enable cash withdrawals around the world. It is currently in the process of raising £40 million from member banks to finance a £100 million spending programme. The objective is to introduce an all purpose electronic debit card that will be issued to 30 million customers by 1986 and about 8,000 ATMs located world-wide.

In this, Visa is embarking on an independent future, operating ATMs itself in countries where its members do not wish to operate the ATMs themselves. It is, therefore, not only linking up existing networks, but also setting up a separate network. It is this almost imperialistic approach that has alienated the Eurocard community, and has deprived Visa of an important entrée into the European markets.

MasterCard MasterCard's strategies are based more on the philosophy of mutuality than Visa's, aiming to provide members with those services that may not be available or provided by non-bank financial competitors. Examples of this are the gold card and travellers cheque.

It does not believe that EFT/POS terminals can be justified on the scale Visa envisage, purely on the basis of potential fraud and credit costs to the issuer. It is, therefore, adapting the design of the card to prevent fraud, through visual security devices and digitized signature verification.

Accordingly, its development of sophisticated authorization and data communication networks, primarily in the USA at the moment (INAS, INET and MACS) allow for reduced costs, flexibility and reliability. It is also establishing its own ATM network in the USA of between 400–600 machines. Indeed, its link with Eurocard, via the European Authorisation Network, permitting credit card transactions to be authorized and processed throughout Europe, and its intention to provide an on-line link to the United States, is an important step in constructing a global mechanism of the same dimension as Visa.

Its professed commitment to payment systems that are paper and not electronically based is not only at variance with Visa but would be highly questionable were it not for the fact that the incorporation of Thomas Cook and Wells Fargo into the system, on a semi-autonomous basis, effectively makes MasterCard the second largest cheque issuer in the world.

Conclusions

- Credit cards and, increasingly, debit cards have become a major element in national payment systems. Their integration into international systems, providing economies of scale and customer convenience contribute hugely to their function and importance.
- The credit card market is still highly concentrated, focussing primarily on JCCC/Access and Barclaycard, but with Trustcard and Amex as other important elements. The concentration of power in the UK suggests that Visa will not fragment the market in the short term, and certainly not through conventional routes. Changing patterns of competitive behaviour and the growing diversity of finance service organizations may, however, provide Visa increasingly with an environment which it can exploit.
- The product ranges of the card companies will extend in line with the parent organizations (e.g. debit cards, money funds, travellers cards and a segmented range of cards). Affiliation will be both a necessity to UK financial institutions, and will also increasingly affect the structure of their activities.
- Secondary financial institutions will wish to become card issuers (e.g. National Provincial and Nationwide Building Societies as issuers of Access), opening up larger markets.
- The proportion of the UK holding credit cards Visa/MasterCard/Access will increase as will the volumes of transactions. This will eclipse the importance of retailer cards. It is, however, questionable as to how much further growth is available to the card companies. Although card holding, reflected in reduced credit limits, is being extended to a wider, less affluent market there are boundaries on this. Most growth will be based on increased usage and greater use of the credit facilities.
- The card companies will be the automatic platform for all the major technological developments (e.g. Barclaycard experiment at Rochester and Norwich with EFT/POS at petrol stations). However, EFT/POS may also act to damage the business conditions for branded credit cards.

The present structure of Access through the JCCC will constrain its development.

Money Market Funds and Cash Management Accounts

Money market funds originated in the USA. Offering gross interest rates tied to money market rates and providing a cheque book so that the account resembled a high interest payment cheque account, they are proving to be spectacularly successful. Their introduction in the UK by a small number of unit trusts, merchant banks and a clearing bank has not proved as successful as in the USA as a direct consequence of mistiming and partly due to the institutional structuring of interest rates.

The retail deposits that the funds were trying to attract tend to be volatile pursuing the best available return. At the time the money market funds were first introduced, offshore roll-up funds were absorbing a good volume of those funds. Although they were offering similar rates, investors were subject only to capital gains tax and not income tax. This tax loophole has now been closed.

The money market funds have certain in-built factors that make them less attractive to large numbers of investors. Most require a minimum investment of £2,500 and a cheque book with a minimum £250 per transaction. However, some accounts have now begun to offer credit cards.

By the end of 1983 these accounts in total had attracted about £500 million in retail deposits. The main reason why the money funds have failed to attract substantial sums of money is because of the building societies. They have the advantages of composite rate and borrowers whose mortgage interest payments attract tax relief. This has given the societies a 3 per cent gross margin advantage compared with typical money market fund rates.

To increase the attractiveness of the funds, in the United States a special overdraft facility has been added to the account, which is secured on holdings of unit trusts and certain life policies. But at least one building society, the Leicester, offers through a connection with Citibank a cheque book and credit facility with no minimum transaction amount.

The move in the States may be an evolution of the money market account towards the more all-purpose cash-management account. The only such account on offer in the UK is through Hambro Life pioneered by Merrill Lynch the stockbrokers. Offering a banking, credit and financial management service it is aimed at the self-employed and wealthy. Its main attraction is that is simplifies financial affairs by bringing them all together in one place. Its features are as follows:

- An interest-bearing current account, with money market rates on £10,000 minimum deposit, but with a cheque book and cheque card.
- An automatic line of credit, from 40 to 60 per cent of the value of investments.
- A Diners Club charge card.
- Administration of buying, holding and selling of shares, bonds and unit trusts. Life assurance and pension funds and an optional portfolio management are available.
- A monthly statement of transactions and evaluation of assets plus an annual summary designed to simplify tax returns.

There are disadvantages: there is no access to cash dispensing machines, and cheques can be cashed only up to £50 at National Westminster and Williams and Glyn's banks. The service costs £60 per annum in addition to the minimum investment of £25,000 cash, shares and financial assets. The account is, like the money market accounts, aimed at the top end of the market.

Conclusions

Whatever the merits and demerits of cash management accounts and money market funds, they do increase pressure specifically on the LCBs' retail deposits, and threaten to replace the all round financial service of the LCBs. It is probable, therefore, that the LCBs, in an endeavour to safeguard their own retail deposits and protect their up-market customer segments, will introduce 'money market' funds, and may eventually be forced into offering packages of services, rather like a cash-management account.

Travellers Cheques

As with plastic cards, the trend in the travellers cheque market is towards consolidation, with a few major issuer groups emerging. It is thought that size, market presence and economies of scale are vital in attracting issuing banks and customers. These same factors are also essential for survival in a period of intensifying competition, as new groups enter the market-place and as volume growth begins to fall with the deregulation of the US market, and the growing sophistication of customers. The main operators in travellers cheques are as follows:

Amex	About 50 per cent market share: it has no captive customer base and relies on other banks and retailers for its distribution.

Bank of America	11 per cent of total market, it has a captive customer base; it has begun also to issue Visa and MasterCard travellers cheques to strengthen the distribution of its product.
Citicorp	11 per cent of market, with strong captive base, relationship with other Citibank products.
Thomas Cook/ETC	14 per cent of total. Owned by the Midland Bank, it is the strongest branded travellers cheque in the UK, and in its partnership with ETC has a 30 per cent share of the European market.
MasterCard	It has only just entered the travellers cheque market, but in its link with Thomas Cook it possesses major market potential.
Visa	It has about 10 per cent of the world market, largely by piggy-backing on Barclays.

About 30 per cent of travellers cheques are used in the US, as they represent a form of national payments system. This explains the predominance of American issuers. The UK is after continental Europe, the third largest market in the world. The main UK clearing banks issue as follows:

Barclays	Visa
Lloyds	Amex
Midland	Thomas Cook
Nat. West.	Nat. West.

The development of uniform Eurocheque threatens the travellers cheque in Europe, as does credit cards. None the less, travellers cheques remain an important part of the international scheme of payment systems. All the banks tend to regard travellers cheques as peripheral to the main services, and it is only Midland/Thomas Cook which seems to be developing an integrated strategy towards international payment system instruments.

Travellers cheques are increasingly being issued by non-banks, such as building societies and money-shops. Often on a non-commission basis, to extend their product lines and improve their attractiveness to customers. Thomas Cook has arranged with thousands of European banks to issue its travellers cheques through a licensing agreement under the Euro-travellers cheque (ETC) scheme, and has gained substantial penetration as a result. The main thrust of Thomas Cook travellers cheques is outside Europe, since

Midland is heavily involved with uniform Eurocheque. The link with MasterCard strengthens the work presence and strength of the travellers cheque, working for the mutual benefit of Thomas Cook and MasterCard.

Bank America and Citicorp only have a limited number of retail outlets through which to promote their product. Visa's pluralistic policy may lead to overall market strength for Visa but means cheque issuing banks compete against each other. However, still in its early stages of development, Visa relies heavily on Barclays.

Conclusions

It is probable that there will be no real further growth in the volumes of travellers cheques, and ultimately there will be a decline in their usage, as credit and charge cards develop global electronic payment mechanisms.

In the short term, however, the travellers cheque market will display all the symptoms of an industry at the stage of maturity moving into decline, with new entrants causing intensifying competition and a consequent lowering of profitability in the industry. It is also likely that further agglomeration will take place in the industry group.

Part IV The Issues

13 Payment Systems

Introduction

The LCBs' oligopoly is based on their control of payment systems. They have built substantial customer franchises on the basis of those services. Their competitiveness is based on their respective market share of current (chequing) accounts. Yet payment systems have been regarded primarily as a means to an end. Payment systems, like the branch network were developed to attract deposits. The growth in their sophistication was, until recently, a long slow evolutionary one; with the LCBs providing only two systems, cash and cheques.

Payment systems represent the key to competing successfully in the retail banking market. The LCBs have used them to build and maintain a customer franchise, through which they have gained cheap retail deposits and provided a range of lending and ancillary services. Yet the provision of payment services has become highly expensive, made more so by the LCBs' failure to price the service rationally, preferring rather to cross-subsidize it through underpricing deposits or through lending and ancillary products.

The growth in the market means that the volume of payments has increased dramatically, exacerbating the problems of cost. To counter this problem the LCBs have introduced additional payment mechanisms, namely credit cards and BACS (automated clearing service) and are in the process of introducing even more capital intensive but efficient payment systems in the form of EFT/POS, in order to reduce the volume of paper and so the cost of operating the systems. In addition they are further automating the existing cash and cheque-based payment system.

An important feature of payment systems is the way in which co-operative policies are imposed in order to facilitate the transfer of funds. The development of the clearing house, BACS and new EFT/POS are all embodiments of this. At another level the agglomeration of credit cards into a few very large companies, the formation of eurocheque and the consolidation of the travellers cheque companies all reflect the necessity of co-operative ventures to reduce costs at the individual bank level and to make the system universally acceptable and workable. But enforced co-operation can tend to result in something akin to perfect competition with uniform pricing policies. The LCBs' oligopoly was partly a consequence of this 'perfect competition' and was influential in producing their common irrational pricing structures. In these circumstances competition has to find other outlets or alternative methods of manifesting itself. It may be that a combination of these factors – irrational pricing, the growing cost of providing payment services, the uncompetitiveness of the LCBs in a universal sense because of their oligopoly, have all contributed to the gradual erosion of their market position in the personal sector.

A feature of clearing banks having established strong customer franchises through the provision of payment services is that payment mechanisms are seen as the key to establishing a profitable market position, and as a consequence competitors will be keen to offer payment services. But in doing this, they are in a strong position to operate more efficient and less costly payments media to their customers which in turn makes them more competitive. The LCBs, to maintain market position, are compelled to match or pre-empt these moves through further investment in payments technology, while simultaneously maintaining existing and less efficient and costly payment systems. It is a dilemma of major proportions facing the LCBs and one of their principal strategic challenges.

Payment Systems: Nature and Function

A payment system can be defined as the collection of instruments, rules and procedures that enables users to meet payment obligations. There are three elements: source, user and payee.

Table 13.1 Methods and volume of transactions: 1983

Form of payment	Millions of transactions
Non-cash	
Cheque	1,050
Standing order	230
Direct debit	170
Postal order	125
Credit card	130
Credit transaction	100
Cash	
Over 50p	2,000

Source: IBRO

Table 13.2 Sources of cash: 1984

	£ billion
Cash withdrawals from banks	24
Cash obtained from post offices	22
Cash obtained from employers	35
Cash obtained from other sources	6

Source: IBRO

There are a number of different payment systems with cash remaining the most elementary, convenient, and cheapest system of all. Cheques come a distant second, but dominate all other payment systems (see table 13.1 and 13.2). Although the use of cash is set to decline over time as existing and new payment systems take a greater share of transactions volumes, the costs of providing the service will continue to be high. In 1984 it was estimated that it cost the LCBs about £500 million to provide the service.

One of the reasons behind the continuing growth in costs for providing this service is the expansion in the banked market. The move down-market netted large numbers of financially less sophisticated customers whose preference is for cash. So although a growing proportion of the population have their wages and salaries paid into a bank account, many withdraw it almost immediately from a bank branch in the form of cash. If the campaign to have social security payments paid into bank accounts succeeds to any level, then the costs problem currently borne by post offices will be increasingly shared by banks. It is one of the difficulties and dilemmas experienced by bank management in extending banking. The advantages of larger customer bases are offset by lower unit profitability, since handling costs and the offsetting value of retail deposits are lower than for other groups.

In an effort to reduce labour intensive handling costs, the LCBs and some building societies have invested heavily in ATMs and fast cash dispensing machines in the front office. The machines are providing greater volumes of cash, and it is expected that by 1987 they will account for some 40 per cent of all cash withdrawals from banks. (ATMs will be discussed more fully in chapter 17).

Paper Based Systems

Cheques (and the eurocheque system), giro transfers, postal orders and travellers cheques have been developed to overcome the shortcomings of cash. The systems have all been developed to be flexible, secure and widely

Table 13.3 Transaction volumes (millions)

	Debit clearing inter- and intra-bank	Credit clearing manual	National Girobank	Postal orders
1978	1,672	184	242	179
1979	1,773	195	260	173
1980	1,947	208	270	155
1981	2,024	212	279	188
1982	2,105	231	300	88
1983	2,200	250	325	95
1984	2,325	265	340	92

Source: IBRO and authors estimates

acceptable. They provide the advantages of a time lapse between payment and an account being debited. Conversely, they require the user to have a bank account, are less convenient, slow and incur charges.

Table 13.3 shows transaction volumes in millions reflecting the inexorable growth in cheques especially, whilst postal orders have declined as a less efficient and convenient payment system. The cheque's acceptability was extended through the introduction of a cheque guarantee card whose limit was raised to £50 in 1977. The LCBs have not increased this limit, despite criticism, mainly because of the level of fraud even at the existing level. It is estimated that fraud is costing some £12 million per annum.

However, this palls beside the physical costs of processing the cheques. It is estimating that about 60 per cent of bank staff are involved in the processing of payments. About £1,200 million in capital costs and between £800 million and £1,000 million revenue costs are tied up. The opportunity costs of providing these systems are evident in the way the banks infrastructures are styled, e.g. the branches and the way recruitment, training and career progression are formulated.

A feature of the cheque and other payment systems is their requirement for a co-operative system. This permits settlements to take place between user accounts. The territorial and temporal distribution of payments calls for the systematic execution of payments made on behalf of customers of different banks. The cheque clearing system in the UK acts as the central mechanism through which debit and credit transactions can be settled. The development of the industry led to the creation of a small group of six full and three functional member banks controlling the clearing house. In addition the clearing banks' ownership of BACS gives them a functional oligopoly in the provision of payment services, with any other bank wishing to provide cheque facilitates having to enter an agency agreement with a clearing bank. Citibank and Chartered Trust have attempted to break this oligopoly by becoming members of the clearing house, but were opposed by the existing members who would not wish to see their current substantial market advantage eroded. However, a recent development is the possibility that the clearing system may be freely opened to organizations such as building societies; this development may be a recognition of the growing impossibility of maintaining an oligopoly in a period of greater competition and deregulation, as well as a perception of a need to change the basis of competitive strategy.

Although the clearing banks form an oligopoly, it is an oligopoly whose members compete strongly with each other for market share. The pricing of payment services is dictated by an intense form of competition leading to grossly irrational pricing. Fee income from the tariff recovers 35–40 per cent of costs. The remainder is recovered implicitly through the value of 'free' retail deposits held on current accounts. The LCBs calculate the cost of these funds at 9 per cent, making it ostensibly uneconomic to have current accounts in periods of low interest rates but conversely boosting profits in times of high interest rates.

Three factors have seen current accounts figure at the centre of the LCBs' activities in the personal sector. The first is that current accounts have been a traditional measure of competitive success providing retail deposits and a basis on which to cross-sell other products. Secondly, substantial investment in automating payment systems and pressures on cost bases, have driven management towards trying to obtain higher volumes of business to produce economies of scale. Finally, social considerations and the changing economics of the market place have made a larger proportion of the population worth pursuing.

The consequent rise in the banked population has broadened the scope of banks' customer bases and in fact complicated their strategic position. A larger, heterogeneous market means that marketing activity and the provision of different services becomes a virtual necessity. Additionally, the economics of operating become changed; firstly, because the characteristics of a current account holder differ widely, in terms of retail deposits attracted and account usage patterns, and secondly, in the mix of payment systems that will be used. For instance, the move down-market means that the account base will have an element that persists in using cash rather than other bank media, especially electronic media, hence pushing up the costs of providing bank services. It should be stressed that at the other end of the scale, competition for up-market customers will force the introduction of new and more sophisticated payment media, ultimately affecting the economics of the business just as much as the move down-market has. In overall terms, increased market share may lead to economies of scale being reached in some areas. However, it will exert pressure on the overall infrastructure by increasing the volume of paper, and the commensurate work-load of branches. The problems of managing a large market incorporating a wide range of payment systems, will also be increased.

It is a situation in which general solutions are not available. The motive to extract profitability from as wide an area as possible means containing costs and trying to serve customers with the most cost-efficient services in a variety of different ways. The growth in the number of payment systems is an outcome of attempting to meet these needs simultaneously. The effect is paradoxically to increase the problems and resource requirements associated with managing payment systems.

One approach to the problem has been to systemize existing payment mechanisms. A solution exists in truncating information held on a cheque. Its appeal is its elimination of paper; against this are the associated problems of introducing common technical standards and operating procedures as well as the question of legal liability of truncated information. Truncation systems are already working in Switzerland, Belgium and the USA, but the imminent introduction of an EFT/POS system in the UK may slow down its introduction. Nevertheless truncation probably offers a key solution in restraining the growth in volumes of paper.

The use of other systems to eliminate paper is worth mentioning. Front office terminals linked to a back office terminal comprise a keyboard, a visual display unit, a card and cheque reader, a printer and in some cases a keypad on which the customer enters his PIN. Counter terminals reduce paperwork and improve data capture. Both banks and building societies use terminals; only 5,000 were in place in 1980, but the growth is expected to rise to 40,000 by 1990. The use of such terminals by some building societies has permitted them to introduce the concept of multi-branching, an idea not yet used by the banks, due to the complexity of banker–customer relationship, and the nature of bank systems.

The use of paper based payment systems extends to the international area. Prior to 1983, cheques supported by a cheque card were acceptable in banks throughout Europe for encashment purposes. Fraud led to its abandonment but reinforced a move towards integration with the European payment system. The clearing banks, with the exception of Midland, have issued a European cheque guarantee card. Midland more ambitiously joined the uniform eurocheque system. Formed in 1968, it is based on pragmatic, unanimous co-operation between members. Although predominantly a national based system, it permits cross-border payments written in local currencies, guaranteeing those payments up to a limit per cheque with the support of the uniform eurocheque card. It benefits from almost total acceptance throughout Europe, and is rapidly becoming the standard paper based system in Europe. By 1984 over 28 million eurocheque cards had been issued reflecting the appeal the system has, although many of those cards had been issued in Germany and the Low Countries. Eurocheque, as with credit cards, reflects the growing internationalization of payment systems.

Branding is an important feature of both cheques and eurocheques, but it is especially so in the travellers cheque market, where customer loyalty is negligible except where the cheques are issued to 'captive' customer bases. Unlike other cheques, each cheque value is fixed and guaranteed by being pre-paid, and can be encashed almost universally. Refund services on lost cheques increase their attractiveness, as does the fact that they are issued in a variety of currencies. An estimated value of $US40 billion were sold in 1983, mostly by retail banks, virtually doubling the volume of sales since 1975. Regarded by some banks as a peripheral fee-earning payment system, the global payment systems of Amex, Visa and MasterCard see travellers cheques as complementary to their plastic card activities, and a central element to payment system competitiveness.

Nevertheless the travellers cheque is a payment instrument which logically should begin to decline with the advent of plastic card payment systems and eurocheques. In addition intensifying competition is leading to consolidation in the industry with six dominant power groups, suggestive of a declining industry. But the example of Thomas Cook, the Midland subsidiary, is interesting, since it has strengthened its position in Europe with a wide-ranging agency agreement under the European travellers cheque (ETC) logo, and in the rest of the world with its affiliation to Mastercard.

Size, economies of scale, brand image and market coverage, pertinent to any payment system, are especially so in the travellers cheque market, and this is fuelling co-operative and consolidatory strategies. The lessons of this market may well be useful in the consideration of future developments in the UK retail banking environment, since it shows the decline of the proprietary branded payment system to a group.

The National Girobank, set up in the mid-1960s to compete directly with the banks, is a state sponsored giro payment system, running a centralized operation based in Bootle but using The Post Office branch network for its physical distribution.

The system has traditionally proved slightly cumbersome and inflexible, as the growth in its transaction volumes suggest. However, the introduction of new schemes, such as Transcash and a generally more competitive and commercial approach to building the business, has greatly enhanced its market position. The most significant of the actions being undertaken is the installation of computer terminals in post offices, linked on-line to the Bootle computer. This will greatly improve the quality of customer service and administration. An intention to share the system with other organizations, such as building societies and finance houses, may contribute to a substantial growth in the payment system and its overall competitiveness. Undoubtedly the National Girobank will become a major force in the payment systems area in the future.

A pseudo-paper based payment system is offered through the National Savings Bank and building societies. The NSB accounts operated through post offices allow withdrawals of cash or cheques in the drawer's favour. Some building societies are more sophisticated. Their computer system allows multi-branching by permitting customers to withdraw money from a passbook account either as cash or as a cheque, either to, or to the order of, the customer. This limited form of money transmission is sufficient to give customers an adequate level of flexibility on the accounts to persuade them to deposit funds with the societies.

In addition, the introduction of limited cheque book accounts from the Halifax and Abbey National and the installation of ATMs further enhance the cash transmission aspect of the societies, suggesting not only a gradual erosion of a demarcation line between societies and banks, but also a remoulding of the competitive structure.

PLASTIC CARDS

Plastic cards do not represent a payment system as such, but act as a catalyst in initiating paper or electronic based payment systems. They also become central instruments to those systems, and grow commensurately in importance. There are two main categories of card: the debit card and credit card. The debit card is used for activating ATMs or front office terminals through an encoded magnetic strip on the card. There is an increasing tendency to incorporate this function into a standard cheque guarantee card. The card will act to debit the customer's account, generally at the end of the working day.

The credit card falls into three sub-categories: the charge card issued by American Express and Diners Club which is settled on a monthly basis; credit cards, as issued by Barclaycard and Trustcard (Visa) and Access (MasterCard), which permit payments up to a pre-authorized credit limit, and finally in-house cards, issued by retailers, which are a mixture of charge and credit card. These cards (especially Access and Barclaycard) can be striped in the same way as debit cards to allow withdrawal from ATMs.

Plastic credit cards were first introduced in 1950, with the Americard. They were introduced into the UK in 1966, originally as an extension to the product line, not as a major innovation in its own right. Many clearing banks originally saw it as unnecessary, but since then growth has been significant, with credit cards accounting for 3 per cent of total transactions by value.

Easy and convenient to use, widely accepted, they are safe and involve no charge to the user, and give free credit. In the case of credit cards and in-store cards, further credit is supplied on demand up to a pre-set limit. They are, however, not universally acceptable. As retailers have to pay a merchant fee on each transaction, some companies such as Marks and Spencer and John Lewis do not accept credit cards and operate their own in-store credit programmes. The introduction of EFT/POS and a reconsideration of pricing policies will change this.

The main problem suffered by credit card companies is fraud with over £12 million lost in 1983 and payments over a certain limit have to be authorized by telephone by the card companies. Nevertheless, it is in this area of authorization that technological applications are being used. Authorization networks are being established by Visa and MasterCard to cover the globe, so that an international traveller, making payment abroad, can have it authorized by his card issuing bank. The new systems being installed will initially permit improved authorization, settlement interchange and the basis for point-of-sale systems and shared ATM networks.

In the UK the credit card companies are looking at the system of transaction telephones to increase customer convenience and to control fraud and the effect of stolen cards. Data on the card is converted into digital electronic form and is transmitted to the credit card company for rapid authorization of payment and for identifying cards that have been stolen on the lost card file. To this extent the installation of transaction telephones and a communications network is limited, since it does not herald a new payment system, but supports the functions of credit cards *per se*. Given the LCBs' intention to introduce a fully fledged EFT/POS system, to which credit card companies presumably will have access, the authorization telephone system seems slightly curious.

The costs of installation are to be shared, but as with any closed co-operative venture there are certain key questions, which are relevant to the overall examination of co-operative payment systems. These are:

—the risk of creating a monopoly offensive to the government
—the distribution of costs and benefits
—the transfer costs for using another company's telephone
—the marketing of a joint venture.

The distribution of plastic cards in the UK (table 13.4) shows the levels of penetration achieved, and how central plastic cards are to payment systems. There are only 12.6 million cardholders, reflecting the relatively high degree of multiple card owning especially in the AB socio-economic groups.

Table 13.4 Distribution of plastic cards in the UK: 1984 (millions)

Cheque cards (including Barclaycard)	17.1
Credit cards	15.6
Store cards	4.7
Travel and entertainment	1.0

Source: IBRO

Table 13.5 Credit card companies (millions)

Access	6.7
Barclaycard	6.5
Trustcard	2.0
Amex	0.8
Diners Club	0.2

Source: IBRO and credit card companies

ELECTRONIC PAYMENTS

As cash has the major disadvantage of being stored and moved in ways vulnerable to theft, and cheques and credit cards are susceptible to fraud and involve sorting on a massive scale, electronic payment systems which totally eliminate the handling of paper, have already done much to cut the cost of payment services, and so hold the key to the mass retail banking market in the future.

The major inter-bank system in operation in the UK is BACS, an electronic funds transfer system offering three kinds of service:

— automated credits for salaries, purchase ledger items, pensions and government benefits
— automated standing orders for fixed accounts including mortgages, rates payments and insurance premiums
— automated direct debits for variable amounts including rates payments and insurance premiums.

Originally BACS accepted data through magnetic tape, cassette or disc, but now also accepts it through telecommunication systems.

BACS transactions cost about a third of paper payments. The use of BACS has not been as fully exploited as it might have been. Poor marketing, limitations on the acceptability of direct debit originators and the opposition of groups such as The Post Office to the payment of social security money

Table 13.6 Automated clearing volume: 1979–83 (millions)

Year	Total	Auto-credits volume	Standing order volume	Direct debits	Intra-bank automated credit
1979	379	70	137	131	41
1980	430	82	153	152	43
1981	485	96	169	173	47
1982	537	115	181	193	48
1983	596	139	190	220	48

Source: IBRO

through BACS have all curtailed its growth. Table 13.6 shows the slow growth in the automated clearing area, despite the significant cost advantages held by these electronic methods.

Electronic funds transfer at point-of-sale (EFT/POS) is the single most radical advance in practical and philosophical terms to be undertaken by the clearing banks in the 1980s. By employing electronic payment methods and by placing a payment mechanism in the retail outlets, the banks are attempting to alter the economics of payment systems, by cutting out paper from payment systems and more significantly by taking administration of the payment system away from the branch.

However, many problems are associated with the introduction of EFT/POS. These stem from the fact that it is an organizationally and technologically driven innovation. It is a joint effort by the clearing banks to retain their functional oligopoly of money transaction, but critically it is probable that non-banks will gain substantially through access to the system, enforced by the government through the Office of Fair Trading. There are three tiers to the problem:

- Agreement amongst banks on the nature of the system to be used, how it is to be managed and how the costs and benefits are to be distributed amongst participants.
- The retailers have to be persuaded that they will benefit from such a scheme. The marketing and pricing of the scheme are crucial, as is the level of consultation with retailer groups. EFT/POS systems, incidentally, lack the flexibility of other payment systems; terminal installation with its associated costs and volume requirements will mean that EFT/POS can only be installed in large retailers. An estimate suggests about 100,000 retailers who will initially be able to justify a terminal exist in the UK.
- The customer certainly needs to be consulted and educated. The new technology will probably mean that only the younger section of the market will employ EFT/POS. The disadvantages of PIN, security and

instantaneous account debiting make the system less attractive, certainly to older customers, although the educative impact of ATM cards considerably reduces this problem.

The overall advantages of the scheme are ostensibly clear: the banks gain from greater efficiency, control of fraud and cost constraint as paper volumes decrease; retailers benefit from faster processing of customers and access to funds paid in during the working day; customers should benefit from its security and safety, and from the freedom of using cheques and cash.

However, although the clearing banks see substantial profits emanating from reduced paper volumes in terms of, less fraud and greater processing efficiency, their faith is based on some assumptions which are unproven: one of the central assumptions is that a competitive barrier to entry will be established through control of the system, which will in turn permit a maximization of profit from the investment. However, it is probable that the OFT will insist that the system is open to other operations. Even if competitors remain outside the system there is no reason why they could not use other payment mechanisms or technology to provide an effective competitive response, thus undermining the massive investment made by the LCBs. The banks overall oligopoly of payment systems will disappear as a direct outcome of the influence of technology and government action.

The ready acceptance by retailers and customers of the EFT/POS system is untested and unproven although it is probable that volumes will rise through time as more retailers have terminals installed and more customers become accustomed to POS payments. EFT/POS, is an organizationally driven response to the LCBs' cost problems in the payment system area. It is one solution out of several, and although it promises a great deal, it is highly ambiguous in the effects it will have on the future of the LCBs' role in the money transmission area.

No EFT/POS system has yet proved economic in the diffuse and heterogeneous North American market. Profitability in the UK seems much more assured, although this will depend largely on the pricing policies employed; the nature of competition between participants in the scheme; the achievement of the requisite volumes to achieve the economies of scale; and, in a strategic sense, upon how the new payment systems will affect the pricing and economics of existing payment systems within the current infrastructure.

Nevertheless, the EFT/POS scheme offers several obvious advantages: lower development costs and reduced capital investment, with no ultimate constraint on the system's size, make it a very attractive system for the future. The system will also accept the currently issued debit and credit cards which have been magnetically striped for use in ATMs, so removing the need to reissue cards. The services offered through EFT/POS will allow for the provision of overdraft facilities, revolving credit facilities, etc., thereby making the system the fulcrum of money transmission and also consumer credit in the future. Indeed, some commentators believe that the introduction of EFT/POS will herald the end for credit cards as an individually branded and marketed entity. Moreover, if the introduction of EFT/POS recreates the framework for oligopolistic (and arguably) perfect competition, the same irrational pricing approach found in the other main-line co-operative payment systems will be self-evident. EFT/POS is inevitable, but its impact is uncertain in its effects and benefits.

Home banking, like EFT/POS, is a delivery system which is also the product. Even more than EFT/POS, its impact is uncertain in the payment system area, since the time scales for its introduction are much longer. Its greater convenience to the customer and its ability to generate fee income in a time when margins on business will be contracted are arguments in its favour. Furthermore, the possibility that it will be able to contribute to the improvement of cost structures through the rationalization of existing delivery systems suggests that its introduction is inevitable.

Against these points in favour, however, are some qualifications: its introduction will depend on the spread of interactive viewdata systems, either through Prestel or cable television; the system also undermines the economic and functional validity of branch networks and allows new entrants into the market, thereby destabilizing in a radical way the existing status quo; the internal problems of managing and marketing yet another delivery system/product will be increased, and like EFT/POS will possibly prove more expensive than first envisaged.

If by the end of the millennium, home banking is a major force in the payment systems area, its effect will simply be to intensify the dilemmas and strategic issues confronting LCB management. More specifically its introduction may well threaten the LCBs' coherence and efficiency of operations in relationship not only to payment systems but also in relationship to the personal sector!

PAYMENT SYSTEMS: THE STRATEGIC ISSUES

The current phase of developments in retail banking brings together antagonistic frames of reference and attitude which threaten to destabilize the status quo in the provision of money transmission. The evolutionary nature of the banking structure and payment systems, within a protected environment, has contributed to strategies that are not market driven. Pricing policies have been developed which are difficult to justify in strictly economic terms. Payment systems have been seen as a means towards an end rather than a product line in their own right by attracting cheap deposits and potential business.

As payment systems are at the core of banking activities, they have determined or modified every other aspect of banking activity, ranging from the delivery systems to the organizational structure. More importantly competitive strategies and long-term objectives have been based on the pre-eminence of payment systems. Maintaining market leadership with payment systems and using payment systems as the method for obtaining market share and leadership remain central to the banks strategic planning, although the tenability of this, and its wisdom given developments in the payment systems and in other areas, is becoming increasingly questionable.

There are three levels to the perception of payment systems within the strategic product matrix:

1 The payment system alone; judged simply by its own cost/benefits, and the need to obtain competitive parity or leadership, not only in terms of the quality of the system offered, but in terms of image, i.e. the need to be seen at the forefront of the market. Examples of this are especially the current account, and to a lesser extent credit cards and travellers cheques.
2 Payment systems as the leading part of an integrated set of different products, serving the interests and needs of the customer and the organization, and marketed to produce income and synergistic effects with other products. Again the current account is the most pertinent example, bringing in its wake irrational pricing policies but whose effect is not fully exploited in the marketing of other products, or indeed whose strategic purpose is misguided through attracting unprofitable customer segments.
3 Payment systems as part of the organization's overall strategic direction contributing and influencing the totality of the bank's activities, through producing a highly complementary product/delivery system – segment mixes, which reflect customer buying characteristics and preferences and the organization's own distinctive competences and strengths.

At levels 1 and 2 the consideration and use of payment systems can work against the best overall interests of the total product range and may unbalance the whole organizational infrastructure and direction.

These problems are currently exacerbated by the degree and speed of change in retail banking. Technology and competition are destabilizing the payment system equilibrium. In themselves they demand coherent responses from the banks. But the question is whether the banks are sufficiently flexible and attuned to the situation to produce the right mixture of responses, and whether, in fact, the investment in traditional payment systems, and the pre-existing organizational culture and ethos, will permit organizations to produce quickly the radical strategies demanded to maintain their market position.

A reflexive response may simply reinforce old errors. The trends in the market-place at the moment against which strategies must be made are:

- Co-operative payment system strategies but with limited competitive scope within those frameworks (e.g. the clearing arrangement and the EFT/POS proposals).
- Attempting to maintain barriers to competitive entry, by building economies of scale, market share and leadership in new payment systems.
- An adjustment in the co-operative structure as organizations move slightly towards unilateralist policies but exploiting the potential of the competitive market-place (e.g. banks' links with building societies and co-operative banks, National Westminster and Midland) leading to new competitive groupings and perhaps ultimately to agglomerations based on partnerships of distinctive competence.
- The entrance of new competitors, exploiting new technologies, and threatening to undermine the present position of the clearing banks.

The forces for change underlying these actions are in themselves understandable. The responses appear to be instinctively reactive and product based because the following set of attitudes and objectives held by banks' management seem to exist:

- Payment systems must justify themselves in terms of gaining interest based income. That is they must serve to attract cheap deposits and act as the vehicle for lending business.
- There is a need to control massively increasing volumes of paper and reduce overheads. Payment systems only recover 35–40 per cent of their operating costs through fee income; since the competitive position largely determines pricing techniques and policies, and transaction balances only make a positive contribution when interest rates are above 9 per cent, operational approaches must be introduced to reduce costs. Technological applications through BACS and EFTS appear to offer solutions. There is, however, a corresponding move towards two types of pricing policy. Either towards rational, cost-recovery or towards using some payment systems as a 'loss-leader' to build market position.
- New systems based on new technologies, offering an ever wider range of choices to the customer, should be introduced to protect their market position and pre-empt competitors.

- The general market position should be founded on obtaining market share in the payment system area alone. This justifies both the existing infrastructure and the potentialities inherent in new payment systems. Economies of scale and the ability to develop incremental advantages through cross-selling into other products are subsidiary justifications. Ambivalent pricing policies are a consequence, with 'irrational' pricing used to encourage use of new systems and build market position or to generate fee income sufficient to recover the costs of operation.
- To adopt co-operative strategies, despite their implicit vulnerabilities, because they promise lower risks, lower investment costs and achievable short-term objectives. Risk aversion, however, can compromise the ability to pursue unilateral, radical approaches to the market with the possibility that they carry on generating substantial profits in the future; it also has the effect of reducing the speed of change and lowering barriers to competitive entry.

The dilemmas facing the banks can be summarized as: how to stop the steady squeeze on profitability, caused by rising transaction costs coupled to a more expensive deposit base, and how to use the new technologies most effectively, and yet ensure that their market position is not eroded.

There are two simple options, in this context; either increase revenue by raising prices or increase revenue by selling more. Each option demands a complex set of interacting sub-strategies. The nature of these sub-strategies can be outlined as follows:

- Market position – how is the customer relationship to be fully exploited, and what customer groups are going to be pursued?
- What mix of services should be provided – how many different payment systems are going to be provided, and to what segments, through what delivery systems, at what price?
- What type of organizational structure should be used to operate and market the payment system?
- What range of delivery systems are going to be used to manufacture and distribute service product mixes?
- What should be the 'political' motivations and arrangements behind co-operative ventures and affiliations to other payment systems, what are the implications behind those choices and actions and what are the economic consequences of those decisions? The main concern is to achieve a balanced membership of different groups, in order to achieve the desired mix of payment systems at an optimum balance of risk, cost and reward, and to maintain the autonomy of the organization.

- What pricing policies should be pursued? Also how to achieve, within the overall product mix, a proper return on payment systems in terms of real investment costs and opportunity costs. These can be measured either in financial terms – that is pricing explicitly to obtain sufficient fee and interest income to make a profit on the basis of the payment system alone – or alternatively, through implicit pricing, cross-subsidizing costs through using the customer relationship obtained initially through payment systems to generate fee and interest income from other products.

The banks position in the personal sector now is that

—the customer relationship is undeveloped
—the marketing resources within organizations are limited
—the pricing function has been largely implicit and unrelated to cost/benefit
—the provision of services has been inconvenient
—services are paper based, personnel intensive and costly
—payment systems are proliferating faster than the ability to manage and market them, and arguably faster than market demand.

The tunnel vision of banks is evident in the way in which market share has been pursued as a central competitive imperative and yet the customer resource has not been used, calling into question the purpose and validity of these strategies in the past. In this light, banks must either use their customer resources fully, or aim to operate their payment systems economically.

The point is worth making that technology allows more marketing orientated organizations to enter the market-place and disrupt the banks' retail business structure and strategy as it is currently based on the current account customer relationship. It is therefore a critical aspect of banks' future marketing to use their customer resource intelligently, to build long-term customer relationships, and so defend themselves against trends of changing and damaging patterns of customer loyalty that will probably otherwise emerge.

At the organizational level, the management of payment systems involves two main considerations. The first is to obtain the best 'deal' for the organization in economic and product terms. The second, especially relevant to the co-operative nature of the payment systems, is the maintenance of organizational autonomy and corporate identity.

At the national level, the banks have paid for the considerable benefit of their close ties through the clearing system with a reduced ability to operate unilateral policies, which would enhance market share and raise the profile of their corporate images. Market share has tended to be static, and corporate differentiation, certainly until recently, was extremely limited. Even so, within the co-operative framework a moderate and stable level of competition has taken place. All these trends are likely to be reversed under the combined influence of new payment systems and greater overt price competition.

However, the increased number of operators and products in the payment system area means that new co-operative conglomerates are appearing, to take advantage of economies of scale and reduced risk; the relationship of some banks and building societies is an example. At an international level the massive global payment systems of Visa and MasterCard, attract members who perceive a strategic need to strengthen their competitive position through the links such organizations offer, but in so doing they are put in a position of enforced consensus. The cost benefit equation therefore is sometimes far from straightforward and can have dangerous implications for a bank's ability to choose its own future.

At an altogether different level, the links with extra-industry organizations such as IBM in the EFT/POS scheme may compromise the best interests of the industry in the long term. The pursuit of short-term solutions may have long-term destabilizing effects. In all cases, the pursuit of co-operative patterns of behaviour is founded on commercial pragmatism, the need to generate profit and survive in the short term. In an environment which has ceased to be evolutionary, the need for political foresight and strategic planning is accentuated.

A mild form of this characteristic is seen in the collective behaviour of the clearing banks through the 1970s. Bound together by mutual interest at one level in providing a standardized, integrated and universally acceptable payment system, the common approach has tended not only to prevail in their dealings with each other, but has influenced their political behaviour relative to other industry groups. They have adopted co-operative defensive strategies. The herd instinct saw them all go into the house mortgage market and pursue the up-market segment. It sees them all pursue common pricing strategies and it determines the approach that they will take on issues such as EFT/POS. It also tends to drive them towards joint ventures such as Access and affiliating themselves with bigger and stronger co-operative groups such as Visa and MasterCard. This is not to deny the commercial sense in what they are doing, but it is vital to see the inhibitions and dangers inherent in such a philosophy and state of mind. The pursuit of co-operative rather than individual strategies has the added danger of making organizations pursue lines of action that are not necessarily the best for them.

Lloyds Bank, of the clearers, reflects a healthy pluralistic attitude towards marketing, co-operation, payment systems and payment system providers. It has links with MasterCard through Access, offers a premium card and travellers cheques through Amex and is developing a shared ATM network that is unaligned to members of either of those two groups. It has the benefits of co-operation, retains its autonomy and identity and serves its chosen markets in the most efficient and effective manner.

Considerations

The preceding description and analysis suggests a number of lines of action for clearing banks and indeed any participant in the payment systems area. These are as follows:

- Any action must be primarily market-led rather than product-led or technology or organization driven.
- As traditional systems will remain pre-eminent and will act as a drag upon the introduction of new payment systems in economic terms, considerable effort should be spent on reducing processing costs and the delivery of those products. Pricing as part of the whole payment system mix should become more explicit and rational, aiming to recover costs and induce the use of more cost effective payment systems, or be used with the specific intention of building a long-term strategic position.
- Payment systems should be used as the fulcrum for competitive and business strategies, pricing for profit and competitive advantage, but subordinating product strategies to business objectives.
- Customer retention should be enhanced through increased quality of service and products, branding of payment systems and the projection of strong corporate images.
- The customer relationship should be exploited fully by maximizing cross-selling opportunities, through improving sale facilities and customer data bases for direct mail and other marketing activities.
- Corporate autonomy should be maintained through prudent involvement in different co-operative payment systems, both nationally and internationally.
- It is necessary to maintain market share and expand penetration in segments that offer the greatest profit potential, rather than expanding into volume markets whose profit potential is limited.
- Coherent strategies based upon organizational strengths should be developed, rather than pursuing lines of action apparently dictated by

market trends, evolutionary processes, political pressures suggesting consensus, or technology driven or competitive action.

- Profitable market positions must be sought, to serve the customer groups that fulfil most effectively the capital and revenue needs and capabilities of the organization.

14 Savings

Introduction

Historically, retail deposit attractiveness to banks and building societies lay in their cheapness and stability. While these characteristics generally remain, changes in industry structure, the influences of greater competition and the introduction of technology are affecting the flow of personal sector funds and the basis on which different sets of financial institutions compete for them.

Banks have relied on large branch networks and payment systems to attract cheap retail funds, in the form of non-interest bearing current accounts and seven-day deposit accounts, priced some 2–4 per cent under money-market rates. A system of implicit, cross-subsidized pricing has compromised the banks' ability to meet price competition for deposits directly. This situation has been aggravated by the building societies ability to bid up the price of deposits and by their systematic expansion of their efficient branch networks.

The strategic importance of cheap funding to the banks has already been discussed in chapter 8; the increasing reliance on more expensive wholesale money to fund asset growth has had the effect of narrowing margins and therefore profitability. The declining efficiency of the branch networks in attracting deposits commensurate with rising costs has further eroded the banks' profitability. The decline in the banks' share of personal sector deposits, described in chapter 3, means that to reassert the banks' role in the personal sector and to maintain a balanced funding mix, as well as to justify the continuation of the branch network, requires some fundamental readjustments in strategic policy towards the savings sector. In the context of liability management, retail deposits have been regarded almost as a form of ballast that did not need to be managed in the same way, if at all, as wholesale funds. Liquidity management, given the inertia of retail deposits, was not important. The concept of maturity transformation, however, implicit in the way highly liquid retail deposits are lent for longer periods (up to 25 years for house mortgages), is central to profit generation and the pricing of deposits, although in a climate of more highly priced deposits, an obvious corollary is to charge borrowers more for the advantage of being able to borrow for a long period.

This leads on to another crucial aspect of retail deposits which is their internal pricing. At the moment retail and wholesale funds are pooled. The effect is that the pricing of lending products tends to be subsidized by retail depositors. When lend-back ratios to the personal sector are about 38 per cent (compared to 86 per cent for building societies) and are priced more highly than for the corporate business sector (ostensibly to reflect the greater costs involved with volumes and risk) it becomes clear that pricing policy discriminates against the personal sector, undermines a proper economic evaluation of the branch networks and distorts a strategic perspective of the retail sector.

Balance sheet management should more accurately reflect the role and cost of retail deposits. Moreover, it should take into account the economics of the market-place. Conventional wisdom has perceived that cheap retail deposits were a structural phenomenon rather than something which had to be actively competed for on the basis of price. Structural solutions (i.e. making the branch network more efficient or improving the quality of product designs) are bound to predominate in an environment where the nature of the balance sheet is so complex, not only in the broad categories of funding and lending maturities, but also by the type of sources of funds and borrowers; and, where the balance sheet structure is made more complex by processes of irrational pricing, cross-subsidization across generic product types and business sectors. But in fact this is a strategic fallacy derived from the 'functional' and non-price competition of interindustry group competition regulated by a cartel.

The problems of the balance sheet management of retail deposits becomes more explicit as not only price competition develops, but as functional or non-price competition also develop. As new product types, such as money market funds and cash management accounts, are introduced, or as different industry groups such as building societies or even retailers replicate payment systems, so the banks' privileged and oligopolistic access to transaction deposits are challenged. When increased competition is added to greater sophistication amongst customers, then the price sensitivity and volatility of retail funds will increase, adding another factor to the demands for a much greater degree of liability management of retail deposits.

To gain a different perspective on the issues it is worth analysing the depositor's motivation for investing funds. Chapter 3 has analysed some of the reasons for the split between different institutions, with price predominating. To recapitulate, there are three levels: transaction, precautionary and speculative, with the last falling outside the ambit of this book. Periods of high inflation and unemployment have driven the personal sector to seek a combination of high return and low risk. Portfolios have also been based on obtaining a mix between liquid, precautioinary balances and illiquid, contractual savings in the form of assurance and pension funds. The first category has been filled largely by building societies. The relative failure of the banks in this area is due to the fact that the growth of transaction and neo-transaction balances, represented by seven-day accounts, has been constrained by the individual's limited need for excessively large transaction balances and his preference for higher earning instruments. This trend is accentuated by greater affluence and financial sophistication. To illustrate this, the average value of current accounts has fallen from £275 in 1981 to £225 by 1983. When the high liquidity and accessibility of building society accounts is compared to the banks' accounts then it becomes obvious why the banks' share of personal sector savings has declined. Building society funds have come increasingly to represent neo-transactionary accounts as well as the traditional precautionary balances function.

The banks are put at an additional disadvantage because as financial intermediaries they rely on sectoral surpluses, whereas the building societies, who operate exclusively in the personal sector, are not so dependent on such surpluses for the operation of their business. The building societies' other advantages outlined in chapter 9 show what a substantial structural disadvantage the clearing banks have.

To illustrate the conditions that are influential in directing the flow of the personal sector's liquid and discretionary savings the following analysis of building society investors provides some consumers' attitudinal and behavioural characteristics that are highly pertinent in the formulation of bank strategy.

In a survey conducted by BRMB in 1982 for the Building Society Association several factors (table 14.1) lay behind the choice of building societies for savings. The implications for a bank strategy are obvious: interest rate, financial relationship (the mortgage) and convenience (table 14.1). The

Table 14.1 Consumer motivation in saving with a building society

Reason	%
Good interest rates	55
Easy to withdraw money	37
Safe way of saving	36
To improve chances of getting a mortgage	43
Easy way to invest	25
Interest paid net of tax	26
Branches conveniently located	19

Source: BRMB

Table 14.2 Savings by age with building societies

Age range	Number of investors (millions)	% of total	Amount invested (£ million)	% of total
16–19	2	8	800	1
20–24	3	11	2,300	3
25–34	5	21	6,300	9
35–54	8	31	19,100	28
55–64	3	14	18,400	27
65 +	3	15	21,700	32
Total	25		68,600	

Source: BRMB

Table 14.3 Regional distribution of building society savings

Region	% of all savings
London	20
Southern	9
Anglia	6
Wales	14
Midlands	16
Tyne-Tees	7
Yorkshire	10
Lancashire	10

Source: BRMB

distribution of savings by age shows how significantly investment is skewed towards the older and generally more affluent (table 14.2). Regional variations also occur on quite a significant scale (table 14.3).

In addition to economic factors, banks have failed to maintain a position in the personal sector savings market at the image level. Whereas building societies have devoted substantial promotional budgets to this end, the banks have seen deposits as a structural phenomenon that did not need to be competed for; building societies as part of an image building process have managed to build a strong relationship through the life cycle. Not only does this marketing success reinforce the societies position, but it makes it more difficult to dislodge them from their market position.

PRODUCT TYPE

The emerging pattern in savings products is of competition within and between industry groups based increasingly on a mixture of price, function and liquidity. The pace of evolution in bank savings product design has increased dramatically commensurate with the growing competition for retail deposits. The progression appears to be towards more integrated product packages, which are tailored to meet specific segment's expectations, either in price or in product features.

Currently the speed of development in the personal savings sector is faster than in any other generic product group, reflecting the urgency with which the LCBs regard their deteriorating share of the market. Another function of the rapid change has been the very marked breakdown of institutional segmentation in the savings sector.

The ambiguity connected with the function of the cheque account (see chapter 13) has resulted in an irrational and implicit pricing system which disguises from banks and their customers the real costs of doing business. The tariff designed to encourage deposits and generate fee income is complex and misleading. It causes feelings of resentment amongst customers, who dislike paying when the bank holds their money. It is probable that eventually, with the advent of more realistic pricing policies, charges will be made on the basis of transactions and interest will be paid on all credit balances, following in the footsteps of the Co-operative Bank's account. It seems inevitable in the competition for deposits that this will occur, even though it will add dramatically to funding costs without providing any commensurate competitive advantage.

A variation on the transaction account, to encourage savings and to make use of the banks' competitive advantage in technology, is a card based transaction/savings account. The Royal Bank of Scotland 'cashline deposit account' is a first step in this direction, with savings balances accessed through an ATM. This is a limited version of the 'functionalist' approach towards attracting savings, which does not seem to offer enough advantages over competing schemes or a strong enough marketing platform to succeed.

Budget accounts and 'save and borrow' accounts give the customer an advantage of obtaining credit readily and saving on the same account, with the bonus of a cheque book so that the account also acts as a payment vehicle. They have primarily been marketed, however, as credit vehicles, with the consequence that savings balances are minimal.

The predominant savings vehicle in the UK has been the time deposit, the seven-day account. Originally a pass-book account it has become a statement account. It is argued that this has been a change for the worse. Traditionally paying interest gross, and often below building society rates, it has not grown at a rate fast enough to match the banks' needs or the expansion in the market. Banks, as mentioned earlier, have wholesale money-market accounts for the personal sector, locked in for various time periods and for sums over £10,000 they do not readily appeal to the mass retail-deposit market.

The banks have begun recently to fill the gaps in their product range by introducing monthly income accounts on sums over £500 or £1,000. The clearing banks pay higher interest rates on these, between 2 and 3 per cent above deposit rate. The products, although packaged to prevent existing deposit monies flowing into them, have had nevertheless the effect of attracting existing retail deposits rather than new funds.

A series of high interest bank accounts offered by unit trusts have arisen. The most prominent are 'Save and Prosper' from Robert Fleming and the Brittania Group's account. Based on minimum investments of £2,500, they incur no bank charges pay a money-market rate and make available a cheque book for paying sums over £250. Both accounts offer monthly income facilities on deposits over £5,000. In addition, Brittania offers a credit card. The Bank of Scotland has produced a similar account, but allows six free cheques a quarter. Schroder Wagg, the merchant bank, offer a seven-day deposit account which provides a return ½ per cent below interbank rate. However, the most significant development is Midland Bank's launch of a similar high interest cheque account, with minimum balance requirements of £2,000 and free cheques. As with monthly income accounts, it is seen as a defensive act to retain deposit money.

In all cases, the accounts are up-market and have generally succeeded exceptionally well, in all attracting over £500 million within a short time span. Most benefit from centralized control and marketing, and are targeted towards a very specific up-market group. It is a market which the banks can participate in only by restructuring their product range and their pricing. Indeed, their entire philosophy towards savings vehicles needs reappraising. The Midland's move is a first step towards such a restructuring. As an incidental point, the overall trend perhaps reflects a more widespread structural change in the top end of the savings market, eliminating the distinction between retail and wholesale funds, and implicitly a central aspect of the retail banking industry.

Two foreign based products point the way to the future. One, the Merrill Lynch cash management account, is of interest because it is an integrated product whose success is much more based on the service element than the aspect of income generation. It combines brokerage and a bank account, offering customers daily interest on account balances, chequing facilities, a Visa debit card and instant loans at brokerage account interest rates. It requires an initial deposit of $US20,000 and charges 0.4 per cent fee for each withdrawal. Many other groups have entered the US market, such as Sears Roebuck, whose minimum investment is $US1,000. The account has been imitated in the UK, by the Hambro Life Assurance Scheme. Requiring £25,000 of cash, shares and other financial assets, it offers an interest-bearing current account offering near money-market rates on deposits over £10,000 with cheque book and cheque card. It also offers an automatic line of credit, a Diners Club charge card, administration of the financial assets, life assurance, a pension plan and an optional portfolio management service. It also gives a monthly statement of transactions. There is no access to ATMs and cheque-cashing facilities up to £50 are available. It costs £60 per annum, plus a tariff on cheques and 2½ per cent over base on borrowing. It is expensive, limited in scope, and targeted towards a rich minority group. Its main threat to the clearing banks is that it will syphon off their better quality customers.

The other example is the Swedish Allkanto or General Account, promoted by Svenska Handelsbank. It offers a cheque book facility, a cheque guarantee card and an ATM card, requires no notice of withdrawal but levies a fee of 0.1 per cent of the amount withdrawn and pays generous interest on the daily balance.

Another innovative account is the American sweep account. Surplus transaction funds are placed in high-yielding accounts on an automatic basis. The sweep accounts offer a one-stop banking service that allows banks to retain affluent customers against the attractions of money-market funds.

What these accounts show are two basic features. They offer a more comprehensive service, so as to accommodate the entirety of the customers financial needs, with fee-income produced from the service element. The second major trend is towards paying interest on all deposit monies, albeit on a scale according to the type of account and the balance held. The loss of margin is compensated for by fee income. The trends that are likely to emerge are therefore:

- The experience of universal one-stop accounts or sets of interconnected accounts.
- The payment of interest on all credit balances.
- The greater application of technology to reduce costs, with a reappreciation of the branch networks' role in attracting deposits.
- The use of relationship pricing, to generate fee income from deposit services.

The banks can therefore see the following elements affecting their funding strategies.

- The deposit mix will become increasingly rate sensitive, more volatile, and more expensive.
- Current accounts will take a much smaller share of the market.
- There will be a shift towards higher interest earning accounts.

The deposit base will become less stable and assured as competitors introduce new packages that directly challenge the banks' market position.

STRATEGIC DIRECTIONS

To summarize, the banks' position in the retail deposits market is highly vulnerable. New directions are essential in order to establish banks as the savings repositories rather than merely providers of transaction account facilities.

With competition intensifying there are two possibilities. One is that the market will become more efficient in its handling of financial assets, so driving the banks share of balances lower (the trends are already to be seen). The second is that specific packages, replicating the banks' erstwhile distinctive competence – the payment system – will appear, threatening ultimately the banks' one significant hold on the market – the current account. These will occur across the market; at the top end through cash-management accounts and money-market funds, and at the mass market level through building societies developing simple but effective payment systems based on the new technologies.

As a direct consequence of all these developments funding costs will increase and the acquisition and management of personal sector deposits will require more resources than have been applied to it before, especially through the development of liability management techniques.

The following lines of action follow from the preceding analysis. Although applied here specifically to the deposits sector, they represent substrategies that need to be incorporated into an integrated product strategy supporting business level objectives.

- Become 'market driven' rather than 'organization driven', responding to market trends rather than relying on established processes and customer inertia.
- Become more committed to the personal sector by providing integrated product lines across the various needs of the life cycle.
- Develop a stronger image in the savings sector based on stressing accessibility, convenience and return.

- Transcend the different liquidity preferences of the personal sector producing products that fulfil transaction and precautionary needs and perhaps even fulfilling speculative needs (e.g. the one-stop cash management account).
- Use existing distinctive competences of the organization – its developed payment systems and infrastructure – to establish competitive advantage.
- Adapt technology to producing more efficient products, and drive down the marginal costs of account operation to make products more price competitive.
- A segmented approach is needed on socio-economic, age and geographic features, packaged and aimed especially at the high income affluent groups both to maximize return and to defend the customer base against competitor inroads.
- Develop asset/liability management techniques for the personal sector, to provide the basis for more accurate and appropriate pricing strategies and product design for the personal sector.
- Generate more fee-income by marketing the service features of products to compensate for the reduction in interest income incurred as a consequence of paying higher rates for deposits.
- Campaign for greater degrees of fiscal neutrality in the market-place, to permit the banks to compete more equally for retail deposits.

15 Retail Lending

INTRODUCTION

The analysis of payment systems and retail deposits suggests two widely different sets of factors determining the banks' approach to the market and indeed arguably leading to inconsistent and divergent approaches. Payment systems remain organizationally or technology determined; the product is provided through an oligopolistic system in which the competitive structure is not fully developed. Retail deposits are at the opposite end of the spectrum; competition is intense and almost wholly driven by market forces. Competition is most concentrated in areas where the attributes of products and customer preferences overlap, and where institutional segmentation has almost disappeared as in the bank/building society sector.

Lending services, at a strategic level, are a hybrid between these two extremes. Products remain largely a consequence of organization driven strategies, although these are now being modified to some extent by competitor action. Some development has been seen in the move away from overdraft lending to reducing and revolving loans and in the introduction of the credit card. The market structure lies somewhere between the still heavily demarcated payment system area and the almost homogeneous liquid savings market. The main competing industry groups are banks (and their credit card companies), finance houses, building societies and retailers.

The personal sector influences the market-place in two ways; rationally it makes portfolio choices in terms of its liabilities, and to date its overwhelming choice has been for the house mortgage liability. Irrationally and attitudinally it has traditionally eschewed other forms of credit, although as chapter 3 demonstrates this is becoming less pronounced as the consumer credit market becomes more developed and mature.

The retail lending market can be divided into two types of market: lending for house purchase and lending for other purposes. The characteristics of the macro market have already been analysed in chapter 3 (see tables 3.2 and 3.7), with the ratio of borrowing to PDI reaching an all time high in 1982. Correspondingly borrowing in real terms for house purchase has grown. Borrowing for other purposes fell sharply from the very high levels of 1972–73 but has subsequently been showing a much steadier level of growth in the last ten years, suggesting a more solid core of consumer borrowing, based on consumer attitude rather than government inducement, (although recent government deregulation has contributed to its growth).

CONSUMER CREDIT MARKET

By the end of 1984 consumer credit stood at approximately £22.9 billion with £4.2 billion new credit extended in 1984. The growth in the consumer credit area is a consequence of three factors:

— increased expenditure on consumer durables
— changing patterns of credit usage
— increasing sophistication of the market.

Table 15.1 illustrates some of these points.

Bank owned credit cards are incorporated into bank lending, accounting for at least 65 per cent of all cards issued and about 80–85 per cent of all

Table 15.1 Consumer credit outstanding by industry group: 31 December 1984 (£ million, current prices)

	1978	1979	1980	1981	1982[a]	1983	1984
Banks	4,741	5,618	6,742	8,792	12,655	15,289	17,408
TSB	84	160	239	331	–	–	–
Finance houses	2,017	2,441	2,767	3,039	1,202	1,790	2,224
Insurance companies	248	240	271	295	317	350	412
Retailers	1,109	1,395	1,425	1,474	1,594	1,715	2,002
Mail order	460	554	716	744	782	833	897
Total	8,659	10,408	12,160	14,675	16,550	19,977	22,943

[a] This figure is change since licensed deposit takers were incorporated into the banking category.
Source: CSO Financial Statistics, Business Monitors SDM 6, SDM 8

Table 15.2 New credit extended by credit cards (£ million)

1978	1979	1980	1981	1982	1983	1984
425	790	1,117	1,461	2,021	2,593	3,190

Source: Financial Statistics

credit extended on plastic cards. Table 15.2 shows how central to bank lending strategies credit cards have become. Tables 15.1 and 15.2 depict

—the considerable growth in consumer credit
—the growing predominance of the banks and within that credit cards
—the relative decline of finance houses
—the small impact of retailers and mail order organizations on market growth.

The shifts can be attributed to some clear cut factors:

- The increased presence of banks in the market-place due primarily to the lifting of the corset in 1980 and more recently hire purchase controls in 1982 leading to more extensive marketing.
- A growth in the banks' market share, due not only to stepping up marketing activity on the basis of derestriction, but equally to interest rate advantages, greater accessibility and the different market perception of banks compared to finance houses.
- The introduction of a better and a greater range of products by the banks.
- The different purposes behind promoting credit usage by institutions. Retailer use of credit is linked to durable sales within stores and its purpose, like mail order credit, is utilitarian and secondary to the retailing function. Finance houses provide a great deal of their credit services geared towards the purchase of specific products. Table 15.3 shows this tendency and the relative rates of growth.

Major growth is occurring in areas where credit is granted for non-specific reasons, and away from the point-of-sale. Nevertheless loans for specific

Table 15.3 Credit extended by finance houses (£ million)

	1978	1984	Annual % change 1978–84
New cars	393.3	966.0	16.4
Used cars	556.4	975.8	9.8
Motor cycles	73.3	62.6	–2.6
Caravans	43.3	49.4	2.2
Household/personal	277.3	418.2	7.1
Home improvements	135.7	276.3	12.6
Other goods and services	116.6	394.5	22.5
Checks/vouchers	135.0	146.7	1.4
Other fixed sums	279.3	980.0	23.3
Total	2,010.2	4,269.5	13.4

Source: SDM 6+Credit (FHA Publication), Financial Statistics

purposes will remain a key element in finance house strategy, but with a shift away from small value, short-term loans. This shift is being induced by competitive pressures from major and in-store issuers of credit cards where economies of scale can be achieved through centralized mass processing.

A key factor behind the changing approach of finance houses to the consumer credit market is the questionable profitability of single item specific product loans. For instance car loans have declined because of competitive pressures within the market to sell more cars. What is being witnessed in the finance house sector is a changing response to factors influencing the entire market; the problems confronting finance houses are a function of a changing market-place. These are:

— greater awareness of the need to be profitable witnessed in the rationalizing of products and forms of delivery
— greater competition leading to a redelineation of institutional boundaries by socio-economic segments
— greater customer sophistication in the use of credit, although the market remains largely insensitive to price.

The changing market holds substantial problems for finance houses. Because the consumer credit market is becoming increasingly segmented by socio-economic groupings, with the banks beginning to dominate the upper-end of the market, finance houses as they move down-market incur higher risks, have to charge higher rates and so are forced by their pricing formula to adopt a new market position. To a certain extent finance houses can mitigate the effects of this process by adopting new marketing techniques, but in general terms the finance houses' current market position and business policy suggests an inexorable decline in their consumer business. This reflects the growing shift away from institutional towards market led forces determining the demand for credit.

CONSUMER CHARACTERISTICS

Segmentation by socio-economic and psychographic characteristics is both institutional and product related. Finance houses are progressively moving into the least sophisticated, highest risk area. Banks are introducing more products and capturing a higher percentage of the more credit worthy, risk customer, through marketing programmes which emphasize socio-economic and life-cycle characteristics. Regional variations in credit as measured by value do not in fact differ markedly, except that there are some marked differences between the more affluent and financially sophisticated South-east and the more thrift-conscious and poorer North (table 15.4).

Table 15.4 Regional credit taking: 31 December 1984

Television region	% population	% all credit
London	21	24
Southern	8	9
Anglia	6	5
Wales and South West	10	10
Midlands	15	15
Tyne Tees	7	8
Yorkshire	9	10
Lancashire	14	12
Scotland	10	7

Source: IBRO

Greater sophistication amongst key customer groups who see credit as a method of managing their finances is one of the prime elements in credit growth. But more important are the elements of deregulation and increased competition which will produce a higher proportion of consumer credit usage by increasing the actual volumes of available credit and by the educative impact of marketing campaigns.

Greater use of credit depends upon the quality of marketing amongst the institutions, and the quality of product delivered. The main motives for credit usage generally occurs in middle income groups in the earlier stages of the life cycle when credit is needed to finance the accumulation of durables. More affluent groups use credit as a short-term device to obtain liquidity since the bulk of their wealth is locked into long-term illiquid investments. New credit products should seek to allow customers to make greater use of their assets, as with Merrill Lynch's 'Asset Access' scheme.

The main factors that determine credit usage are availability, flexibility, cost and convenience. Cost is a major influence in more affluent groups and availability to less affluent groups. Other important determining features of credit choice are the prior relationship with an organization, the status of the lender (e.g. a bank has better standing and a higher market profile than a finance house), the availability of unsecured credit, the term of loan available and service charges.

Products

There are five principal types of consumer credit offered by institutions. These include fixed and variable rates of interest; and fixed and non-fixed periods of repayment. Credit can be further broken down into that type which is available at the point-of-sale and that which is available as a universally acceptable credit line, with the latter typically linked to a payment system.

The most common kind of credit available, is the fixed term, fixed rate loan which represents by far the greater volume of consumer credit outstanding. Available at the point-of-sale or separately it is often used to finance specific purchases and remains the most popular form of credit.

Revolving credit facilities, like fixed term, fixed rate loans are available from finance houses and banks, and in the latter case are normally linked to cheque-book facilities. A regular monthly payment entitles the account holder to borrow a multiple of the monthly payment at a variable interest rate. A variation on this theme is the 'save and borrow' aspect, where credit monies receive interest.

The overdraft facility enables customers to overdraw their account up to an agreed limit: it is a convenient, flexible and effective method of providing credit, although it has been largely supplanted by the packaged reducing or fixed term personal loan.

Plastic credit cards, such as Access and Barclaycard, are option cards, allowing customers to settle only part of their outstanding debt and make use of an extended credit facility for the balance. The main advantage of these cards is that they are multi-function cards. They can obtain credit at the point-of-sale and can be used for obtaining cash from bank branches or ATMs and for accessing other bank accounts. They are virtually universally acceptable. They have shown the most dramatic growth of all lending instruments, rising by 28 per cent in 1983–84 and representing some 14 per cent of all consumer credit in 1984.

House Mortgage Finance

House finance in the UK benefits from fiscal advantages. Interest payments are tax deductable and there are no capital gains on the appreciation of value on property. Housing has benefited from the availability of long-term loans, often at negative real rates of interest. A prevailing ethos, extending to greater proportions of the population, is the desirability of home ownership. The market is a substantial one, and although the size of the market has traditionally been believed to be determined by price, recent trends show the market growing relatively price insensitive, absorbing all the mortgage finance available. Whether this was a release of pent-up demand created by the building society monopoly or a genuine shift in the market behaviour is debatable.

For reasons already examined, the UK market has developed in curious ways, mainly because the clearing banks remained absent from the house finance market for so long. Without competition, the market developed anomalies and imperfections. Queues for finance developed as did differential rates for mortgages over certain sums, which were only eliminated when the banks entered the market on a large scale.

The business was clearly profitable to the building societies who were virtual monolopy suppliers of mortgage finance. The rudimentary balance sheet management of building societies is made relatively easy by their ability to vary rates on both deposits and loans in line with the market. This, together with their ability to tap the market for funds, gave them a high degree of liquidity by enabling them to demand manage the situation. Different cost structures and fiscal advantages gave the societies an extra edge in the market ensuring that they generally possessed considerable price advantages in the competition for retail deposits.

Table 15.5 illustrates the changing shares of the market in the period 1978–84 and shows how dramatically the banks burst of activity changed the pattern of market shares, and more interestingly how quickly the market absorbed the extra volumes of finance made available for house finance. The building societies lost market share even though their loans reached record levels.

The motives behind the banks' entry and subsequent exit are arguable and varied. The prime motive for entering the market may well have been directly competitive, extending the competition against building societies from the deposit sector into the lending sector and in so doing, changing the pattern of product-market competition away from institutional to market related factors. The second reason was probably an evolutionary one. Banks had never before apparently contemplated entering the house finance market because of their traditional aversion to long-term lending, the existence of profitable markets elsewhere and their prevailing commitment to the corporate as opposed to the personal sector. Competitive pressure and the existence of a large, apparently profitable and stable market, whose risks were low, however, must have seemed very attractive to the banks especially as the eventual removal of the 'corset' allowed them to enter the market as part of a realistic portfolio adjustment strategy. What is surprising, however,

Table 15.5 Mortgage balances outstanding by industry group (£ million)

Year	Building societies	Local authorities	Insurance companies	Banks	Other public sector	Total
1978	31,715	2,900	1,623	1,805	500	38,543
1979	36,986	3,193	1,854	2,403	574	45,010
1980	42,708	3,654	2,117	2,996	821	52,296
1981	49,039	3,906	2,204	5,441	1,169	61,759
1982	56,894	4,447	2,365	10,714	1,494	75,914
1983	67,798	4,103	2,489	14,353	1,516	90,259
1984	82,328	3,894	2,701	16,667	1,431	107,021

Source: Financial Statistics – Supplementary Tables and Table 9.2

is not so much the rapid growth of their presence but the subsequent pulling back from the market.

There is an underlying mix of reason and irrationalism in the banks' move into the house mortgage market. For example, there was an apparent, implicit faith in the idea that by competing with the building societies on both sides of the balance sheet the banks would win back personal sector deposits and re-establish the banks as the pre-eminent force in the personal sector market. While house mortgages represent a fundamental part of the relationship with the personal sector market the analysis on retail savings showed that the structure of the deposits market, by value, is not related to house mortgage provision. It may act to establish a relationship, but even then it is highly questionable whether the provision of house mortgage finance substantially, in itself, acts to attract deposits. Rather, mortgage finance acts as only one element in a range of factors that attract personal customers. It should more realistically be viewed as the touchstone to earning fee income in related areas, such as insurance, house broking and conveyancing, personal loans and so on, and probably also as a validation of other product strategies in the personal sector.

The profitability of house mortgages to banks is also debatable. So long as banks follow the 'market' rate as dictated by the Building Society Association, their profitability must be impaired, since the banks' funding costs and overheads are different and more expensive than the societies. If balance sheet growth is to be funded from the more expensive wholesale markets, a corollary must be that a market exists that can sustain rates marginally unaligned with and higher than those of the building societies, and which reflect the real cost of funds to the banks. When rates for both banks and building societies are the same, there will be times when house mortgages are overtly unprofitable to the banks. However, there is a compensating factor that in periods of falling interest rates there is a time lag between falling money costs and mortgage loan rates which will provide the banks with a counter-cyclical lending bonus. Nevertheless, the banks cannot compete by price with building societies for business on both sides of the balance sheet. Rather they have to rely on excess demand or the inability of building societies to satisfy demand if they are to make a significant profit in the house mortgage area.

The slowdown in the banks' activity in the market since 1983 was probably governed by four factors:

- —portfolios had been adjusted to accommodate the required volume of mortgage lending
- —capital adequacy considerations
- —profitability, for reasons outlined above

—the failure to assert themselves in the personal sector market as quickly and as strongly as was wished, through house mortgage finance.

The low profitability aspects of the mortgage lending were exacerbated by the unwillingness of banks to create their own market. Additionally, house mortgage lending was probably regarded as an all-embracing solution to the problems of the personal sector and not as one component in an overall scheme. Finally, the huge investment in the mortgage sector has not been used to maximum effect, with the potential incremental fee income to be derived from the sector not fully developed through the packaging and marketing of related ancillary services.

Bank Strategies in the Retail Lending Sector

This chapter has outlined the existing situation. The market is more diverse and uncoordinated than either the payment systems or retail deposit area. The market is still largely segmented on institutional lines (although this pattern is changing with greater levels of competition across the market), which in turn reflect different product market segment requirements. For instance, finance houses provide instalment credit facilities at the point-of-sale for white and brown goods. The alternative, the credit card, is not used by the less sophisticated market, to which finance houses are geared, although as the market grows more affluent and sophisticated, the traditional finance-house market will be further substantially eroded.

The market structure reflects the various degrees and needs of sophistication of the customer, from vouchers the cheques to overdraft facilities. It has also necessarily tended to be institutionally segmented by socio-economic risk characteristics. At the one end crude and expensive credit instruments serve an unsophisticated and undemanding market. Greater sophistication and cost sensitivity is shown in the middle and affluent market, who, incidentally, may pay greater fee income but carry less risk than other groups. It is a market in which the choice of position is more crucial than in any other as it influences pricing, product design and delivery system and therefore the long-term profitability of doing the business.

The components of retail lending, house mortgage finance and the different types of consumer credit provide banks with a range of portfolio options. Ideally, they should be managed at the personal sector business level as an integrated line, the overall commitment to the personal sector having been decided in the portfolio choice at the group level.

In the management of a portfolio, decisions should be based on a long-term commitment to provide a service. Opportunistic drifting in and out of the market, as the banks did in the housing market, without properly defining the long-term objectives of such a move, is alien to portfolio management and its connected purpose of building a resilient market position. The absences of coherent strategy saw the herd instinct asserting itself both in entrance to and exit from the market. In such conditions it is impossible to maximize yield in terms of interest and fee income. Establishing a competitive market position and then realizing profits are necessarily long-term objectives especially in the developing consumer credit market.

In terms of the retail lending market there are three pressures: competition, regulation and the market environment. At the present state of development, the main forces in the market are the banks and building societies. Finance houses and retailers are in real terms seeing a decline in their position. It is unlikely, given the dimensions of the market, that the balance will substantially change, except in terms of what the new technology may do by encouraging retailers to extend the provision of credit although the Consumer Credit Act will limit the expansion of the market by institution.

Building societies, who are currently limited by statute from offering personal credit, are side-stepping this by linking with finance houses or credit card companies. With deregulation it is probable that they too will become much more active in this market. However, the banks' advantages of delivery systems, established portfolios and distinctive competence in this area will ensure their pre-eminent position.

The biggest obstacle in this respect will be the regulatory environment. The history of credit control and the use of banks as a tool of monetary control mean that any balanced lending strategy is vulnerable to curtailment through government policy. Direction in terms of what volumes can be advanced and to which sectors can easily upset policies centred on the personal sector (except for politically sensitive house mortgages) which is especially susceptible. Prudential requirements in terms of capital adequacy and liquidity requirements will also restrict balance sheet growth.

The market environment is the third aspect. Although macro-economic factors should determine the volume of credit taken up, growing sophistication amongst the UK population and the historically underborrowed position of the UK market for consumer credit suggest that massive potential for expansion exists. In fact in both the consumer credit markets, and especially the housing market, expansion will be limited not so much by demand but by capital adequacy, portfolio choice and the ability of organizations to market and deliver lending products with sufficient profitability to the market. This situation will, however, be increasingly susceptible to increasing competition for the lowest risk areas by institution and product; this may have the effects of driving margins down as consumers become more price sensitive.

In the US, consumer credit as a proportion of consumer expenditure has not fallen below 22 per cent in the last 4 years. Although the US market is fiscally boosted, the UK by comparison is much less developed, with less than 10 per cent outstanding, although it has been steadily rising in the last 5 years. To establish itself successfully in the market a bank needs to:

—be competitive (for the chosen market) on price
—have an established customer relationship
—provide rapid credit decisions
—be successful at marketing and possess a good corporate image
—have an integrated range of unsecured credit products
—offer a choice of different loan maturities
—provide ease of access to credit.

At the organizational level, as already stated, there are several key features behind the structuring of the portfolio to obtain an optimum choice of assets by volume and type. For just as the banks, to be successful, have to judge the portfolio requirements and preferences of customers, they have to put into the organizational context portfolio choices belonging to the retail sector, which will also be largely determined by the organization's chosen market position. These will hinge on:

—the preferred growth of the balance sheet
—the preference for different business options (e.g. which sectors to lend to)
—the degree of risk aversion
—the costs of funding the business
—the relative profitability and risks of alternative business options.

Capital constraints, exposure limits and regulatory requirements will act to provide further modifying influences.

The main concern is to maximize profit with the lowest degree of risk. The three main components in creating a portfolio are risk, maturity and yield. Risk can be managed in two ways; firstly by achieving a diversified portfolio, ranging from house mortgages which are long term and secured, to personal loans which are short term and unsecured. The second is through scale of operation. By pooling a large number of loans in each category, an organization can reduce its overall risk. In this instance there are economies of scale. The 'pool' can be managed centrally, with statistical evidence about behaviour providing the guiding principle thereby reducing the need to learn about each borrower in depth. Lending policy should therefore be determined by its scale. Differential pricing techniques based on credit scoring analysis can, for instance, be applied to the mass retail credit market.

A portfolio choice should also be founded on the basis of a choice of compatible, different income streams. Reducing and revolving accounts income profiles, for instance, are different, as are their capital setting-up costs and maintenance costs. Different asset types will also respond in slightly different ways to market stimuli such as interest rate changes or economic conditions. A product 'pool' therefore should be chosen not only on its expected return but also on how its yield will move in relation to other 'pools' within the portfolio.

CONCLUSION

Differentiation is less important in the lending market than market position, visibility and quality of products by type and range. Competition is less immediately influential in the credit market in determining volumes, although its impact is far greater in determining margins and product offering. It is probable, however, that this situation will change as competition intensifies and the market grows more mature.

Decisions on pricing and the choice of product offering should be based on market led influences, rather than on cartel based decision making. Portfolio choice and management, on a scale equal to liability management, should be undertaken. Firstly, at the corporate, organizational level and then at the retail banking business level, with specific product as opposed to sectoral choices being made.

Long-term commitment to the personal sector requires long-term product plans and objectives, rather than short-term pragmatic or opportunistic decision making. New products should be developed which allow consumers to make much greater use of their assets. 'Asset Access' from Merrill Lynch in the USA illustrates how home equity and insurance equity can be used to release funds.

The management of competition through market positioning is crucial in determining the long-term profitability of a bank's consumer lending, and the formulation of integrated relationship banking and pricing policies.

16 Ancillary Services

Introduction

Ancillary services describe any service offered by the banks that are not payment services, lending or deposit facilities. They generally lie outside the scope of traditional mainstream banking, with the result that they have developed on an *ad hoc* basis.

There are several strategic issues in the development of such services for banks. Generally, ancillary services have developed on a non-strategic basis, often producing fee-based incremental profit by exploiting the in-built selling advantages of the branch networks. However, their development has generally not been structured; the levels of distinctive competence in ancillary services are low in comparison with other mainstream banking services and these services have not been properly marketed to develop their full potential.

The banks are faced by strategic dilemmas in the formulation of what can sometimes represent diversification strategies. These ancillary services are increasingly being seen as a solution to reduced profitability, induced by excessive infrastructure costs, and also as a means to extend the range of services offered to consumers. In other words, ancillary services are being seen as a future justification for large branch networks, whose value is declining principally because of the increased automation of services, and the pressure of overheads, rather than as any planned strategy for extending business activity.

The high degree of staff–customer contact that ancillary services require suggests another reason for their introduction: automated services tend to lower customer contact and loyalty, and the provision of ancillary services would help to lock in the customer and even provide a key feature in a relationship pricing formula. Similarly the development of ancillary services lends itself to the concept of a one-stop financial supermarket, exploiting a full range of retailing possibilities. This theme also underpins the idea behind the development of financial conglomerates offering a full range of financial services to the customer.

ADVANTAGES OF DEVELOPING ANCILLARY SERVICES

The advantages in developing ancillary services in organizational and marketing context can be identified as follows:

- To improve the profitability of existing bank products by 'bolting-on' fee-earning ancillary services that will generate incremental income. The provision of insurance on bank loans is a good example.
- To provide greater customer convenience by providing a package of services through the existing infrastructure. Both the organization and customer will benefit.
- Diversify, through an established customer relationship, into new areas, offsetting the problems of remaining in a business where intensifying competition will erode margins and curtail business development; and also to provide a mechanism for adapting the existing infrastructure to new and more profitable purposes.
- Create new differentiated market positions, through developing new business opportunities and by providing a 'unique' set of segment/customer packages.

All these opportunities, however, need to be seen in an objective way, as any diversification strategy carries with it risks different and incommensurate with those associated with normal banking activities, and which may lie outside the bank's organizational and marketing capabilities.

THE DEVELOPMENT OF ANCILLARY SERVICES IN RETAIL BANKS

There is an assumption that the financial market is homogeneous and that expansion into a related service area is logical. Certainly, the historical evolution of the banks' service to cover non-deposit investments, such as the sale of shares, safe holding and investment advice, has taken place as a natural extension of banking business. However, more recently the move into ancillary services has been more positive: the provision of more specific advisory services in the branch, with the introduction of personal bankers by Barclays and by the use of 'credit counsellors' amongst 'money shop' operators, is an example of this. This move towards selling bank products and services and providing advice and guidance on branch premises is a first step towards using the branch as a retailing space rather than in its historically developed role.

Subsidiary Companies

To overcome the practical problems of operating in areas where banking expertise is insufficient or where there are regulatory or legal considerations, the banks have established subsidiaries in a number of areas. Trust companies which handle executorship and administer estates and trusts are a particular, specialized example. In 1983 the bank trust companies dealt with about 10 per cent executorship work in the UK, in addition to related taxation and investment services.

The problems faced by the trust companies, however, are indicative of those faced elsewhere when entering other business areas, particularly when running and marketing an ancillary service through a separate and largely autonomous subsidiary. These problems can be identified as follows:

- The market is competitive, and fee income is hard to generate.
- The service provided is only for a very limited part of the bank's customer base, and is seen as expensive and élitist. This can create problems of image and market positioning for the bank as a whole.
- There are difficulties in marketing a separate company's services through the medium of the branch network. This is indicative of organizational and image problems associated with retailing 'subsidiaries' services, as well as the general problem of selling extra and more complex products through the branch.
- Legal problems in the relationship between the parent and subsidiary raise doubts about the integrity and impartiality of the bank providing such a service.

SERVICES

Apart from trust companies the most important subsidiaries that have been developed by banks are: life assurance and pension funds, unit trusts and investment services, insurance services, insurance broking and travel services.

Life Assurance

The life assurance subsidiaries are small compared to mainstream companies. Banks normally sell policies over the counter rather than through the normal life assurance channels of sales representatives. Typically the policies sold through banks are generally linked to equity or property funds, gilt edged stocks, building society shares, money market funds or a combination of these. Given the scale of funds entering the assurance market and its inherent profitability, it is strange that the banks have not extended the business to much greater proportions or extended the range of their other savings and investment products to become more complete savings and investment institutions.

Unit Trusts

Unit trusts, linked to assurance contracts or as special portfolios of industry shares, are similarly managed by special management subsidiaries and sold to bank customers.

Insurance Services

Insurance services and insurance broking are probably the most central of ancillary services to the banking operation. Either producing their own insurance policies or acting as brokers, the bank is able to provide insurance options on loans to personal customers, thereby, producing incremental income. In the area of house mortgages, assurance cover on the contract and structural insurance act as incremental fee earners and probably ensure profitability for this particular facet of business. Insurance cover for holidays and for house contents are also available through banks. Two major financial groups, Amex with the Firemen's Fund and Sears Roebuck with its Allstate Insurance, operate full insurance companies. The problems of acting in a secondary area are illustrated by Amex's experience with Firemen's fund, where underwriting losses in 1983 wiped out a quarter's entire profit for the group.

Travel Services

Travel services can also be provided: only two organizations, Midland's Thomas Cook and Amex's travel subsidiary, operate full package holiday subsidiaries, although the motive behind these was probably based on the fee income derived from selling travellers cheques and foreign currency. Again substantial problems are evident; Thomas Cook operates in an intensively competitive market with the consequence that its profit contribution to Midland has not always been commensurate with its investment.

Although there is some logic behind the connection in financial services terms, the operation of a so-called 'related services' subsidiary, and the way it is managed within the business matrix, begs several questions: does it 'fit' into the overall dimensions of the business in a mutually enhancing way?

Does it complement the business activities of its parent? Does it obtain economies of scale and synergy of operation? And does it offer real potential for positive business growth into the future?

Problems of Diversification

These issues are pertinent to the whole range of issues surrounding the problems of diversification. Essentially they derive from recognizing the logical connections with the core or parent business, and assessing the resultant difficulty in managing and marketing what is essentially an unaligned subsidiary. This has clear implications for any business diversification strategy.

Nevertheless, there are various logical areas for expansion by banks capitalizing on both the intrinsic needs of the organization and extending services in a gradual way to fit in with business opportunities inherent in an existing or new mainline product. These can be fulfilled by integrating that service within the existing infrastructure, establishing a new business unit in the form of an autonomous subsidiary within the organization, or using another organization's products and obtaining commission income from the arrangement.

Given the scale of investment and its central place in the economy the housing market represents the most obvious and immediate scope for diversifying business and earning substantial fee income. At the moment, this is largely limited to insurance adjuncts but Lloyds have extended the rationale with the formation of the Black Horse Estate Agency. It has bought up existing agencies and united them under a common name, and used communication technology to achieve greater customer convenience, efficiency and economies of scale. In Lloyds' case, the decision to diversify by buying up existing businesses with existing expertise, rather than attempting to initiate the business, was both pragmatic and logical with the result that it has proved profitable and entirely satisfactory.

Moreover, there is further scope for increasing fee income in the establishment of 'Real Estate Brokerage', as Sears Roebuck have done through their Coldwell Baker subsidiary. The integration of conveyancing and surveying into a single package facilitated by a recent act of parliament, either through subcontracting to a selected group of solicitors and surveyors, or by setting up an internal team to manage the operation is a feasible and commercial proposition. Similarly renovation and repair work could be centrally controlled through subcontracting work to builders.

CONCLUSIONS

Ancillary services as a generic product-service group represent a key area for growth in the retail banking sector. There are several organizational as well as commercial reasons for this. The growth in new systems will outpace the ability of management to organize the overall restructuring of the branch network. Pragmatic and profitable solutions to fill the service and profit gap produced by this change will be needed. Ancillary services will absorb surplus staff in their marketing, and will help to shift staff resources towards new business activities. Similarly the branch network will evolve towards a new, more retailing-based role. The selling of integrated packages of services to a highly segmented customer base, will help banks retain personal contact with their customers and reinforce customer loyalty. If its ancillary services are developed as part of the banking relationship and pricing philosophy, then the business and profit base of banks will grow, and the infrastructure will move towards a new function.

In a period of narrowing margins and greater competition, ancillary services will boost fee earning and incremental profit and raise the quality of the service offering of the bank, giving it a position of greater market strength and incidentally contributing to the process of creating greater corporate differentiation. The process of building on a position of strength in the financial markets is logical and necessary given the large infrastructure of the banks and their retailing strength compared with the often fragmented nature of competitors in the market and their different styles of business.

However, although the ancillary services provide obvious solutions to the banks' problems there are several caveats to be made against an *ad hoc* diversification strategy: ancillary services may be seen to provide a set of cosmetic solutions to problems which are in fact more fundamental and structural. Banks and building societies may be seduced into a wholesale ancillary service strategy because of an excess capacity of branches. The second issue is whether the ancillary services are inherently profitable in the long term and are not simply being used to bolster up a more serious decline in operating profits and an erosion in the customer base. The third issue is whether they are viable in business terms; does the customer really want them? Finally, are there sufficient management resources and skills to develop, operate and control these new areas?

A second set of issues revolves around the nature of the different ancillary service markets. The issues belong to any new business development. In strategic terms, it is a question as to whether mobility barriers are low enough within the different industry areas to permit banks or building societies entering them. For instance, the assurance market is large, well developed and dominated by a few large organizations; market penetration could prove difficult, whilst in the investment market of shares, unit trusts and investment trusts, the banks are in a very strong retailing position when compared to the strength of stockbrokers.

The insurance market appears substantially unexploited by the banks, with the market generally fragmented, and the banks with centralized marketing well able to dominate the market, especially when selling insurance in conjunction with established product lines. The development of ancillary services based on house finance is another obvious route.

Throughout the analysis it is clear that new ancillary services must be compatible with existing business practice. Management control will be unduly stretched if widely divergent and technically sophisticated financial (and non-financial) services are introduced; indeed these could damage the integrity of the business. Not only do new ancillary type products have to fit existing product lines (and ideally be incorporated into them with packaging) but in broad terms the ancillary service, if controlled by a separate subsidiary, should fit into the business portfolio matrix and be capable in image and organizational terms of being properly marketed. It is worth considering whether such subsidiaries should enter into a wholesale restructuring of the personal sector business. Building societies' enthusiasm to expand into new areas means that the risks they will be carrying will be greater and incommensurate with the risks and style of business they have been used to conducting. The same is true of banks. It is also true that while management may be stretched, the staff who have been trained to perform routine tasks will be suddenly expected to perform more demanding and complex activities, and this will require substantial training programmes.

The examples and indications seem to argue for a gradualist approach to the development of ancillary services. Vertical integration into new areas should ideally first be through agency agreement and then perhaps for the organization to offer the product themselves after building up sufficient competence. Services should be seen to complement and enhance existing product lines. It may not seem worthwhile to step beyond the current parameters of the business and infrastructure when the strategies for ancillary services are designed to fill deficiencies within the existing business framework. Ancillary services, to be viable, must be manageable and use existing distribution lines in the short to medium term.

The most promising way forward appears to be to shift the retailing structure towards ancillary services, by changing product design, training, infrastructure (e.g. branch design) staffing (more staff dedicated towards providing advice and selling products) and management control. The move requires a steady change in business philosophy and culture. Any strategy must rely on compatibility with existing business styles and feasibility and should not attempt to duplicate systems or provide a service that is far removed from existing operations.

Ancillary services are a vital and important part of retail banking's future strategies. Their introduction will have to be slow and concurrent with the culture change within the retail banking sector and the ability of the banks to adapt their organizational structures, images, retail infrastructure and marketing to the needs of what will represent a significant and fundamental shift in their business.

17 Delivery Systems

Introduction

Delivery systems represent the methods by which banks and other financial service organizations communicate with and make their products available to the market-place. Branch networks in the UK have traditionally fulfilled both of these functions with considerable success and patterns of business activity and competition have correspondingly been established on the central role of the branch network.

The pre-eminence of the branch is due to the difficulties associated with marketing financial services. The branch provided a highly effective mechanism for administering, collecting and delivering cash as well as providing the wide range of associated lending and ancillary services. Branch networks historically arose to attract cheap retail deposits through the convenience of the branch location itself and through branch based payment systems. Indeed, the relationship between the customer and the branch underpins the banking process.

However, the branches exclusive function is tenable so long as the assumptions and conditions that determined its historical position hold good. The first of these assumptions is that the market will continue to respond to it; the second, that it will remain the basis for patterns of competitive behaviour, and connected to this is the final point, that more effective and economic delivery systems do not emerge.

The banks' branch networks have succeeded in obtaining a high penetration of the adult market in the area of payment systems, to the extent that the market is now effectively saturated. In retail deposits, however, the banks' share has declined dramatically despite the existence of their massive networks.

Patterns of competitive behaviour are also changing, away from the idea of competing networks, providing high degrees of customer convenience, to more price based competition. This is exemplified in two ways: the first is at the level of retail deposits where the building societies' possession of cheaper cost structures, fiscal advantages and a unique control of their balance sheets has enabled them to dominate price competition. The second is in the area of current accounts, where banks offering more favourable tariff terms are attracting higher levels of accounts, away from the main LCBs. The move from non-price competition, or rather implicit price competition, to explicit price competition marks a shift away from the 'functional' competition of branch networks to 'economic' competition. Branch networks in these circumstances have to begin to justify themselves on the basis of financial performance, and therefore have to improve the efficiency of their operation.

The problem of interbank and interindustry group competition is compounded by the emergence of alternative delivery systems based on electronic technology. These are of two sorts: those that complement branch functions, such as ATMs, front office terminals and cheque truncation, and those which offer alternative forms of networks, namely EFT/POS, plastic cards and home banking. To date, technology has tended to support the continuation of the branch networks, with the development of 'bank office' computer terminals and ATMs which permit the branches to process greater volumes of business, and so in functional terms make them more efficient. The nature of price competition, based on established cost structures, and the general availability of this technology means that no decisive competitive advantage is available.

However, the new technologies are more crucially affecting the competitive equilibrium by permitting new entrants access to a market from which previously they had been excluded by their lack of branch networks. The most pertinent examples of this are the plastic card organizations, especially the non-bank American Express, and highly centralized financial service groups such as money-market funds and cash management accounts. The future development of technology may well allow international organizations such as Citibank or Merrill Lynch, or non-aligned groups such as insurance groups, data processing companies or retailers, to offer financial services in the UK, eroding the banks' domination of payment systems and so ultimately their ability to control a strong market position. In this situation, radical strategies are required to build strong market positions on different or adapted barriers to entry.

The effect of the new technologies and competition has been to fragment the market-place and to break down the homogeneity of the banks' products. The two are causally related: as delivery systems begin to offer specific types of service packages, the traditional interdependence of savings, payment systems and lending products and their relationship to a single unsegmented market must inevitably break down. In essence diversity breeds diversity.

The ability of the branch concept to cope with this change is limited. It is static, expensive, difficult to manage, difficult to adapt to market requirements and not really suited to deliver the range of products necessary if the bank is to maintain its full relationship with the customer. In image terms bank branches have also to adapt to a changing market and therefore a marketing need, making their appearance less anachronistic and intimidating.

The issues of delivery systems, and especially branch networks is fundamental to a strategic appreciation of the personal sector market. The quality and effectiveness of retail banks lie in their ability to deliver products competitively and profitably. Because bank branch networks as they are currently organized are no longer able to meet fully this strategic requirement then inevitably new delivery systems will be introduced to complement and supplement the existing infrastructure. The emphasis in strategic terms will be away from managing a branch network to managing a mix of delivery systems. The choice of delivery systems will be determined by a number of factors:

—the availability of capital to invest in new systems
—the need to build competitive cost structures
—the choice of market segments
—the influence of the existing delivery systems (the present level of investment in staff and infrastructure cannot easily be discounted).

In turn the choice of a delivery system mix will determine:

—the bank's competitiveness in terms of product range and price
—its ability to occupy and manage a market position
—the scope of its relationship with its customer and hence profitability based on the principle of relationship pricing

THE DEVELOPMENT OF DELIVERY SYSTEMS IN THE UK

The development of large branch networks in the UK is a consequence of largely evolutionary and unplanned growth. The mergers of 1968 saw the formation of a group of four major clearing banks whose networks had grown under the influence of 'functional' competition, since the cartelized oligopoly restricted price competition and yet provided a rate of return that encouraged physical expansion. Partly as a result of the mergers creating over-large networks and also because the emphasis of competition has changed slowly to price competition the networks have begun gradually to contract. However, table 17.1 illustrates that network size was the major factor in determining market share.

There are some distinct trends taking place: the major clearing banks' number of branches has fallen from 12,315 in 1968 to 11,068 in 1984

Table 17.1 Numbers of bank branches

Bank	No. of branches (mid-1984)	Market shares current account
Barclays	2,889	18.9
National Westminster	3,234	18.0
Midland	2,308	12.9
Lloyds	2,316	12.7
William and Glyn's	321	1.2
Yorkshire	214	2.9
Co-operative	63	2.2
Trustee Savings Bank	1,640	18.8

Source: MINTEL, BCMB and Annual Reports.

Table 17.2 Comparison by nation of branching: 1983

Country	No. of branches	Population per branch
Belgium	9,252	1,064
Canada	13,150	1,779
France	34,161	1,604
Germany	43,953	1,395
Italy	12,104	4,695
Japan	41,505	2,780
Netherlands	5,753	2,434
Sweden	3,804	2,182
Switzerland	4,781	1,318
USA	90,215	2,398
UK	17,200	3,250

Source: IBRO

(excluding TSB), of which 3,370 were sub-branches. In marked contrast there has been a slow growth in the number of TSB's branches to 1,640 by mid-1984. Money-shops have grown from virtually nothing in 1972 to approximately 340 in 1983, representing an opportunistic though largely unsuccessful incursion by North American companies into the personal finance sector. However, when the UK is compared with other countries it appears that it is by no means overbranched (table 17.2).

The size of networks should also be measured in terms of the demographic characteristics of a country as well as the homogeneity of the financial system. The urbanization of the UK and the tradition of reciprocal agency agreements amongst the banks makes the level of branching seem higher still, and so especially prone to universal rationalization.

The pressures on branch networks arise from two sources. The first is that individuals are seeking both greater control over their financial affairs and greater convenience. Greater affluence and sophistication has led to much tighter management of finances, with the consequence that people are seeking better returns on their money and only tending to keep transaction balances with the banks. The second derives from the vulnerability of the branches to excessive increase in costs; labour and fixed costs of maintaining premises mean that the branch becomes less economic to operate. This situation is exacerbated by the low levels of cost recovery on payment systems (estimated to be about 30–40 per cent in the UK). Emerging technologies, giving birth to new delivery systems, that are able to cope in economic terms with bank branches, further contribute to the growing problems of the branch concept.

Building society networks are used to illustrate the deficiencies of bank branches in terms of style and operating efficiency. However, although their situation is in many respects analogous to the banks, it is much simpler. Simpler because of the limitations of their product range and inherent cost advantages and analogous because the societies' branch expansion under the protection of a cartel arrangement is similar in some ways to the banks' growth prior to 1971, although the element of non-price competition is greater than in the banks' case. The growth of the societies' networks has, in its own right, undermined the banks' competitive advantage of convenience and has had the incidental effect of providing a mechanism for direct price competition against the banks.

The banks' branch networks still possess powerful advantages. Branches remain a potent barrier to competitive entry, although this advantage is diminishing. Branches remain the best method for occupying and servicing the market; the ability to project corporate image and especially the customer convenience of a branch are powerful factors in its favour. Branch networks can benefit from the introduction of new technologies to make them more efficient and enable them to channel more business through them, so that they can begin to achieve economies of scale comparable to other delivery systems. The introduction of branch controller equipment, as Midland Bank has done, enables the branch to automate much of its business processing, administration and routine customer service. The addition of front office terminals and ATMs in and outside the banking hall lower the branch's clerical manpower requirement and modify its function from an administrative centre to a marketing centre. Information technology will permit branches to increase the range of services offered to customers, building upon the existing relationship and so extending the value of the existing infrastructure.

The almost evolutionary functional adjustment in the branch's role is seen in the way some of the clearers have begun to alter the style of their branches.

Barclays, Lloyds and Midland have all introduced open plan branches, allowing much higher degrees of contact between staff and customers for marketing purposes, as well as improving the ambience of the branch.

However, these developments obscure the disadvantages of branches. At a strategic level they inhibit changes in business direction; their scale effects the nature, degree and speed of response available to banks. It should be noted that, as the basis of industry competitor behaviour remains the branch, the forces for change will tend to be gradualist and evolutionary, with each protagonist seeking to improve its relative cost position and customer service. The main threat will come from non-branch competitors who have yet to make a move; it is against these that the branch based financial service organizations have to make pre-emptive moves. The other major disadvantage with branch networks is the cost of adapting them to new needs; the capital requirements for complete infrastructure renewal are immense and probably well beyond economic justification, as the banks' consumer business is currently directed.

It is against this background that some form of branch rationalization is taking place, to bring the networks back into a state appropriate to prevailing market and economic conditions. Both Barclays and Midland have embarked on such programmes. Both sets of schemes are based on a hierarchy of branches, ranging from a large central full service branch to a smaller branch orientated purely to the personal sector. The Midland Bank under the 'Branch Network Reorganization' scheme developed clusters of service type branches around central administrative and management functions. Midland have applied this idea wherever feasible and are now in the process of reducing the numbers of branches. Barclays envisage a 25 per cent drop in the numbers of branches by the end of the millennium, introducing this hierarchal principle, with the mass of branch reductions occurring in the medium-size branch.

Rationalization of branch function is beginning to take a further step with the development of self-service fully automated branches. The German Verbraucherbank has introduced a small network of such branches, and in the UK National Westminster have introduced such a branch.

The Impact of Technology

The need to make branches more efficient by automating their services, to counteract inexorably rising revenue costs through front-end capital investment and to extend customer and quality of service by providing 24 hour facilities, have led to the wide scale introduction of ATMs, which

Table 17.3 ATM distribution by bank

	1979	Mid 1984
Barclays	131	739
Lloyds	819	1,574
Midland	24	771
National Westminster	131	1,428
William and Glyn's	–	175
Yorkshire	–	115

Source: Banking World

also have mitigated the decline in branch numbers. As table 17.3 illustrates the growth in ATM numbers has been spectacular.

The examples of Barclays and the Co-operative Bank against this backdrop are interesting. The Co-operative, because of its large supporting network of Handybanks in Co-operative stores has, in effect, no need for ATMs. Barclays reluctance to introduce ATMs was based on a lack of conviction that ATMs were the most cost effective way (ATMs cost about £30,000 each) of servicing the personal sector. Their Saturday opening campaign runs contrary to other clearers who have put their faith in ATMs. Indeed the National Westminster/Midland ATM sharing agreement was initially a defensive response to Barclay's Saturday opening.

ATMs primarily provide cash dispensing services, but also balance enquiry, statement and cheque book request services and in some cases deposit collection facilities. In addition marketing messages can be flashed up on the ATM screen as well as personalized messages. ATMs can be used for providing these services through striped debit or credit cards.

There is now a general move towards ATM sharing agreements in the UK. After the Midland and National Westminster agreement, Lloyds, Barclays, Royal Bank of Scotland (including Williams and Glyn's) and Bank of Scotland are setting up a shared network. Some building societies are also discussing the possibility of introducing a shared network. It seems that these agreements represent a move towards new power-groupings, and represent a further aspect in the need for the banks to establish unique market positions on the basis of strategies different from those they have historically pursued.

The themes of co-operation and competition, recurrent in payment systems, are also a feature of delivery systems. This will, at least into the medium term, guarantee the future of branch networks, because while other delivery systems will tend to be co-operative ventures, the branch will inalienably define and identify the individual bank. The reason for co-operation in new delivery systems are self-evident: given that a bank can build and maintain a customer franchise by virtue of a branch network, it will seek to reduce both variable and fixed costs implicit in the new system and simultaneously seek to spread the inherent risks associated with it. However, to join these co-operative alliances often requires a large pre-existing commitment and/or a readiness to input significant amounts of capital, as with the ATM sharing schemes and EFT/POS.

The development of EFT/POS, which although essentially a payment system may also be described as a delivery system, works on the same principle as ATM sharing. The joint development of an EFT/POS network creates a joint barrier to the entry of other groups and maintains the market position of individual institutions in the same way that a cartel or the payment system oligopoly does. It is, however, likely that the OFT will insist that the system is open to other financial service providers, so undermining the idea of building a competitive position based on EFT/POS. The introduction of EFT/POS is a major step towards using technology to control the growth in overheads. But a paradox of its introduction is that while EFT/POS is a 'functional' or service adjunct to branch based banking, in the same way that ATMs are, dependent on an established customer franchise, it weakens the role of the branch operation and the strength of the relationship between bank and customer. In this respect, EFT/POS may be seen as the first major technological step away from the branch concept, and one which will ultimately act to introduce significant rationalization in the branch network. The growth of EFT/POS systems, accessing an account on which automatic credit facilities are available, or simply in a debit capacity, will undermine the existence of branded credit cards, which are used by the same customer group that is likely to use EFT/POS.

The establishment of EFT/POS may well change patterns of financial behaviour, but if the evidence of ATM use is an indication, use will tend to be limited to younger customer segments. EFT/POS exists principally as a system attractive to banking organizations for curtailing rising costs in the payments area. Its attraction to retailers and customers is unproven; its value to the banks is ambiguous, especially as other methods of cost curtailment exist. Its introduction will progressively disrupt the existing business structure at considerable financial cost; it will begin to undermine the economic and functional validity of large elements of the branch network yet it will not act to build customer franchises and will provide an entrée to competitors. EFT/POS fully embodies the strategic dilemmas of the new technologies in a traditional industry.

Home banking is perhaps the most significant new delivery system, although its full effect is unlikely to be felt until the 1990s. What is common to all the delivery systems is that they all rely on an established customer franchise and marketing base. They are all offshoots of the common branch network. Home banking, however, will not depend on those prerequisites.

The possibility of developing home banking was dependent on the availability of interactive communication networks. The production of videotext systems based either on telephone lines using packet switching techniques or on cable television systems, with their ability to carry up to 200 communication channels simultaneously, provides the bedrock for the development of home banking. A number of experiments are already in operation; Verbraucherbank in Germany using the Bildscherintext system and the Nottingham Building Society in link with the Royal Bank of Scotland through the Prestel system are working very effectively. What is interesting in both cases is that both organizations have very limited branch networks, and are using home banking as a branch surrogate.

The services that could be available through such systems are payment services, financial management services, reporting services, professional and home business services and administrative services. The main problems facing an organization wishing to enter the home banking market will be in developing a software package that will deliver an appropriate product mix and which will permit a high degree of interactivity between the customer and the bank.

The advantages to the financial organization and the customer are joint and considerable. Although the installation costs will be relatively high, home banking will further reduce banks' dependence on inflation prone networks, allow them to invest in highly efficient systems and will in turn generate fee income. The last point is especially critical since the ever increasing presence of information technologies and consumer sophistication will make retail deposits increasingly volatile and highly rate sensitive, compressing bank margins and making profit from the retail sector especially dependent on fee income. The customer for his part will receive a greatly enhanced level of convenience and service.

Given an adequate demand for the enhanced videotext service of cable television, banks will have to offer home banking facilities simply to preserve their customer franchise and establish a strong position as providers of financial information. The liberating effect of information technology (and money is simply alphanumeric data) will mean that the barriers to competitive entry will be very low and will require pre-emptive defensive strategies by banks to maintain their market position.

Although the implications of home banking are considerable, it is strategically vastly different from other forms of EFTs by not being dependent on an established customer franchise and not being dependent on co-operative schemes with other financial institutions. It will nevertheless require the intermediation of a communications company.

The motives behind its introduction will be twofold: firstly, as a strategic act to defend market position against other competitors who may introduce home banking facilities, and secondly to use the economies of scale and fee income implicit in the system to build more effective and therefore more competitive cost structures. This second element is central to all banking strategies of the future and by necessity indicates the end of the branch concept's pre-eminence.

Other Forms of Delivery Systems

The branch, ATM, EFT/POS and home banking are primary forms of delivery system, with plastic cards representing a hybrid between a payment system and a delivery system. Plastic cards, however, require a supporting communications infrastructure, represented either by the postal service, for paper based payments or the telephone system for electronic based payments. The existence of highly efficient systems has permitted the development of centrally run operations that have no captive customer base or retail network. Not only do credit and charge card companies use such systems, but their availability means that other competitor groups, especially money market funds and cash management accounts are able to attract substantial volumes of business by working on radically different cost structures operated and required by established competitors. This trend has spread to insurance companies and building societies, with centralized operations controlling fairly substantial customer bases.

The main threat posed by these groups is in their ability to attract the most profitable customer segments away from banks, by undercutting them in price and offering relatively higher degrees of service and convenience. The threat is marginal, but sufficiently great to disrupt the economics of retail banking based on competition between groups with reasonably similar cost structures and infrastructure.

The banks are, however, in a position, to use mail and telephone based delivery systems in their own right. The 'ownership' of large customer franchises with a commensurate store of information about their financial habits (albeit in an often unstructured way for marketing purposes) places them in a situation where they can exploit direct mail and telephone selling techniques. Both are highly cost efficient methods of developing customer relationships and levels of produce use through specific and focussed communication programmes. There are inherent dangers in such an approach but in a changing delivery system environment, they will represent important communications media to a customer base whose direct contact with the branch network grows less through time.

The Strategic Issues

The choice of a delivery system mix represents the principal strategic issue confronting bank management. The eventual choice will influence the banks product range and its ultimate interaction with the market. Both of these factors are major factors in influencing market share. A more crucial determinant, however, will be how the choice influences the cost structure and hence the bank's price competitiveness and overall profitability. Implicit in this choice, therefore, is the banks' overall ability to operate successfully in the retail market. The choice of a delivery system mix will be based on:

—maintaining a strong market position through attracting and retaining a large, profitable customer franchise
—introducing new delivery systems to counteract the cost characteristics of the branch network
—building a delivery system mix that can respond flexibly to changes in competition and the market-place
—exploiting fully the benefits inherent in the existing infrastructure.

Within these choices lie a number of key issues: the most important, is that the clearing banks have an established, dominant market position based on the possession of large branch networks. To move to a different strategic delivery system position would require an evolutionary and gradualist approach, as the branch structure and its attendant investment in staff and systems will act as a major constraint on change. Similarly there will be a need to ensure that the organization maintains its customer franchise during such a change. This will, to an extent, depend on the ability of new entrants to gain access to the market via new delivery systems. Market pressures will also develop from the greater range of options available to customers and from the customers own increased financial sophistication.

Technology will become the principal arbiter of change and strategic direction, providing a choice to financial institutions of products and delivery systems in addition to altering the economics of the market-place. Perhaps, after a long period of gradual evolutionary change, the banks will no longer be able to determine internally their strategies, but will have to produce strategies based explicitly on options provided by technology, and in response to competitive and market forces. The time frames available for such adjustment are uncertain, but it is probable that the speed of change will quicken dramatically.

Against this backdrop, banks will have to change their assumptions about operating in the retail bank market-place and to look at delivery systems, particularly the branch networks, as functional rather than central aspects of their business. There are three main features to delivery system strategies:

—provide more efficient delivery
—increase customer convenience
—increase levels of fee based income.

Future branches therefore will be seen less as a combination of retail deposit collector and payment system provider. New delivery systems will tend to take payment systems out of the branch. Retail deposits will grow more expensive and will tend to be attracted on the basis of explicit price rather than convenience. Under these circumstances, therefore, the underlying economic justification of branch networks changes, and has to be replaced by a more plausible, functional rationale.

Retail banking, at whatever stage of its development and whatever the influence of new technologies, will need to fulfil certain essential requirements in order to survive. These include the necessity to occupy the market; to acquire new customers; and to service relationships. The new delivery systems, including home banking which is potentially the most compelete of them all, tend towards the third category by providing a simple range of services. The important elements of market occupation, through tangible manifestation, and acquiring new customers, through physical location, are functions which branch networks can more successfully accomplish as compared with alternative methods (e.g. agents, direct mail, etc.). The existence of ready-made networks argues for their development into new directions.

In choosing an overall delivery system, therefore, the following criteria will need to be observed:

- Service delivery must be matched to market requirements (e.g. POS and ATMs will be preferable for customer convenience over the less locationally and functionally convenient branch for payment and obtaining cash).
- Locational convenience for high volume transactions must be increased (e.g. increase the availability of ATMs and 'thin' or self-service branches).
- Service should be differentiate by location, optimizing delivery cost and improving locational convenience according to the characteristics of the chosen market.
- There will be fewer locations provided for infrequent transactions.

The retailing system mix will combine the advantages of the branch concept with those of electronic technology. It will consist of:

—full service core branches
—satellite service or 'thin' branches
—remote self-service banking points
—point of sale
—home banking.

Point of sale and home banking have already been discussed. Self-service stations will consist either of ATMs or self-service fully automated branches along the lines of Verbraucherbank's banks of lobby ATMs. These fulfil a number of objectives, enhancing the level of service and convenience provided to customers and improving internal performance through reduced costs thereby increasing the bank's competitiveness and its ability to respond strategically to changes in the future. The self-service points will provide withdrawal and payment services, deposit and funds transfer facilities and inquiry functions.

The manned 'thin' branch will serve just the retail market with a limited number of personnel in a small high street unit, offering the same services as a self-service branch, it will provide loans and mortgages, new account opening and customer services. The full service, traditional branch will market the full range of services, to include financial planning and investment advice services, trust services and safe deposit facilities. It will also be responsible for dealing with corporate business. The ratio of full service branches to satellite branches is difficult to ascertain but will probably be of the order of one to three.

The continuation of the branch concept is under many pressures; competition is intensifying and is becoming far more orientated towards price. New and competing delivery systems are being produced, and the traditional basis of business, the attraction of cheap retail deposits, is no longer a realistic strategy or purpose for branch networks. In the scheme described above, the branch has an important functional role to play, but where competitiveness will increasingly be based on efficient cost structures this will not be enough to ensure the persistence of large networks. Rational pricing of products will help, but the purpose of the branch must be extended to incorporate a wider range of services.

A number of different ideas have been postulated, from selling much more extensively the so-called ancillary services, such as insurance, investment and pension schemes, to providing more diverse information services, covering travel and estate agency. All of these will contribute to the relationship concept which will come to dominate personal banking in the future, and will, as an aspect of this, generate substantial levels of fee income, so ultimately giving the branch economic as well as functional validity.

CONCLUSIONS

The delivery system question is central to the whole development of retail banking. There is no doubt that the effects of electronic technology, competition and an increasingly sophisticated market will effect a dramatic change in the way that banks deliver their products. Branch networks will be modified by number, organization and function, but will remain central components in the retail bank sector. The networks will be complemented and to an extensive degree supplemented by new delivery systems. The long-term effect for banks will be to make them more efficient and competitive, but will change some of the fundamental aspects of their business; customers will benefit from greater levels of convenience and service. Home banking will provide the most substantial threat to the branch networks, but even this will in measure depend on the branch network to provide a customer base.

The greater number of delivery system options will allow banks to pursue segmentation strategies with a much greater refinement than at present through their currently styled branch mechanisms. Different delivery systems tailored to meet different segmentation strategies based on the purchasing characteristics of those segments will produce a much more differentiated arrangement of clearing banks, with this differentiation leading to possible wide divergencies in profit performance.

The only real certainty, however, is that whereas delivery systems in the past have been the product of long-term evolutionary processes, the delivery system mix of the future will require rigorous and sophisticated strategic management as the size of branch networks contracts under the combined pressures of cost and the emergence of new delivery systems.

The development of new delivery systems will contribute to the formation of new power groupings in the market-place which will differ markedly from the present arrangement of industry groups. This will be prompted by the need to pool distinctive competences and capital in the development and maintenance of delivery systems, and to exploit fully their inherent economies of scale.

In the short term the strategic implications of these changes for the London clearing banks can be summarized as follows:

- Strategies will be developed that move away from the centrality of branch networks by building strategies that progressively adopt new delivery systems and new products.
- There will be a move towards establishing competitive market positions by carefully selecting 'partners' in an endeavour to maximize both economies of scale and the choice of financial products to customers.

- New organizational structures will be created that facilitate the introduction of new delivery systems and the management down of branch networks.
- Differentiation strategies must be built that use the capabilities of the branch for projecting corporate image, and the existing infrastructure must be adapted to:
- Provide genuine retail service in terms of hours and greater interface between staff and customers.

18 Pricing

INTRODUCTION

Pricing and delivery systems are the key components in retail bank strategies. However, although pricing within the retail banking sphere is seen more as a marketing tool than as part of the general strategic process, the evolved method of pricing within the business compromises both the functional and strategic role of pricing. Often purely qualitative issues such as convenience are central to pricing considerations. This is principally due to a lack of knowledge about the cost–profit characteristics of products and customers. As the market becomes progressively more price driven then a much greater degree of accurate and specific pricing for profitability and long-term market positioning is needed.

Pricing is, of course, a function of market opportunity and, bearing in mind the nature of the banks' evolution and their cartelized oligopoly, pricing in the personal sector tended to be a covert and implicit activity rather than overt and explicit. Implicit, since the true cost of a particular service to the customer can be disguised through cross-subsidization from other products and services, and covert because the underlying cost (if known) is often not truly reflected in the price charged.

Cross-subsidization, lying at the heart of implicit and irrational pricing, exists at three distinct levels. At the marketing level in the cross-subsidization of products within a given sector, at the business level in the cross-subsidization of borrowers at the cost of depositors, and at the strategic level in the cross-subsidization of sectors, arguably the corporate sector, at the direct cost of the personal sector. These distortions in pricing policy naturally affected the way the business was structured and directed. Following the line of least resistance, it tended to concentrate on asset formation in the corporate sector rather than pursuing the higher margin, but more diffuse consumer business.

The rationale behind this derived both from the evolution of the banks' business and business mechanisms, and from the structure of the competitive market-place. Competitive action was focussed and modified through the LCBs' cartel and oligopoly of the payment system. The banks' prime interest in the personal sector and the principal reason why payment systems and branch networks developed was to collect retail deposits. Both acted to provide the personal customer with a service, whose cost was partially discounted in the lower rate of return that the depositor could obtain relative to other, less attractive forms of investment. The cartel was built upon the common basis of similar business styles and philosophies and more importantly similar cost structures. This produced a state where competition could only be manifested in what might be described as non-price competition, as the price for deposits and the tariff for payment systems was pre-set. In fact, it can be more accurately described as implicit price competition, as the quality of service and convenience was a major feature of the competitive 'pricing' syndrome. The nature of interbank competition, judged on this basis, was more intense than might have been thought. Certainly the focussing of attention and energies within a limited and very powerful competitive circle tended to eliminate the threat of serious competition from other industry groups.

However, with the slow fragmentation of the oligopoly and the inevitable emergence of new competitor groups, pricing mechanisms founded on oligopolistic principles become less tenable, and the philosophies of business based on the unequal distributions of cost and price must be questioned. Firstly, principles of cross-subsidization become unsound when competition is extended beyond an oligopolistic industry group as price becomes the ruling competitive norm, and secondly, pricing should, if it does not reflect the cost characteristics of an individual product, reflect the cost characteristics and profitability of customer and business segments.

Moreover when the very structure of banking business is undergoing radical change through the introduction of new products and services, and when the scope and nature of the market itself is changing, traditional formats of pricing must also necessarily change. More rational and competitive pricing strategies, based more on underlying costs, must be introduced.

These competitive pricing policies will have substantial implications for the organization of banks: with the removal of cross-subsidization and the links between corporate and retail business becoming less fixed, more independent strategies and structures, based on the cost, price and profitability of different business sectors, should be constructed. The logical extension of this approach would seem to support the argument for a division of corporate and personal business.

Background

As outlined in the introduction, pricing exists at three distinct levels: the strategic, the business and the functional or marketing level. At the strategic level, pricing is related to portfolio preference and balance sheet management. In banking, profitability is essentially based on interest income which is largely determined by efficient maturity gap management and risk transformation. Fee income has become more important to banks as interest margins have diminished, but still remains a relatively minor contributor to profit. Fee income tends to be associated with explicit service features, which reflects some breakdown in the homogeneity of cross-subsidized pricing towards a more explicit programme of pricing and cost recovery.

At the strategic level, however, payment systems are a component of funding, although the 'cost' of gaining and maintaining these funds is not seen as a funding cost, but as an overhead to be deducted from operating income. The same irrationality is seen in the way retail deposits are 'underpriced' both in relation to the consumer and to the organization. Such underpricing at the strategic level distorts a proper evaluation of the business. The correct pricing of retail deposits in internal and external terms is a fundamental aspect of any future retail bank strategy.

At the strategic level pricing tends to represent an equilibrium between internal portfolio choice, market preferences and regulatory control. Portfolio choice will be based upon the risk–return trade off of the business measured against other business options, the level of market demand and the costs of funding that business, measured in direct and opportunity costs terms. The level of demand for that business will be determined by the market's choice of instruments, its expectations of return or cost, its maturity preferences or liquidity requirements and finally its choice of institutions.

At the business level there are more specific objectives behind pricing. Within the LCBs the structuring of the business, as stated in the introduction, tends to make such pricing objectives difficult to achieve. The high degree of cross-subsidization between sectors compromises any pricing decision, since they are not based on a true assessment of the inherent cost associated with servicing a sector. Hence the prices required to achieve profitability, and more importantly the profit potential of the sector measured in competitively achievable prices, tend to be difficult to achieve or, indeed, difficult to assess.

A product pricing decision should be designed both to achieve particular objectives in its own right, and at the business level to fit in with a complex interactive arrangement of other product/market pricing decisions. The prevailing homogeneity of product groups and delivery systems makes the choice of specific product pricing strategies, built upon underlying cost and market demand, difficult to achieve. However, the following pricing motives, taken singly or together, can apply to a sector or a group of related products at the business level strategy just as much as at the single product level: pricing for market share – this is based on cost leadership and whether a bank is prepared to build market share at the direct cost of short-term profit. If this is a widely adopted competitive strategy, industry profit can be undermined. The similarity of cost structures and profit expectation amongst the London clearing banks makes this an unlikely strategy at the business level, although it may be adopted by new entrants seeking a market niche or by other industry groups exploiting different cost structures for competitive purposes.

Pricing to Encourage Use

This is a strategy to be used when a range of different products are available to a bank, and when it wishes to encourage the use of more efficient and inherently more profitable products. This is especially relevant to the payment system area, where technology is making available electronic mechanisms such as BACs and EFTs which are both more efficient and less costly to operate than the paper based systems.

Pricing Based on Cost

Pricing can theoretically be based on marginal incremental cost or on average cost. This, however, raises a number of questions. Firstly, how are those costs to be calculated? It has proved extremely difficult in banking to allocate costs to products on a average cost basis and even with marginal cost pricing, calculating cost components such as cost of funds, distribution, delivery and service costs, etc. has proved just as difficult. Secondly, how to cost realistically the qualitative aspects of a financial product? A service tends not to induce increased usage itself relative to other systems. But this form of pricing will become an increased part of bank strategy with increased price competition leading to rational pricing policies.

Ascertaining direct costs often requires knowledge of the true cost of funds. Given the cross-sectoral nature of the banks' business and the different sources and costs of funds, a single pool of funds concept seems the most obvious and simple approach averaging out cost and providing a basis for calculating product profitability.

However, this approach militates against an accurate evaluation of sectoral profitability judged by its contribution to and use of funds. Such an evaluation process, for instance, could well award the consumer sector a notional profit for its contribution, less use, of cheaper than average funds. A refinement of this idea would then be to decide whether consumer lending profitability should be evaluated on the basis of the cost of sectoral funds or on the basis of average cost of funds. This concept of evaluating sectoral profitability lies at the heart of future corporate level strategy and will determine the importance it assigns to formulating strategy and organizing the customer sector.

Pricing as a Component of Service

This is appropriate where price is based on the specific service attributes of a product, and the uses made of the service by an individual. The current account, under the present pricing tariff employed by the LCBs, uses both a blanket mechanism - a minimum deposit balance requirement - and a separate item tariff when that balance is not maintained. The tariff specifies different charges for paper based and EFTs transactions and so does attempt to recover the cost of operating the service. The 'blanket' method is extraordinarily crude, since the profitability of such a scheme is questionable if there is high account activity and only a relatively low deposit balance held.

Secular trends show that the real value of balances held on current account are declining, as customers grow more price sensitive and sophisticated. A move towards a more precise charging framework seems inevitable. For instance pricing factors could be based on:

—a maintenance charge for a basic service
—account service
—balance position
—exception handling

Such a change would mark a shift towards obtaining income from service fees rather than interest income. The appearance of the cash management account exemplifies this move towards a service fee based on an inclusive product.

Pricing Based on Perceived Benefit

A supplementary issue in costing and competitively pricing products is the degree of value-added benefit the individual receives from them. Availability of service and convenience have been reflected until recently by the banks in the implicitly charged costs of access and in the traditionally low returns offered on deposit accounts. Pricing on this basis can only be subordinate to other pricing decisions in a highly priced competitive market.

At the marketing or functional level, many of the features of business level pricing apply to individual products and product group pricing decisions. The difference between business and functional level pricing decisions tends to be one of specificity and degree.

The marketing of individual products is complicated by the existence of factors peculiar to the industry. The first is that financial products can be replicated within a short space of time and so competitive advantage will be short term. The second point is that many products are related to co-operative systems between institutions, most especially in the area of payment systems, with the effect that this curtails flexibility in the pricing area. Finally, because of a range of different objectives operating simultaneously, pricing decisions tend neither to be straightforward nor autonomous.

At the functional level, and bearing these factors in mind, pricing decisions relate either to the introduction of new products, or to changing the price of existing products and reacting to competitor action. The two embrace quite separate sets of decisions.

In launching new products there are three main objectives: getting the product accepted, maintaining strength in the market-place against competition and creating profits. There are also two distinct pricing options referred to as skimming pricing and penetration pricing: skimming pricing is operable in circumstances where it is the first product to the market and so is unaffected by competition. Higher prices can be obtained from less price sensitive customers, potential demand can be determined and the bank can maximize the profit opportunities. Within the retail bank market it is more realistic to obtain market presence first and make profit later with penetration pricing. The characteristics of the market which make this the preferred option are the availability of economies of scale, the threat of competition and a market where the quantity of 'products' sold is relatively sensitive to price.

Changing the price of existing products can be necessitated by changes in the organization's cost structure or product range, or more frequently by changes in the level of market demand and competitor action. The aim will be to maintain or improve market position or to obtain competitive advantage, and to maintain or maximize profitability from a product line. Elasticity of demand, environmental and institutional factors will all complicate the situation.

Pricing in Retail Banking

There are four specific product groups which all have to be considered separately in pricing decisions despite the high degree of interrelationship. These are payment services, lending services, deposit services and ancillary products. Traditionally banks have levied a single-part tariff, generally an implicit charge, by typically giving no interest on transaction balances and low rates of interest on short-term deposits. The alternative to this was a service charge for each transaction. In lending products the costs were rolled up in the interest rate charged, and ancillary services were either provided free or priced independently.

There is now a growing move towards multiple part tariffs made up of a combination of implicit charge, service charge per transaction and account maintenance and other flat fees. Cash management accounts and premium credit cards adopt this approach. Credit cards are an interesting case since they both have an implicit charge to the card holder in high interest costs (and in N. America also charge a maintenance fee) as well as charging the retailer a merchant fee.

The traditional pattern of irrational cross-subsidization of products means that it is more difficult to move towards coherent strategies of profit maximization, by basing prices on individual product profitability or through obtaining the greatest return on the totality of the bank customer relationship. It is this feature of financial services, the bank's traditionally central function in the individual's financial affairs, based on the provision of payment services, that acts as a key factor in pricing strategies. The profit opportunities available to a bank, through a pricing policy that reinforces the essential homogeneity of bank services through a rational but perhaps implicit pricing strategy, are considerable and represent the bank's main competitive advantage in the market-place. The current situation does not fully exploit this situation as figure 18.1 illustrates. A reconstructed and rational pricing policy would have the following effect: by fully exploiting an established customer relationship through cross-selling and up-selling into other products on the basis of rational, i.e. full cost recovery pricing, the bank maximizes its profit and reduces the operating costs of customer recruitment and business expansion through promotional media (figure 18.2).

Figures 18.1 and 18.2 both tend to represent extreme cases. There is some room for 'loss leaders' in attracting new business. The payment system can be priced close to cost in these circumstances. However, relationship pricing requires highly detailed data on the underlying costs of the products that make up the potential relationship, so that pricing decisions and profit objectives can be based on the sum of products, taking into account factors such as the synergy resulting from the interaction of products in such a relationship scheme.

Relationship pricing, as its name suggests, will mean that pricing policies will be based on achieving particular matches between product ranges and customer segments. To optimize on profitability through attracting particular segments and encouraging the use of specific products, sophisticated differential pricing techniques will be needed. Differential pricing is used to a limited extent at the moment in encouraging the use of particular products at a general level, and in fact tends to reflect underlying costs such as that found in tariff difference between EFTs and cheque transaction. But differential pricing in relationship terms will be designed to attract segment groups, and to encourage the use of an interrelated product range.

Relationship pricing has many advantages; it increases customer loyalty and should maximize the bank's return from a customer relationship. Through differential pricing techniques it will apply with equal validity to up-scale and down-scale customers. In these terms pricing will be a function not of individual product profitability objectives but of segment profitability objectives. Relationship pricing in an increasingly competitive and sophisticated market represents a paradigm to which retail banks must aim.

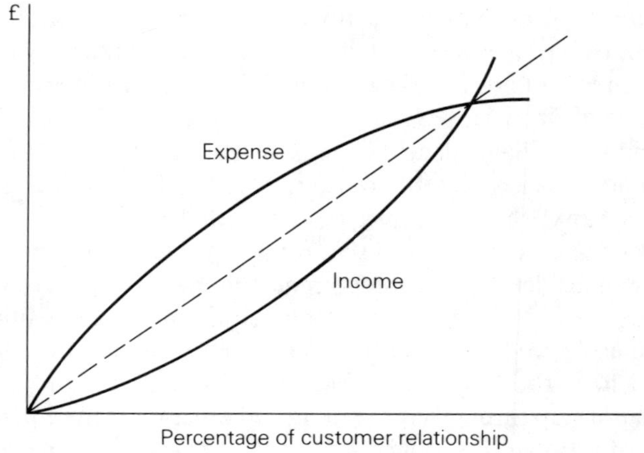

FIGURE 18.1 An illustration of current pricing policy

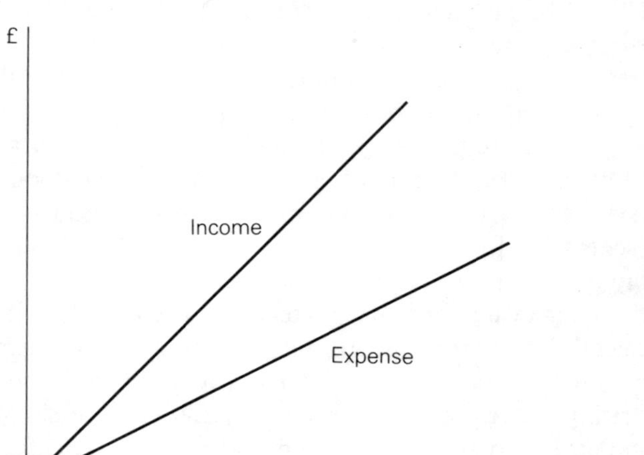

FIGURE 18.2 An illustration of an ideal pricing policy

CONCLUSIONS

As the market becomes more competitive in terms of the products and services offered and more orientated towards price competition, and as the introduction of new technologically based products breaks down the traditional homogeneity of bank products, so banks must necessarily move towards a position where they either adopt largely explicit and rational pricing policies, or alternatively introduce policies that both reinforce customer loyalty and obtain a substantial long-term return from the totality of the relationship with the customer.

Prices will have to become aligned to industry conditions, not just those of the industry group. This has major implications for banks' cost structures, the way in which they price their products and how they organize their business activities. In this situation, the banks can only expect the market to pay a reasonable price for a reasonable service. Business and marketing strategies will need to become more efficient in selecting, attracting and servicing customer segments in the most profitable way. Major policies to achieve these objectives should be:

- The use of differential pricing to induce the use of new services, to attract specific customer segments and to make the bank's relationship with those segments one which maximizes its profit.
- Pricing must reflect specific costs, whether the intention is to obtain profitability on an individual product basis or through a relationship.
- Pricing should recognize the absolute industry requirement for fees to counteract diminished interest margins.

19 Organization: Management, Personnel and Structures

Introduction

Discussion of organizational issues in retail banking is complicated since it has either not been seen as a central problem specific to the development of retail banking or indeed as a strategic issue in its own right. There are several reasons for this, but the most powerful is connected with the way the LCBs have developed through building large branch networks. Organizational forms tended to follow on from the business imperatives produced by these networks with mechanistic, formalized, administrative systems at all levels to control the operation of the branch networks.

Organizational form has also tended to be seen as the consequence of strategic decisions at the functional business level, as most actions have been taken without consideration for a coherent organizational framework in which to manage them. Organizational forms should, to an extent, reflect the sum of separate decisions which ideally should be based on matching the business opportunities and environment to the capabilities of the organization. Nevertheless, there is a stage when a coherent organizational format becomes a condition for success. Then the decision of what structure to employ becomes a central and key element in the implementation of successful business strategy. A philosophical shift has to take place between allowing organizational form to be produced almost accidentally or pragmatically by environmental forces to internally structuring the response to the environment by deploying resources in a specific way. Concern with organizational form is really a function of industry maturity; simple patterns of organization tend to reflect relatively simple business environments. The environments tend to become more complex as the industry moves to maturity. This necessitates not only a more sophisticated response but a better deployment of resources to capitalize on profit-making opportunities, which themselves become less obvious the more sophisticated the business environment.

What has happened within the retail bank market, and to the LCBs especially, is that organizational forms developed in periods of industry growth are now confronted by a much more complex set of issues. The fundamental aspect of their business, the branch, is growing less relevant: more centralized management functions, such as business development, marketing and control of the balance sheet, are shifting the focus of the organization from the diffuse and largely unstructured branch network towards the centre. Developments in telecommunications and electronic technology are the main arbiters of this shift. Communication and information permits a much greater degree of central management, and hence strategic control of the business. In effect, the banks are now in a position to structure thier response to the environment, rather than, as in the past, the environment tending to dictate the organizational form.

The dimensions of a retail bank strategy are now far more wide ranging and complex than in the past. The environment and market have grown more sophisticated, affecting the underlying economics of the industry. With the capabilities now available to bank management for controlling the business, the strategies should both reflect a greater degree of central direction and redistribute resources through organizational forms matched to environmental necessities. Organizational forms should embody strategic choice and direction in a way that will actively contribute to the implementation of those strategies. In essence this means that bank management should critically review the appropriateness of its organizational forms in the changing environment, and be prepared to restructure on the basis of achieving the best match between organization and environment.

It is worth analysing, in this context, the main components that make up organizational form and relate these to the issues confronting bank management. There are three dimensions: management, personnel and structure. Personnel and structure represent the resources behind implementation and management represents the dynamic force behind the manipulation of resources. Successful organizational form therefore depends on an efficient interaction between these elements.

The quality of the relationship between the organization and the environment has been mentioned; successful organizations are those that achieve the best match between the two. However, there is a third element, similar to the management function, which is intangible and yet a powerful force within the dynamics of the business. This is the set of organizational norms, represented by its myths, beliefs, ideas, values and goals. This is typified by the political balance of power within an organization at all levels. It can more accurately be described as the corporate culture: it influences strategic choices and their method of implementation. To achieve strategic (and organizational) change requires cultural change.

Background

The chapters on the environment and the clearing banks have illustrated the trends and forces for change in the retail bank market. Their history is one of conservation and relative stability. Their growth has largely been evolutionary; organizational structures have reflected very broad categories of business, being divided into domestic, international and related business categories. Domestic business, with which the study is primarily concerned, was founded on the long-established branch network and its heterogeneous collection of business activities.

The structure of the business has naturally affected the nature of management and the business. Management skills are established on prudence and caution; skill at lending and at branch administration were and are regarded as key competences. The LCBs' oligopoly of money transmission gave them a natural market dominance, which tended to shelter them from the rigours of external competition. This created a concentration on low-risk asset formation as the main dynamic of management, with money transmission seen in administrative and functional terms, and the collection of deposits either an incremental aspect of the system or provided through a treasury function via the wholesale markets.

This situation was compounded by the fundamentals of the business, the branch network. The complex but parochial branch environment produced distinctive attitudes towards business and acted as the main influence on structure. Its operation produced rigid, formal and hierarchical management structures. The business tended to be propelled more by formal, administrative factors than more dynamic market issues. Recruitment, training and career progression were also geared to the idiosyncracies of the branch environment.

The norms produced by this environment encouraged slow evolution rather than radical change, formal range than flexible approaches, conservatism and the status quo rather than the dynamic and creative, and a cautiously prudent approach opposed to risk taking. The organizational structure and its associated norms have tended to produce a management style which is increasingly less fitted to the changing business environment.

Reasons for Change

The ramifications of industry change are crucial since they question the established assumptions about running a bank. The changing structure of the industry is in turn changing the economics of the market-place. Competition and technology are challenging the pre-eminence of the branch and eroding the LCBs' protective oligopoly, so exposing them to a more dynamic business environment.

The communications and information revolution mean that central management is in a stronger position to dictate business strategy and overcome the inertia of the branch network, and this entails a greater emphasis on marketing based skills and a greater sensitivity to the full range of environmental variables. The need for greater awareness of the dynamics of a business exerts greater strains on the entirety of management.

External factors, in turn, multiply the complexity of the problems facing management. Increased competition leading to reduced profitability and larger, more diverse and more sophisticated markets requiring greater levels of management act still further to stretch the existing organizational form.

It is this shift from self-determined to market determined organizational forms that lies at the crux of the problems facing the LCBs. Organizational norms and the dynamics of management were introspective and slow to develop under the influence of growing markets and an oligopoly. As soon as the industry reached maturity, and its oligopolies begun to disintegrate as a consequence, organizational forms became exposed to the full force of environmental issues. Organizational forms must therefore respond by adapting themselves to the new set of business imperatives.

The branch structure and branch ethos are obvious victims of this change in direction. Branch networks are a major element of the cost base, yet difficult to control in financial or management terms. The appearance of more efficient, competing networks and alternative, more economic, delivery systems puts pressure on the continuation of the traditional bank branch. The propensity of customers to use different delivery systems (e.g. ATMs, plastic cards) and the failure of the networks to attract retail deposits commensurate with their investment increases that pressure. The management of the delivery system mix is one of the major factors forcing a change in organizational forms. The problems of managing several systems simultaneously, and managing down the branch network while introducing new systems arguably lies at the heart of organizational change.

The last major factor in the need for change is the market. The physical growth in the size of the market, as the banks went down-market, has produced problems of scale and scope and profitability, as income per unit has declined. The increased size and sophistication of the market, along with increased competition for that market, has undermined the ability of the LCBs to service all sectors of their market with the resources available to them. An answer to this has been the adoption of segmentation strategies, selecting those customer segments that can most efficiently and profitably be serviced by the bank. Improved management information means that those segments can be identified and their needs supplied. But segmentation strategies are more easily employed when distribution and delivery systems are broadly aligned with market needs. The problem here reverts to the issue of delivery systems. Branch networks and their management are not, in their traditionally conceived role and style, capable of supporting segmentation strategies. This suggests another powerful reason for change in organizational form.

The Limitations of Change

Cultural and organizational change, however necessary in changing environmental conditions, are difficult to achieve, especially in an industry that has a long and successful history, and to whom the crisis of environmental change does not seem imminent or is at least capable of being absorbed through slow adaptation. However, it could be argued that the retail banking industry and its environment are already in the middle of radical restructuring that requires a radical philosophical and organizational adjustment.

There are three prime constraints. Firstly, at the strategic level is the question of the overall dimension and speed of change. In other words, to what extent and in what way should the organization react. Secondly, at the structural level the existing systems of distribution and delivery represent such a major investment that management may be inclined to adapt rather than abandon them in response to changed conditions. Especially in a period of reduced profitability, the limited availability of capital needed to fundamentally change the nature of the structure acts as another major constraint. The third and final factor is political and cultural, and is intrinsic to the character of management and personnel. There are two facets to this, the first is founded on the branch banking ethos where particular skills and attitudes were promoted and which naturally limits the ability of an organization to change. The second, and connected factor, is resistance to change at the personal level. This is exemplified in management adherence to the status quo and in union resistance to technological change. Change in organizational forms disrupts social patterns, changes the status of individuals, changes working relationships and threatens job security. The cultural and personnel implications of a changed organizational form are massive and necessarily have to be dealt with over an extended period of time, say 10 to 15 years. Recruitment, training and the nature of career progression are all fundamentally altered. Often, because these problems seem insuperable management can tend to let things run their course in a pragmatic way that ultimately dilutes organizational success.

Organizational Forms for Retail Banks

The preceding discussion has outlined the background to the LCBs' organizational forms and the reasons for and constraints on change. It is, however, apparent that market pressures have gradually eroded the LCBs' position, and that the future promises even more dramatic upheavals in their business. The problems are extrinsic and intrinsic, formed out of the processes of historical development. Extrinsic conditions have caused a restructuring of the market and the LCBs have to some degree failed to match those changes. Their intrinsic problems revolve around their cost bases, the nature of their markets and their organizational forms.

The LCBs' domestically designated operations, working through branch networks, combine a huge variety of functions, serving a variety of different sectors with a massive range of different products and services. The branches are managed through regional head offices which in turn are subordinated to central management. Head office tends to be composed of divisions that support rather than direct the branch network, such as personnel, business development, marketing and computer operations. The system, although ostensibly cohesive through its focus on branch networks, is in reality highly fragmented. Firstly, because branches are inherently not a unified entity, and secondly, because the range of sectoral markets served are growing progressively dissimilar in the demands they make in the banking industry. Segmentation into business sectors is only a partial solution, when each of those business sectors demands increased specialization and dedication of resources, which can only be achieved by serving selected segments through particular, refined combinations of product and delivery system. Segmentation of business sectors is an insufficient response, when each of those sectors demands increased segmentation and contingent specialization.

The problem is capable of several solutions all of which are different from the existing organizational forms. There are essentially two main pressures exerted on the LCBs: one is market based and the other is technology based. Some North American banks, notably Citicorps and Bank of Montreal, have developed structures which reflect the sectoral nature of banking business. They have organized their banks into personal retail business and corporate business, developing thoroughgoing strategies and organizational forms to correspond with this decision. The other radical solution is to build a structure that would be responsible for introducing and managing technologically based distribution and delivery systems, separate from the branch network. The second solution has the advantage of an uncompromised approach to the slow run-down in the branch system and the introduction of new systems. At this level it is interesting to note that some LCBs are beginning to rationalize their branch structures through reducing numbers and producing a hierarchy of branch types, from the small personal branches to large branches that accommodate both personal and corporate business.

The shift in the emphasis of management will be away from the branch network towards central control and towards sectoral (e.g. personal and corporate business) rather than general management. Integrated domestic strategies will be based on balance sheet management, with control of margins and maturity transformation, which will be reflected in sectoral management through a mixture of explicit, rational and relationship pricing policies. Contingent to the sectoral management through the balance sheet will be the control of the cost base. Here the concern will be to find the most effective balance between maintaining market position and maximizing profitability, through, for example, segmentation strategies in the personnel sector complemented by an appropriate mix of delivery systems and marketing activities. At this level, the simple pressure of economic rationale will determine, to an extent, the choice of strategies and organizational forms.

However, as the banks are not able to control the speed of change and so assure their market position, action is required to redress the balance in a radical way. New strategies require new organizational forms. The growth in market pressures and the ability of electronic technology to go some way towards providing solutions, in the form of more cost-effective delivery systems, in the provision of more detailed management information and in the provision of more effective communication systems, suggest that organizational solutions will derive from the centre rather than being dictated by the branch networks. This spells the eventual disappearance of the branch management ethos.

In cultural terms, the hierarchies' strict management of the past will no longer be adequate. The divisional style of management will become more orientated to the matrix style (reflecting the industry transition from growth to maturity). The emphasis will be towards more organic and dynamic management and away from the mechanistic, formal approach necessitated by the branch network.

This combination of environmental, business and organizational factors will necessitate an entirely new range of skills and perspectives. Management will have to become more dynamic as the business structure becomes more open and flexible. The general calibre of individuals will have to be much greater as the business in general moves away from being labour intensive to being capital intensive.

As the range of business options is extended and as the problems become increasingly uncertain and long term, the strategic options available to bank management will become more risk prone, and this in itself will require a cultural change. In general terms, radically new approaches to recruitment, training, career progression and motivation will be necessary.

Finally, organizational forms in themselves will reflect the increasingly sophisticated strategies required to operate in the market-place. Matrix management focussing on product and segment management will determine the nature of delivery/distribution systems which will in turn be subordinate to the key objectives of each business sector relating to size, position and profit.

Conclusions

The choice of organizational form with which to support strategic objectives will be the central issue facing bank management. It is probable that organizations will be run much more from the centre, but that the personal and business sectors will develop their own strategies and infrastructures to accommodate the growing complexity of the business and market-place.

Under the pressure of multiplying business options, the growing fragmentation and sophistication of markets, the LCBs will become increasingly differentiated. This will be a result of pursuing different segmentation policies which will be dictated by their specific arrangements of distinctive competence and weaknesses. Successful retail banks will be those that produce market-led organizations, while simultaneously controlling their activities through balance sheet management, control of cost bases and the proper allocation of resources.

20 Image

INTRODUCTION

Within the strategic business matrix, the question of customer attitude tends not to be viewed as a central element in its own right. It is seen often as an adjunct to the marketing of the organization, within whose power lies the ability to change, as required, the response to and from the market.

However, in a service industry and especially in a retailing industry, the reaction of the consumer to the organization is critical. Especially when that response is connected to a complex series of interrelated reactions formed by product features, the quality of its distribution, its price, etc. In fact the image the bank has in the consumer's mind is the most important type of branding that it can offer, and should, therefore, be the central component within any marketing strategy.

It is worth making the point that marketing as an activity lies at the interface between the organization and the market, communicating and responding to the market. In such a salient position, the quality and effect of this activity will be coloured by the ambient image the organization or industry possesses. However, it is an issue that has only gained recognition slowly and still remains a problem; not only are images 'sticky' and difficult to dispel or change, but the tangible aspects of an organization, most especially those of banks, are profoundly difficult to alter as they become imbued with traditional attitudes and forms of behaviour in the consumer's mind.

Any strategy, therefore, that attempts to provide the conceptual foundations for business success in retail banking must consider not only the rational and analytical factors, but also the subjective and emotional factors when dealing with the crux of the problem.

AN OUTLINE OF THE PROBLEM

The clearing banks have had a long presence in the retail market, longer than any other competitor group. However, it has been a presence moulded by certain characteristics which inevitably continue to make a substantial impact.

The banks have traditionally serviced the upper-end of the market. The quality, substance and style of the service and the way in which it was presented were all fashioned by the assumed needs of a particular, rather than a mass market. The combination of personal, commercial and corporate business in one branch accentuated these remote qualities, producing an emotional gulf between customers and the banks. They embodied British qualities of security, probity, reliability and coldness. Virtues which were deemed critical to the functioning of a financial system but, nevertheless, damaging in many other respects. Consumer response and attitude at the micro-level is the prime determinant of macro-market behaviour. Banks have 'discovered' the virtues of the retail/personal market, more or less simultaneously with the recognition that competitor groups, of which building societies are the key group, have overtaken them and are rapidly widening the gap between the banks and their personal customers. The banks within their own industrial sphere have also begun to compete more actively against each other for personal sector business. The consequence is intensified competition and an appreciation amongst the banks that they must bridge the emotional gap between themselves and their personal customer market.

There are degrees in the solution of the problem, corresponding at the macro-level with factors that shape the physical ability of the industry to compete and at the micro-level with the problem of attracting and persuading the individual towards the organization. Each level possesses a particular approach, although within the defining boundaries of image they are all interdependent. The different aspects can be listed as follows:

—corporate identity —public relations —advertising —design of distribution and delivery systems —products and product features	} corporate image and competitiveness

CONSUMER ATTITUDES

Consumer attitudes have been modified by two principal factors. Firstly, the expansion of the banks' customer bases has meant that banks are more in the public eye and have contributed to changed perceptions about money and financial institutions. Secondly, the process of social change is greatly contributing to changed perceptions and expectations from service organizations.

The prime factor behind this social change is higher educational standards. This has led to a greater sophistication in the important (i.e. most wealthy and account-active) groups and a demand for higher levels of service and responsiveness at the individual level. Organizations, in the age of consumerism and individualism, must react more positively at the personal level. The changes in life-style both by type and number of consumers also demand a much higher level of responsiveness from banks.

In some market surveys conducted in 1980 by Opinion Research Centre and MORI, some interesting viewpoints came to light but which were deceptive. Generally 93 per cent of customers were satisfied with banks, and banks ranked slightly higher than building societies in overall estimation of their standing. They stood for honesty, efficiency and helpfulness. The apparent reason for the satisfaction was that customers were happy with the main services the banks provided. However, the majority of customers were unaware of the vast array of services available and so were not in a position to make a proper judgement.

On closer analysis (see table 20.1) the levels of usage by these self-same customers of bank services revealed some disparities. Although cheques and standing orders had fairly wide use, loan facilities were not used by the majority of bank customers, and in terms of savings the banks had a less than healthy position.

The banks may have considered themselves as unique suppliers of financial packages, but in fact they were being primarily used as providers of money transmission services. This had led clearly to their decline in the savings market and, until recently (and probably this is still the same), was partly responsible for their position in the personal lending market. People may express satisfaction, but they go elsewhere with their deposits and borrowing needs. The rational response of satisfaction, couched in the cold terms of efficiency and trustworthiness, reveals an absence of any kind of emotional attachment

Table 20.1 Levels of image in 1980 by bank product

Type of service	%
Cheque book	79
Standing order	52
Deposit/saving account	49
Cheque guarantee card	45
Travellers cheques	39
Access/Barclaycard	31
Personal loan	28
Overdraft	18
Budget account	9

Source: ORC and MORI 1980

to the organization. Forty-two per cent of people felt frightened in 1980 when they went into a bank: 'bank services are complex and difficult to use'.

To compound the problem some saw banks as neo-institutional, flairless, inflexible and huge. There are incipient feelings of hostility and intimidation. Building societies, by contrast, have bridged the emotional gap: the simplicity of product and service coupled to the branch design has achieved that which the banks have so palpably not.

The problem is much more acute with the less sophisticated new-to-banking or unbanking market who view banks with suspicion and alienation. They are generally regarded as not particularly easy to use, not suitable for the less well-off and not particularly cheap. The banks are still in a position where they are product led, not market led.

The criticisms and feelings of intimidation are soluble. The impersonality, authoritarianism, arrogance and patronizing effect of the banks are violently antipathetic to the modern age. Customers expect recognition, courtesy, value for money and guidance. Clearly a more reciprocal, confidence-giving relationship is required by the customer.

Communication is the key; if banks are to make the important psychological step in attracting the customer's full loyalty a radical change in philosophy is needed that will affect the whole gamut of products, services, premises, opening hours and locations, to produce customer contact.

Image Creation

As previously outlined there are four interconnecting aspects in the development of a corporate image that will make the organization competitively more recognizable and stronger, and will assist in the communication of ideas to customers.

—corporate identity
—public relations
—advertising
—delivery systems

Corporate Identity

This is portrayed by the panoply of visual symbols and colours that identify branches by the fascia, advertisements, by their logo and typeface, and all the promotional and administrative activities of the organization. It unifies and brands all that the organization does. Without the signal of corporate identity there is nothing for either staff or customer to respond to in a coherent way.

Yet corporate identity programmes are much more than a simple signal; they can articulate a great deal of information about an organization through the style and colouring of the logotype and typeface and the applications and adaptations it is put through in the corporate communication exercise. Intelligently used it can attract customers on a large scale. An appropriate example has, unfortunately, to be drawn from outside the banking syndrome. Marks and Spencer's 'St. Michael' brand is synonomous with a number of positive characteristics. These are the product of years of successful and unobtrusive marketing. But that brand communicates a variety of wholly good qualities about the organization. It is an objective that the retailing banks must aim for.

However, the corporate identities of the banks, symptomatic of their relative inexperience in retailing and in competitive differentiation, tend to be seen as a cluster rather than a group of organizations stridently competing against each other. As competition increases, both as a function and an aspect of that increased competition, corporate identities will become more important in the development of retail strategies.

Public Relations

This is concerned with the issues that give rise to broad changes in the regulatory, legislative and attitudinal environment that affects the banks. It is concerned with the creation of favourable attitudes to banks. As communication to the market-place has improved in line with the growth in media coverage and in the growing sophistication of the market by consumerism, so the banks have necessarily had to improve the quality of their public relations activity.

The main groups to whom public relations must address itself are the media (press and broadcasting), the political structure (politicians and civil servants, and the pseudo-governmental groups like the National Consumer Council) and the competitors, shareholders and finally employees.

Action and the statement of opinion must be expressed to the most influential groups. The groups outlined above are in many ways becoming more influential, more anti-bureaucratic and pro-consumer and therefore more potentially influential and in need of more careful consideration than ever before. The banks, as indeed the whole financial sector that is heavily involved in the retail/personal market, are vulnerable to accusations of unfair practice. Incompetent public relations may therefore lead to a disfiguring and damaging reputation.

The onus is more clearly on the retail banks to understand the importance of public relations in mitigating or adjusting political and media comment and the attitudes of opinion formers in an age of more critical and questioning audiences. It is vital, if the retail banks are to be successful, that public relations activity works so that the principles of free-market private enterprise are not detrimentally compromised by public expectations.

Within this, retail banks need to develop public relations systems that are effective in monitoring and responding to significant shifts in the public's expectations of banks and that are also effective in educating the opinion formers of the future.

Advertising

Advertising is simply one aspect of marketing. In the context of this section it represents the most salient method of communicating information and persuading the market-place. It is a key aspect in an image-making strategy, and as such has played a leading part in establishing current bank images.

Advertising can be a highly effective method of attracting business. Its function in a service industry, and especially a retail-service industry, is open to question. The problems of selling financial service products is most evident in advertising. How is a service given concrete definition? How is it made to last as a concept in the consumers mind, given immediacy or predictability? These are questions that have been largely evaded by banks' advertising which has tended to promote 'generic' images such as the 'Listening Bank' or the 'Black Horse', rather than information about particular products. It is difficult enough to gauge the effectiveness of specific service advertising, but when it is lifted on to the level of nebulous corporate qualities it becomes almost impossible to correlate expenditure with effect. Nevertheless this has not deterred the banks and building societies from investing huge budgets in advertising (see table 20.2). Banks and building societies are regularly seen amongst the top ten highest spending organizations. The breakdown amongst the banks in 1983 is shown in table 20.3.

The common element amongst bank and building society advertising has been to give information, build awareness and give comprehension and reassurance to prospective customers. This has tended to concentrate on image building and development rather than raising product awareness. Most advertising has acted as a collective promotion, although in the last few years a greater onus has been put on specific product advertising, gaining tremendous effect as with Lloyds Junior Saver Package. Very little advertising has been done to gain instant response through coupon or telephone reply.

However, advertising, although recognized as a vital part of the marketing mix, remains an expensive, unquantifiable and volatile activity. In common

Table 20.2 Advertising expenditure by industry group and bank, total advertising expenditure: 1980

	£ million	% rise 1970–80
Building societies	20.9	+641
Insurance and assurance	12.4	+311
Unit trusts	2.8	+66
Credit cards	4.5	+2,499
Banks	17.8	+583

Table 20.3 Expenditure on personal bank advertising: 1983

	£ million
Midland	4.4
National Westminster	13.0
Barclays	4.1
Lloyds	4.8

with all other elements of the banks in the area of image building it is still at a formative stage. Marketing departments are beginning to make massive strides in their willingness to try more imaginative and creative approaches and yet they still remain uncertain and slightly diffident about the results. Nevertheless budgets continue to rise in the conviction that mass-media advertising is a substantive solution to the problems of establishing a significant and winning position in the market.

Promotion

This is a key feature to the marketing mix. It is concerned with the availability of services, the types of services offered and the manner in which they are delivered. This clearly extends far beyond the scope of this section in terms of general branching and ATM strategies, product design and delivery, etc. Certain aspects of it, however, do fall under this heading, particularly the issues of branch design and the quality and convenience of service.

Building societies have progressed, more by accident than design, in the form and function of their outlets. Certain money-shops also have tried to pursue the route of providing a relaxed, convenient and comfortable ambience in which to do business. The intimidating and off-putting baronial style halls of some bank branches have definitely not helped the retail bank cause.

The design and manning of banks to provide a cash transaction service, rather than an environment for consultation, advice or even selling of other bank products, is as unprofitable in real terms as it is anachronistic. Some banks are changing their ways; Barclays has introduced some open-plan offices, dispensing with traditional teller positions and also providing in both these and its more traditional branches, personal bankers to serve customers as counsellors. Other banks are beginning to follow this route, but in much more limited forms.

The point-of-delivery is the most crucial area for the banks, yet the most problematic. Since, in terms of resources available and profit expectation, the renewal of their branch infrastructure and extra personnel, in an intensively cost conscious world, is massively expensive, this makes the banks very cautious in redressing the balance between profit and customer expectation. Yet it must be an equation that will swing towards the consumer; increased competition, the obligation properly to fulfil the role of a retail bank and the changing needs of the consumer are all contributing to a reassessment of the bank's style and image in the retail market.

CONCLUSIONS

To build stronger market positions in a period of intensifying competition, the LCBs, as a fundamental part of their consumer strategies, will have to differentiate themselves in the market-place more strongly than in the past, primarily through a coherent communications programme, incorporating integrated public relations and marketing campaigns, to both customers and staff. The main components of this for the banks will be as follows:

- To develop coherent corporate identity campaigns that help bridge the gap between them and their customers. It will often be necessary to produce particular identities and images for the consumer market, but in turn this will contribute to the corporate identity and ethos.
- The quality of customer service should be improved significantly through training programmes, personnel recruitment and the design of the branch.
- The external appearance and internal design of branches should more fully fulfil their retail purpose, and should act to breakdown barriers between staff and the customer.

Selected Bibliography

BOOKS

Aaker, D. A., *Strategic Market Management*, Wiley, 1984.
Armstrong, Rt. Hon. Lord of Sanderstead, Challenges in the 1980s in *The Banks and their Competitors*, Cambridge Seminar IOB, 1980.
Arnold, D. R., *Strategic Retail Management*, Addison Wesley, 1983.
Cowan, N., Effects on staff and organisations, in *The Banks and Technology in the 1980s*, Cambridge Seminar IOB, 1982.
Crosse, H. D. and Hempell, G. H., *Management Policies for Commercial Banks*, Prentice Hall, 1973.
Frost, T., Effects on wholesale banking, in *The Banks and Technology in the 1980s*, Cambridge Seminar IOB 1982.
Gluek, W. F., *Strategic Management and Business Policy*, McGraw Hill, 1984.
King, S., How the public sees banks, in *The Banks and the Public*, Cambridge Seminar IOB, 1981.
McIver, C. and Naylor, G., *Marketing Financial Services*, IOB, 1980.
Nicholas, T., Effects on retail banking, in *The Banks and Technology in the 1980s*, Cambridge Seminar IOB, 1982.
Parker, R. C., *The Management of Innovation*, Wiley, 1982.
Reed, C. N., Coping with change, in *The Banks and their Competitors*, IOB, 1980.
Rose, H., The British financial structure, in *The Banks and their Competitors*, IOB, 1980.
Seebotim, F., The marketing programme, in *The Marketing of Bank Services*, Cambridge Seminar IOB, 1971.
Williams, L., A competitor's view, in *The Banks and their Competitors*, Cambridge Seminar IOB, 1980.
Wilson Committee to Review the Functioning of Financial Institutions, Report and Appendices, Cmnd. 7937, HMSO, 1980.
Zawadzki, K. K. F., *Competition and Credit Control*, Basil Blackwell, 1981.

ARTICLES (No specified authors and miscellaneous)

Across the counter – retail banking in Britain: a survey, *The Economist*, 8 Dec. 1979.
Automation opens up new opportunities for managers, *Bankers Magazine*, 1982.
Automation trends – 1984 – a survey, ISBI Survey, Savings Banks International, Mar. 1984.

Bank marketing in the eighties – an introduction, in *The Marketing of Bank Services*, European Journal of Marketing, 1982.
Banks: Charges for money transmission services, *House of Commons Paper 337*, HMSO, 1978.
Banks in cash point link, *The Times*, 15 Mar. 1983, p. 17.
Banks join forces to create ATM networks, *Bankers Magazine*, Nov. 1982.
Branches are still part of strategy, *Bankers' Magazine Survey*, May 1982.
Building Societies: markets to the fore, *Banking World Survey*, May 1984.
Competition, Innovation and Regulation in British Banking, *B.E.Q.B.*, Sept. 1983.
Midland thinks again on Ops Centres, *Bankers Magazine*, Aug. 1982.
National Consumer Council, *Banking Services and the Consumer*, Methuen, 1983.
New perspective on EFTS, *Bankers Mag.*, Aug. 1982.
Payment Clearing Systems, Review of Organisation, Membership and Control, (The Child Report), Banking Information Service, 1984.
Technological change, Special Account, *Banking World*, Nov. 1984.
The changing role of the banks, Briefing Note, Barclays Bank Group Public Relations Dept.
Time to reappraise the drive into automation, Special correspondent, *Banking World*, July 1983.

ARTICLES (with specified authors)

Abramson, Bernard, Automating the branch, *Banking Technology*, June 1984.
Behan, P. S., Marketing for deposits by the banks, Manchester Business School, Management Course – 12.
Bennett, Tony, Barclays Bank to re-structure branch network, Barclays Bank, plc, Public Relations Dept., June 1983.
Blanden, M., New names drawn to the City, *the Banker*, Nov. 1982.
Boleat, M., Competition between banks and building societies, *National Westminster Quarterly Review*, Nov. 1980.
Brandenberg, M., The changing face of High Street banking, *Accountancy*, Aug. 1979.
Brooks, J. A., Retail banking and the future of large branch banks, *The Magazine of Bank Administration*, Nov. 1982.
Buckroyd, Keith, Bank advertising: the switch to services, *TSB Review*, April–June 1984.
Burr, Rosemary, Radical restructure means closures at Barclays, *Retail Banker International*, 11 July 1983.
Cassell, M. and Lofferty, M., Banks and building societies set for High Street battle, *Financial Times*, 14 June 1980.
Cockcroft, J., The Saturday 'Network', *Banking World*, Dec. 1984.
Conover, C. T., Is there a future in banking, *Bankers' Monthly Magazine*, July 1984.
Crawley, F., Competition in retail banking, *Long Range Planning*, Vol. 15, No. 3, pp. 71 to 79, 1982.
Crawley, F., Technology and the challenge of the future, *Lloyds Bank News*, Mar. 1984.
Croisdale-Appleby, D., Target marketing of financial services, *The Banker*, April 1984.
De Petra, Giulio, The banks and information technology, *Savings Banks International*, Mar. 1984.

Drury, T., Finance houses, *Journal of the Institute of Bankers*, Oct. 1981.

Drury, T., Finance houses – Operations and Markets, *Journal of the Institute of Bankers*, Feb. 1982.

Drury, T., Finance houses – a happy new year? *Banking World*, Jan. 1984.

Fairlamb, David, This London's a wonderful sight, *Banking World*, Aug. 1984.

Farley, Rob, The marketing of financial services – using the branch network, Speech given to the International Financial Services Conference, 2–4 April 1984, W & G Bank, Deregulation and Service.

Fielding, Stephen, Housing finance: vast changes in train, *Banking World*, Sept. 1983.

Frazer, Patrick, Revolution in the banking business, *The Accountant*, Mar. 1982.

Frazer, Patrick and Vittas, Dimitri, The forces of change in retail banking, *The World of Banking*, July–Aug. 1983.

Friedman, A., Breaking down barriers for the unbanked, *Financial Times*, 27 Sept. 1982.

Garrard. Garry, Cable banking, *Banking Technology*, Oct. 1984.

Graham, John, The human face of banking, *Banking World*, May 1984.

Green, C. F., The future of the banker/customer relationship, *Journal of the Institute of Bankers*, Aug. 1980.

Grindley, R. C., New challenges in retail banking, *McKinsey Quarterly*, Spring 1978.

Grollman, Julia, Looking for a niche in the community, *Banking World*, Sept. 1983.

Hammond, C. Running a profitable branch network, *Brankers Magazine*, July 1981.

Handscombe, R. S., Marketing in banking: how is it to-day? *Journal of the Institute of Bankers*, Oct. 1982.

Hannaford, Peter, Strategy for the future at Societe Generale UK, *Banking Technology*, Oct. 1984.

Hindle, Tim, Branch banking in the 1980s, *TSB Review*, Jan. 1980.

Hopton, D., Electronic fund transfer systems: the issues and implications, *Bangor Occassional Papers in Economics*, 17, University Of Wales Press, 1979.

Ireland, J., Out of the banking hall, into the parlour, *Guardian*, 29 Jan. 1983, p. 20.

Irons, Ken, How to manage services, *Management Today*, Nov. 1983.

Jones, D. National Girobank goes for the unbanked, *Bankers Magazine*, Nov. 1982.

Jones, David, Challenge from the building societies *TSB Review*, July–Sept. 1983.

Jones, David, Fraud: inherent danger in automated payments, *Banking World*, Sept. 1983.

Jones, David, Bringing banking back to the branches, *Banking World*, Jan. 1984.

Jones, David, EFT/POS – backward bankers? *Banking World*, Mar. 1984.

Kay, W., Abbey Habit spreads to cheque books, *Sunday Times*, 16 May 1982, p. 49.

Kendall, N. F. H. and Sheridan, T. J., Foreign banks in Britain – the opportunities ahead, *The Banker*, Nov. 1982.

Kirkman, Patrick, Current and future developments – changing payment patterns – 5, *Management Accounting*, Sept. 1984.

Kitching, D. W. C., Rationalizing branch banking, *Long Range Planning*, Vol. 15, No. 1, pp. 53–62, 1982.

Kodman, C., Bank automation – review and preview, *Savings Banks International*, Mar. 1984.

Koolman, Cornelis, Banking automation – review and preview, *Savings Banks International*, Mar. 1984.

Lewis, B. R., The personal account sector, in *The Marketing of Bank Services*, European Journal of Marketing, 1982.

Llewellyn, David T., The Green Paper: an exercise in competition policy, *CBSI Journal*, Nov. 1984.

Lugg, Anthony, The Big Four's marketing push, *Banking World*, May 1984.

Matcroft, S. R., The diversification of banking, *Journal of the Institute of Bankers*, Oct. 1982.

Maycock, James, E., Third Force challenge: the development of 'third-force' banks, *Canadian Banker*, April 1984.

Meidan, Arthur, Bank marketing strategies, *International Journal of Bank Marketing*, Feb. 1983.

Morison, Ian and Frazer, Patrick, Shaping the future of retail banking, *Long Range Planning*, Vol. 15, No. 4, pp. 105–115, 1982.

Morris, A., Information technology and bank services, *Journal of the Institute of Bankers*, Aug. 1982.

Morris, R., Moves towards one-stop finance centres, *Bankers Magazine*, Aug. 1982.

Nadler, Paul S. Banking's next 100 years, *Bankers Monthly Magazine*, Jan. 1984.

Page, K., Big challenges ahead for Britain's banks *Times*, 1 Feb. 1983, p. 13.

Park, R. and Read, C., A management perspective and banking from home, *World of Banking*, Jan.–Feb. 1982.

Quinton, J., Banking in the 1980s – key strategic issues, *Journal of Banking*, Oct. 1982, p. 155.

Reid, Margaret, The end of the banking GP? *Banking World*, June 1984.

Rocker, Christopher, Establishing and managing a corporate bank marketing strategy in the UK, *Banking World*, Sept. 1984.

Rogowski, Robert J. and Simonson, Donald G., Prospects – and problems – of banking and technology, *Bankers Magazine*, May–June 1984.

Roman, Murray, *Bank Marketing – A New Frontier – from Telemarketing campaigns that work*! McGraw Hill, 1983.

Stainer, Gareth, Marketing and finance – working together, *Accountants Magazine*, Jan. 1984.

Stopp, Christine, The brisk growth of the Co-op Bank, *Bankers Magazine*, Aug. 1982.

Stroud, D. and Todd, P., Technological development: the long-term impact of banking *The Banker*, April 1981.

Turnbull, P. W., The role of the branch manager in the marketing of bank services, in *The Marketing of Bank Services*, European Journal of Marketing, 1982.

Vander Weyer, Deryk, What future for the High Street branch? *Banker's Magazine*, Aug. 1982.

Walden, Herbert, How building societies see their role in the financial services revolution, *The Banker*, Mar. 1984.

Watson, J., The adoption of marketing by the English clearing banks, in *The Marketing of Bank Services*, European Journal of Marketing, 1982.

Watson, J., Some current issues in UK bank marketing, *International Journal of Bank Marketing*, Vol. 2, No. 1, 1984.

Index